What Readers Say about *Grounds for Marriage*

FROM PILOT THERAPY GROUP PARTICIPANTS

"In *Grounds for Marriage*, Stone shares scripture regarding truths that many faith communities have failed to address. It's a valuable investment of time for those of us thirsty to know God's heart and his desire for us in both successful and failed relationships. It's not an easy read, but it is life-changing. It is relationship-changing. It's a "Wow!" book—a book of freedom and hope."
—Lynne Lemke, Hair Stylist, Mom, Grammie

"This book has helped me to see and understand marriage as a covenant and to accept my and my husband's brokenness. Stone challenged me to grapple with uncomfortable truths, to do the 'heart work' that comes with acknowledging relational failure. It introduced me to a wide array of references for further study and examination. I leave the book with awe at God's wonderful design for marriage and hope for my future, even though my marriage has ended. This is one of the most compassionate, grace-filled books about marriage I have ever read, and I am thankful for it."
—Judy Estabrook, Counselor-in-Training

"I am truly grateful for this book and its timing in my life. I had a huge cloud of shame over me as I experienced my own relationship failure. This material helped me to move forward and release shame, find truth, and it gave me words for my own process in ways I could not articulate. It gave me permission to be honest about what was already true in my own toxic marriage, and gave me a new picture of covenant with God and people."
—Kristin Schultz, Mom

"This book has changed my marriage in ways I hadn't been able to hope for. We went from 'one last try before divorce' to the best relationship we've had in the entire seventeen years we've been together. We have learned what a good relationship looks like, and how we can take responsibility for our part in it. Thanks, Jade."
—Rod Clemmer, Field Service Engineer

"I came into the group hoping to get Biblical justification for divorce. I'm leaving the group feeling like I want to be married forever. I didn't think this was possible. We have a lot of work ahead of us, but now at least we know what we need to do."

—Kristie Clemmer, Hospice R.N.

"*Grounds for Marriage* gave me a fresh perspective in a troubling time when I was searching for understanding and answers. It has humbled me to my part to the pain in my marriage."

—Glen Moore, Housing Developer

FROM PEOPLE-HELPING PROFESSIONALS

"I found *Grounds for Marriage* to be a beautiful blend of biblical insight, professional understanding, and personal story regarding what is required to form and maintain a covenant relationship. Stone has the ability to speak both to the mind and to the heart, and she does so with compassion, honesty, and courage. I highly recommend this material and eagerly await its publication so that my clients may benefit from it as well. This unique material is both theologically sound and highly unique and powerful. I have searched for a book like this for many years and have yet to read its equal."

—Cindy Brosh, Licensed Professional Counselor

"*Grounds for Marriage* is a call to live on the high plane that esteems *covenant relationship*. While offering practical help and guidance, *Grounds* holds out hope for true intimacy, offered in the empathetic voice of one who has grieved through great loss yet courageously pursued the hard work of personal healing and intimacy with God . . . at any cost."

—Donna J. Noble, author of *Standing on the Heights: Building a Platform for True Beauty*

"Jade G. Stone has put together a book about marriage that is unique. I am impressed by the interweave of theology, psychology, and personal life experience. Each section brings to life the living nature of the written Word combined with real life experience, struggle, and pain. This book is not for the faint of heart, written to those who take the covenant of marriage seriously. It is controversial as it calls us to consider a higher view of marriage and forces us to tell the truth about destructive and traumatic relationships. To every seminary student, to anyone who wants to truthfully re-evaluate their marriage covenant, to those who are currently in marriages that are close to the brink of dissolution, and to those on the other side of divorce, this book should be studied cover to cover."

—Dan Cox, Licensed Professional Counselor

"Stone's brave and compelling book invites the reader to fresh engagement with the issues of covenant marriage. She presents a high view of the significance and purpose of marriage as she explores underlying theology in comprehensive but accessible ways. This theology is richly held in the context of story as Stone explores the compelling questions that enlarge our minds as well as our hearts. You will be stretched, you will be challenged, and you will be touched."

—Ruth Dirks, Licensed Professional Counselor Intern

"As a Licensed Professional Counselor working with Christian couples and individuals, I often recommend books that can provide foundational information about relationships and can challenge personal assumptions. In *Grounds for Marriage*, Stone has written a carefully crafted and readable blend of professional insight from years of counseling experience, carefully researched theological foundations, and remarkably vulnerable personal experience about marriage. This is a book I have been hoping to have available for my clients, not because it will 'fix' them, but because it has the potential to help them to think differently, and that can lead to profound and positive change."

—Susan B. Zall, Licensed Professional Counselor

"In Grounds for Marriage, Stone points out the kind of relationship God designed for marriage: a covenant formed by love. She also opens our eyes to compassionately recognize a trauma bond, the counterfeit of a covenant marriage. A trauma bond challenges the individual's and the couple's emotional and spiritual health. While not all trauma bound marriages play out alike, Stone's own story woven throughout the book offers an inside glimpse of her conscientious journey through a trauma bond. It is an important book for Christians considering marriage or those already suffering in a trauma bond."

—Gaylie Cashman,
Certified spiritual director with an embodied approach

Grounds for Marriage

Grounds for Marriage

A Fresh Starting Point for Couples in Crisis

JADE G. STONE

WIPF & STOCK · Eugene, Oregon

GROUNDS FOR MARRIAGE
A Fresh Starting Point for Couples in Crisis

Copyright © 2011 Jade G. Stone. All rights reserved. Except for brief quotations in critical publications or reviews, no part of this book may be reproduced in any manner without prior written permission from the publisher. Write: Permissions, Wipf and Stock Publishers, 199 W. 8th Ave., Suite 3, Eugene, OR 97401.

Wipf & Stock
An Imprint of Wipf and Stock Publishers
199 W. 8th Ave., Suite 3
Eugene, OR 97401
www.wipfandstock.com

ISBN 13: 978-1-60899-810-4
Manufactured in the U.S.A.

Scripture taken from THE MESSAGE. Copyright © 1993, 1994, 1995, 1996, 2000, 2001, 2002. Used by permission of NavPress Publishing Group.

Some of the anecdotal illustrations in this book are true to life and are included with the permission of the persons involved. All other illustrations are composites of real situations, and any resemblance to people living or dead is coincidental.

All rights reserved. No part of this manuscript may be reproduced, stored in a retrieval system, or transmitted in any form or by any means—electronic, mechanical, photocopy, recording, or any other—without the prior written permission of the author.

*To my former husband:
May we both find the healing and wholeness—
for relationship with God, ourselves, and others—
that we didn't find together.
I imagine and look forward to the day,
either in this life or in the next,
when we're reconciled.*

You'll always have a special place in my heart.

Contents

Acknowledgments xiii
Introduction xv

PART 1   FOUNDATIONS—THE SPIRIT OF ANCIENT PAST

1   Happily Ever After—A Match Made in Heaven?   3
       A True Treaty

2   Happily Never After—Mates By Mistake?   17
       A False Treaty

3   God's Love Languages   47

PART 2   HONEST EVALUATIONS—THE SPIRIT OF REALITY PRESENT

4   E.Q.: Don't Be Home Without It   69

5   'Til Homicide Do Us Part   85

6   Naked and Unashamed   107

7   A Decalogue to Diagnose Hardening of the Heartery   138
       A Toxic Condition

PART 3   DECISIONS—THE SPIRIT OF WHOLEHEARTED FUTURE

8   Repentance: Surprisingly Soft and Shame-Free   169

9   To Have and to Fold   189

10 Grounds for Parenting: What about the Kids?   211

Epilogue   Head and Heart: Reunited, and It Feels So Good   221
Afterword   Happily Ever After?   229

PART 4 GROUNDS FOR MARRIAGE STUDY GUIDE
How to Use This Study Guide 235

Introduction 238

1. Happily Ever After—A Match Made in Heaven?
   A True Treaty 242
2. Happily Never After—Mates By Mistake?
   A False Treaty 247
3. God's Love Languages 250
4. E.Q.: Don't Be Home Without It 252
5. 'Til Homicide Do Us Part 255
6. Naked and Unashamed 259
7. A Decalogue to Diagnose Hardening of the Heartery
   A Toxic Condition 263
8. Repentance: Surprisingly Soft and Shame-Free 268
9. To Have and to Fold 271
10. Grounds for Parenting: What About the Kids? 275

Epilogue   Head and Heart: Reunited, and It Feels So Good 278
Afterword   Happily Ever After? 281

PART 5   PRACTICAL TOOLS—APPENDICES
Appendix A: Active Listening Skills 287
Appendix B: Trial Separation Agreement Form 288
Appendix C: Sample Confrontation Letter 291
*Appendix D: The Decalogue (Ten Commandments)
    of Honest Appraisal and Personal Responsibility* 314
Appendix E: Twin Parables 318
Appendix F: Annotated List of Resources 331
Bibliography 341

Acknowledgments

PEOPLE WHO KNOW ME often ask me how long it took me to write this book. "Thirty-nine years," I tell them. We smile together because they know that I'm thirty-nine years old.

To acknowledge everyone who's contributed to the fabric of this story would be impossible; I'm sure there are some people who've woven threads into the tapestry of my life that I don't even realize. Tennis great Althea Gibson said, "No matter what accomplishments you make, somebody helps you."[1] That's the way it is with this book: it's a community effort that finally culminated in something printed.

To my friends and colleagues: You have, in various measures, believed in me, gave me my start in the field of counseling, witnessed the final demise of my marriage, and watched me come alive again—Dan Cox, Brian Cox, Norma Tucker, Byron Kehler, Cindy Brosh, Kristi Parker, Ruth Knott, Cathie Berry, Michael Plummer, Naomi Mandsager, Gene Hiehle, and Motor and Cathy Berghoff—I've been able to rest in your presence because you seek out the good in me. You've watched and listened to me wrestle with issues of faith and relationship, and you've held me up along the way.

To George Berry: Guess I waited for you after all. . . . Our time reading this book together continues to prove invaluable in countless ways. I'm grateful for you.

To the tireless participants of the critique group—Dan Cox, Cindy Brosh, Ruth Dirks, Susan Zall, Gaylie Cashman, and Kathy Querin—and to the courageous members of the pilot therapy group—Rod and Kristie Clemmer, Kristin Schultz, Lynne Lemke, Judy Estabrook, and Glen Moore—thanks for every suggestion and counterpoint you offered. I've weighed every one.

---

1. Applewhite, Evans, and Frothingham, *And I Quote*, 4.

To my former husband: I am both grateful and sorrowful for your sacrifices as we went through life. I know you were lonely, and I'm deeply sorry.

To Mom: I'm grateful for your sacrifices, too, those that mothers make silently because of their love. Thank you for your blessing of this work and for your commitment to the truth of this story, even though it hurts. I admire your courage to have this story out in public.

To my counselors: You will always be precious to me because you helped me become human again. John, wherever you are, you introduced me to a new view of spirituality through your character and through compelling books. Kyle, you asked soul-searching questions, gave probing homework assignments, and wisely refused to rescue me from my pain.

To Larry Crabb and Dan Allender: Your tag-teamed efforts put me on my spiritual journey, and I cannot thank you enough for that. Larry, *Inside Out* gave me the courage to live authentically, to never pretend about anything. Dan, *The Wounded Heart* gave life back to me, and helped me to face disappointment, to identify my self-protective failure to love, and to continually seek grace and forgiveness. Your written materials, seminars, and seminary classes left me more honest, vulnerable, sorrowful, free, hopeful, and well prepared for working as a therapist and living in wonder.

To Hannah Selleck: Your copyediting made this book more efficient and effective. I'm grateful.

To my God: I'm in awe.

Introduction

A THEOLOGICAL PERSPECTIVE

Why I Use The Message

I WAS BORN AND bred using the King James Version of the Bible, and I'm glad for this when I recognize allusions from this translation in our cultural literature. Most of the time, however, I'm drawn to more contemporary translations because I have to do fewer mental and emotional gymnastics to hear God. Although I realize that the harsh doctrines of the denomination in which I was reared were due more to faulty interpretations than to faulty translations, the KJV reminds me too much of the pain generated by that denomination's strange misinterpretations. I can hear God better when I'm not hearing ancient voices of preachers whose "teaching has messed up many lives" (Mal 2:8).

When I became a Jesus-follower at the age of twenty-six, I was ravenous for the scriptures, and I devoured various versions of the Bible, starting with the New International Version. At the time, I was teaching high school Language Arts, so when the summer came, I spent almost every free moment between its pages. Then I discovered parallel Bibles, then Bible software. Then I went to seminary for my counseling degree, and I discovered a wealth of Hebrew and Greek helps. Then, just last year, I discovered *The Message*. I was impressed with how and why it had come into being, and I found myself spellbound by its easy readability. Within three months I had read *The Message* from cover to cover, using colored pencils to highlight themes as they jumped off the pages. Then I went back and typed out, by theme, the verses that I had color-coded. The document turned out to be fifty-two single spaced pages, which I printed out and bound for personal use.

I've been sold on *The Message* ever since, but I realize that others may not be. Because this version is so readable, some wonder if it's an accurate rendition. I can't make that determination for anyone other than myself. I can only say that I've been more blessed by this translation than I have by any other. That's why I use this version in this book: it's like one long sermon, and if you can approach it like most approach sermons (inspired by God and applicable to everyone who hears), you might be blessed by *The Message*, even if you're skeptical at first. If you're uncomfortable with *The Message* for any reason, I encourage you to look up the given verses in your favorite version as you read *Grounds for Marriage*. (I've noted when I use a translation other than *The Message*.)

Personal Pronouns for God

It may also be disconcerting to some that I've chosen not to capitalize pronouns for God (He, Him, His, etc.) so as to emphasize the intimacy that we can have with him. As this book is about our covenant with God and others, I wanted to stress the closeness that is possible with Abba Father. No disrespect is intended; in my view, intimacy engenders both increased familiarity *and* increased respect.

In contrast, you will also notice my use of the Tetragrammaton[1] YHWH (הוהי) at times. This is the Hebrew name of the God of Israel, sometimes pronounced Yahweh. Eventually, the Jews considered the name too holy to pronounce, and instead said Adonai, or Lord. Even YHWH, however, reminds us of how near God is to us as it is linked with the verb היה (hayah), *to be*, probably referring to the presence of God with his people (Exod 3:12). That God dwells with his people as an intimate partner is a foundational concept of Grounds for Marriage.

I hope your experience of this book will draw you into deeper intimacy with God.

Prescriptive Interpretation vs. Descriptive Interpretation

The kind of relationship we have with God depends on our God-concept, and our God-concept depends on how we approach scripture. Allow me to describe two approaches to understanding scripture: a *pre*scriptive approach, and a *de*scriptive approach. A purely *pre*scriptive approach is based on the idea that the way life was when the Bible was written is the way it's supposed to be now. It *prescribes* a specific manner of liv-

---

1. The term Tetragrammaton comes from the Greek word τετραγραμματον, combining *tetra* meaning *four* and *grammatos* meaning *letters*.

ing. A purely *de*scriptive approach is based on the idea that the way life was when the Bible was written is not necessarily the way it needs to be now. It *describes* a cultural manner of living. I take a middle-of-the-road approach, in that I believe there are parts of the scriptures that are prescriptive and others that are descriptive. The way we approach the scriptures and interpret them, our hermeneutic, will help us make these judgments for ourselves.

In *Grounds for Marriage*, I refer to the scriptures primarily from a *pre*scriptive standpoint, because most of the people who will read this book have been taught this approach. However, there are a growing number of people who also incorporate a *de*scriptive approach where scriptural passages seem to be steeped in culture. Even those who would condemn a descriptive approach in favor of an exclusively prescriptive one often dismiss or re-interpret scriptures that seem to be based in cultural context. For example, most who subscribe to an exclusively prescriptive approach do not accept the practice of polygamy, although some of the great men of the faith were polygamous. From a descriptive approach, we can understand these practices from a cultural standpoint and realize that just because they did it then, doesn't mean that they *should* have, nor does it mean that *we* should today. We all interpret descriptively at times, so it's important to be honest with ourselves when we do. We can't have integrity if we don't have honesty.

A Brief History of Hermeneutics

Much of the confusion regarding what the scriptures say about marriage, divorce and remarriage stems from the various ways people approach scripture interpretation. Your own hermeneutic will determine how you make sense of various passages regarding relationship.

Interpreting the scriptures isn't an easy task. For most of human history, this job was left to the religious leaders, some of whom were conscientious and many of whom were not, judging by the biblical prophets who often condemned the false teaching of their fellow prophets and religious leaders. However, since the seventeenth century Reformation, when the scriptures were translated into the common language and mass printed, and since educational institutions foster literacy more than ever before, the common person is able to engage in interpretation right along with the scholars.

The possibility of misinterpretation became a major debate during the Reformation when church leaders, such as Martin Luther, felt that the risk of misinterpretation was less important than the risk of leaving the people without the scriptures. Luther and others who believed that people could think critically for themselves were in good company. Jesus said, "Don't set people up as experts over your life, letting them tell you what to do. Save that authority for God; let him tell you what to do.... And don't let people maneuver you into taking charge of them. There is only one Life-Leader for you and them—Christ" (Matt 23:8, 10). This echoes the sentiment in Proverbs 14:15: "The gullible believe everything they're told / the prudent sift and weigh every word."

Certainly, the scriptures provide warning after warning to and about false teachers, such as we find in Malachi 2:7–8: "It's the job of priests to teach the truth. People are supposed to look to them for guidance. The priest is the messenger of God-of-the-Angel-Armies. But you priests have abandoned the way of priests. Your teaching has messed up many lives. You have corrupted the covenant of Levi." According to James 3:1, those who teach the Word are held to a higher standard than others, so it is incumbent upon Bible teachers and theologians to be especially careful with the scriptures.

Because it's so easy to misinterpret and lead others astray, we must have guidelines (hermeneutics) to increase the likelihood of sound interpretation. Here, I lay out my assumptions so that you can decide for yourself whether my approach is sound.

My Approach

I come to the scriptures with the core belief that the scriptures are inspired writings, a phrase that has many different meanings to many different people. Although God uses many methods of revelation, a primary mode of understanding for me has been the Bible. However, most people throughout human history didn't have personal access to scripture; in fact, few people were literate prior to the last several centuries. Instead, the scriptures were presented orally and infrequently. In an era when the written word is so accessible, it's easy to forget that during most of human history, people were connecting with God in ways that didn't include Bible study. So can we, and we'll refer to some of these methods throughout this text.

More important than spending all of our time studying scripture is putting it accurately into action. If we all would only *practice* Jesus' instructions to love God and to love our neighbor as we do ourselves, we would connect with God in an intimate way. It's not what we *know* that gives us trouble; it's how to *practice* what we know that is so difficult.

Unfortunately, when the scriptures are poorly interpreted, people can accept a view of God that obstructs a conversational and intimate relationship with him. While I wouldn't trade the privilege of living in this era when the scriptures are readily available, I also recognize the great dangers associated with irresponsible scripture interpretation. When I hear erroneous interpretations, I often wish that access to the Bible were not available. At least then fewer people, without tools to study wisely for themselves, would be damaged by the faulty interpretations of irresponsible religious leaders.

This, I fear, is what has happened with regard to the subjects of marriage, divorce, and remarriage. Because teachers have not taken the time to study carefully, they've presented doctrines that "have messed up many lives" (Mal 2:7–8), and it's heartbreaking to see people in bondage to what they've been taught is truth.

A Brief Lesson in Hermeneutics

Some say that a "plain reading" of scripture leads to clear doctrines and practices. By this they mean that if you just read scripture and take it at face value, its message is clear. However, many of those who espouse this view differ on what scripture "plainly" teaches about this or that topic, and it becomes apparent that a "plain reading" doesn't yield clearly defined results on any but the most basic doctrines.

The "plain reading" concept arose out of the Reformation. The Roman Catholic Church was convinced that commoners would distort the meaning of scripture if it were accessible to them, so translating the scriptures into the vernacular was sometimes punished by death. Martin Luther and other reformers risked their lives when they translated the scriptures into common languages, believing that the benefit of getting the Bible into the hands of the people would outweigh the risk of distorted interpretations.

Luther didn't claim that *every* doctrine in scripture was equally clear, but that everything we need to know *with regard to salvation* is clear. This idea was called *sola Scriptura*, meaning that Scripture alone, without church leaders, is enough to lead us to a relationship with God. Eventually, this debate led to the Westminster Confession, which reads: "All things in scripture are not alike plain in themselves, nor alike clear unto all, yet those things which are necessary to be known, believed, and observed, for salvation, are so clearly propounded and opened in some place of Scripture or other, that not only the learned, but the unlearned, in a due use of the ordinary means, may attain sufficient understanding of them."[2]

In other words, there are many concepts in scripture that a "plain reading" doesn't make clear. To read the scriptures responsibly, we need to determine some principles to follow to help us reach interpretations that are reasonable. "With the right of private interpretation comes the sober responsibility of accurate interpretation."[3] This is the task of hermeneutics: the responsibility of careful interpretation.

The first task of the careful interpreter of scripture is to find out what the text *meant* in its original context. Only after we've done that task can we try to understand what it might *mean* to us today. This may be the first hurdle for those who've been introduced to a method of understanding scripture that doesn't take into account the historical and grammatical context in which a particular book or passage was written. It's easy to forget that the original text wasn't written to you or about you. But the first task in good interpretation is to determine to whom the book or passage was written and what may have been going on in their world. The first rule of hermeneutics to remember is that "a text cannot mean what it never meant."[4]

A second consideration regarding context is the book or passage itself. When we lift a verse or passage from the verses and chapters around it, or from the canon as a whole, we run the risk of making it mean what it never meant, often simply using the scriptures to "prove" what we have already concluded is true. This is called "proof texting." To prevent such misuse of the scriptures, here's another helpful axiom: "context is king."

A third consideration when trying to interpret responsibly is to understand the genre or style of a book or passage—its literary context. If a text is a letter to an individual or to a group of people, you'll ask different questions than if the passage is a poem, a prophecy, proverbial saying, or a historical account of an event. There are many good resources that

2. Instone-Brewer, *Divorce and Remarriage in the Church*, 148.
3. Sproul, *Knowing Scripture*, 36.
4. Fee and Stuart, *How to Read the Bible for All Its Worth*, 30.

describe differences between one genre and another, so I'll only address these issues with regard to the specific passages for our study of covenant. For a more detailed discussion of Biblical genre, I recommend *How to Read the Bible Book by Book*.[5]

A PERSONAL REFLECTION

Making Sense of License Plates, People, and Scripture

As mentioned, scholars are not the only people who engage in interpretation. We all do. Let me illustrate.

At the ripe young age of thirty-five, I purchased my first car of choice—a 2003 "sundown orange" convertible New Beetle. I felt guilty for spending so extravagantly on a car for myself, so when the dealer asked if I wanted vanity plates, I declined. But when my then-husband, whom I'll call Chip, asked, "Are you sure?" I rethought my decision. That started the process of determining what I wanted my plate to say. My first choice, "IN AWE" had been claimed exactly one month prior. All of my other choices (such as *whimsy, wonder, wow, peace, gr8ful, bugged*) were taken, too, so my choices narrowed to "N AWE" or "AWE." I went with "AWE," which turned out not to have been wise. Now I have to explain what my license plate means when people ask or I have to simply smile politely when they interpret it to mean "Awwwww," which is what happens most often. A friend's five-year-old grandson who has Down syndrome calls my car the Awemobile. I'm pretty sure he thinks AWE means "Awwwww." I can't blame them; the car is cute as a baby's cheeks!

There's no harm done when people misinterpret the meaning of my vanity plate. What it means to them isn't what it means to me, but the mistake is inconsequential. They don't know that I chose this word because I wanted to be constantly reminded of my spiritual core, which is often in awe. Adults sometimes ask whether "A," "W," and "E," are my initials, and I say, sort of wistfully, "No, I just live in awe most of the time." They give me a condescending "That's nice, Honey" look. Or, as I live in Portland, Oregon, where the slogan is "Keep Portland Weird," maybe they think I'm just doing my part. My close friends know what my vanity plate means, though, because they know *me*. They know that

---

5. Fee and Stuart, *How to Read the Bible Book by Book*.

my license plate and my car are expressions of who I am: I love to play and I love to feel the wonder of life.

As it is with vanity plates, so it is with scripture. You have to know the author and the whole context in order to fully understand the meaning of the text. I wish misinterpreting scripture were as benign as misinterpreting license plates, but it's not. Misinterpreting scripture has the potential of imprisoning people with partial truths. Many of the problems that I treat as a Licensed Professional Counselor, working mostly with Christians from the evangelical tradition, stem from poor teaching about what God is like. I would give up my job in a heartbeat if it meant that poor interpretation would stop. Church leaders have just as much responsibility to "do no harm" as do medical professionals who are bound by the Hippocratic Oath. Faulty interpretations can cause emotional, spiritual and physical damage. May we carefully consider how our interpretations impact people before we share them with the public.

Hermeneutics and Covenantal Relationship

I must admit that I didn't want to write this book because it required summoning and putting words to deep pain. I didn't want to publish the book, either, because like my vanity plate, it could be misinterpreted and misused, and with great consequence. My intent is to invite people in troubled marriages (and those who help them) to take a look at covenant from a fresh perspective, so that they may experience fundamental change and require themselves and their spouses to keep the promises they made, or to accept the consequences of not doing so.

Most believers understand marriage to be a covenantal relationship, based on God's covenant with Abraham and then later with his people through Moses. But the idea that covenant is conditional? That broken covenant has consequences? Few believers have heard this part of the story addressed from the pulpit or anywhere else. With the emphasis on love's patience, kindness, and humility, there has been little room for love's inherent conditions for relationship, at least not for the marriage relationship. A covenantal approach offers hope, healing, and freedom for those in relationships in which covenant promises and conditions have been irreparably broken. This book is a call to love more fully, a call to change our hearts, which sometimes looks unconventional. Ultimately, our approach to making sense of the Bible, our hermeneutic, influences our theology about and practice of relationship.

Poor Interpretive Methods Cause Confusion

My ride on the hermeneutics carousel began in a church that refused to call itself either a *church* or a *denomination*. Because the Greek word for *church*, *ecclesia*, refers to a gathering of people, not to a building, it was considered spiritually uninformed to talk about "going to church." And because they claimed to be God's assembly in modern times, those whom God called out from the errant world of denominationalism, they denied being a mere denomination. This denomination still exists and still claims to practice as closely as possible to the first-century church (as do many others). All of these denominations make this claim based on how they interpret various passages of scripture, passages that they say "clearly" teach their practices and doctrines. They make these claims based on their hermeneutic—their approach to interpreting scripture.

Growing up in an environment that claimed to have the corner of the market on truth was frustrating and confusing, especially since it forbade questioning and rewarded conformity. I wondered, however, how I could know what the scripture really meant when well-meaning people interpreted it in very different ways. For example, the church of my youth set up special rows of seats for unbelievers, outside the circle for those "in fellowship," based on a verse that mentioned the "room of the unlearned" (1 Cor 14:16, KJV).

Adding to my confusion was the chaos of my family situation, which included physical, emotional, verbal, spiritual, and sexual abuse. All of this was in a family that claimed to be Christian, but our church addressed none of these abuses. When I was young, I prayed to God for wisdom to survive my family environment. I hadn't claimed to be a Christian at that point, and I'd been taught that God doesn't hear the prayers of unbelievers, but my prayer for wisdom was all I had, and I cried out in desperation. Perhaps this book signifies a belated answer to this prayer.

I can only imagine what it would've been like if the wisdom of Proverbs 25:5 had been applied to my father to remove him from his leadership position in the family until he could demonstrate the character required of a godly leader. I remember longing that my parents would divorce; I just wanted the fighting to stop. Of course, this would've required my mother to have had the strength and courage to defy our faith sub-culture and the teaching in her own family of origin, as well as seek help outside of a closed system that shunned everything offered in "the world," especially counseling. And she would've had to do all of this while living below the poverty line. So instead, my siblings and I paid the price for the poor choices of our parents and for the faulty interpretations of our denomination.

Growing up in a system that seamlessly wove truth with falsehood created tremendous confusion in me, and shortly before I came into my own relationship with God at the age of twenty-six, I cried out to him in desperation again. "God, if you even exist," I pled, "I need to know it. And if you do, will you please erase everything I've ever been taught about you and teach me the truth yourself from scratch?"

Perhaps God answered my prayer and continues to answer it in many different ways, including my seminary training several years later, when I wrote a paper critiquing the hermeneutic of my childhood denomination. What a freeing experience! During this time, I learned how to read and interpret the scriptures using methods that made sense to me.

I'll never forget one assignment in my New Testament Genre class. The professor had each student bring an email or a letter to share with others, and in small groups, we read our letters aloud, while our groupmates tried to interpret the meaning of the letters. Knowing neither the context nor the relationship between the writer and the receiver, it was impossible to understand some of the details in the letters, even though we knew our classmates well. It was a good lesson in humility when I considered how easy it is to misinterpret what one person writes to another. And these were letters in my own language and in my own historical time period. It was clear to me that to carefully interpret letters, such as the epistles in the New Testament (and any literature, for that matter), it would require a lot more study than I had previously required of myself. Understanding the original languages and the world of the text (the grammatical-historical context) would be critical for sound interpretation. Anything less would be irresponsible.

A THERAPEUTIC REFLECTION: THEOLOGY AND HERMENEUTICS IN THE COUNSELING OFFICE

As a mental health counselor, I've been discouraged by the poor biblical teaching (based on poor hermeneutics) and the spiritualizing (avoiding pain by using spiritual-sounding words) that I encounter. Even more discouraging is that the people who are most confused by what they've been taught are people who desire to please God. Unfortunately, many haven't been presented with a God who can be *pleased* (a biblically legitimate concept), but one who must be *appeased* (a biblically illegitimate concept) by our following the letter, not the spirit, of the law. From this shame-based ideology, it's possible to have a performance-based relationship with God, but not an intimate one.

For example, as I worked with a client who is an elementary school teacher, it became clear to me that his punitive view of God was keeping him paralyzed and confused. We compared his relationship with his students to God's relationship with his children. He agreed that he'd be *pleased* if a student volunteered to help clean up the room, but wasn't sure how he'd feel if that student were simply performing his expected duty. "Joe," I asked, "Is it possible that there is *neutral* territory—territory in which you aren't *pleased* about something specific, but you aren't *displeased*, either?" Joe nodded, and he also acknowledged that if he'd been displeased with that child for, say, stealing another child's lunch, a genuine apology for that hurt would be enough to restore the relationship with him—the child wouldn't have to constantly try to *appease* Joe to assuage his anger. Joe acknowledged that humility and genuine sorrow for the harm done, a repentant heart, would restore the relationship.

Given that there is much poor teaching on the character of God, I find myself encouraging my clients over and over again to study the scriptures for themselves, not to simply accept the interpretations of others. We must accept responsibility for our own lives, realizing that a personal relationship with God doesn't include other people. Certainly, scholarly tradition is important, particularly when there's controversy over how to interpret a passage. But ultimately, you must decide for yourself who your mentors will be when believers disagree on passages that can be responsibly interpreted in various ways.

As mentioned, another hermeneutical error that has caused much pain is the practice of spiritualizing problems to minimize them or to avoid dealing with them. Although you would never know it by the way we use trite phrases, such as "forgive and forget," with one another in the community of faith, the scriptures never call us to pretend that our situation is better than it is.[6] We are enjoined to expose the deeds of darkness (Eph 5:11), to make judgments that aren't based merely on appearances (John 7:24), and to deal with truth in a loving manner (Eph 4:15).

6. Crabb, *Inside Out*.

If God were interested in cheap grace, he wouldn't require confession and repentance as a prerequisite for reconciliation. But many of my clients have been taught that they should overlook gross harm and continue in hurtful relationships instead of confronting offenses in themselves and in those with whom they are in intimate relationships. If we allow the scriptures to apply to our marriages as they do to all other relationships, we would behave in an entirely different manner—not allowing ourselves or our spouses to have a blank check to treat each other disrespectfully.

On this journey, may we avoid the error of the Israelites who worshipped idols they made with their own hands about whom God asked, "Don't they have eyes in their heads? Are their brains working at all?" (Isa 44:19). And may we avoid the error of the Pharisees, who placed God in a box the size of their own rules, and whom Jesus warned his listeners to avoid (Matt 23:8). May we seek to hear with our hearts and with our spirits the voice of the God of ages past, who is also the God of the twenty-first century.

WHY WRITE THIS BOOK?

As mentioned, this book almost didn't see the light of day because I was resistant to writing it. It would've been much easier to simply live out what I've written here, which has been hard enough. In fact, I resisted beginning to write the book for several months until my internal wrestling required that I take up the pen. Sometimes we do what we need to do because of our desire. Other times we do it because we can't be at peace until we do. Writing *Grounds for Marriage* came from the latter motivation.

After I began writing, I still resisted from time to time. Writing a book is hard work, especially one that requires the kind of soul-searching that this one demanded. But each time I resisted, I found that it was better just to sit down and write, so that my spirit could settle down and stop nagging me. I would write until whatever was locked inside of me came out, and then I could go on again in peace . . . until the next time my spirit started harassing me.

The resistance I experienced was because I knew that birthing the next paragraph or the next chapter would be painful, rending my heart until I was completely exhausted. This book is a patchwork of pieces of a broken heart that came together to form something that's meaningful and needs to be said, even if it's not well-received by everyone.

Ultimately, I wrote this book because I'm brokenhearted and desire healing for relationships. As a Jesus-follower, I mourn for the state of broken covenant that we see in our marriages, between couples who claim to have an intimate relationship with God, but who don't share an intimate relationship with each other. As a therapist whose work is informed by her own relationship with God, I lament the way believers choose "loyalty to a way of being that comes from a wounded past"[7] over loyalty to their intimate covenant with their spouse. Our hearts are hard, and I long for our faith community, one believer and one couple at a time, to humble itself, to seek God's presence, and to turn from its idols, so that God might restore us to health (2 Chr 7:14). I long for the day when that passage, spoken in ancient times to a wayward Israel, could describe the global faith community in modern times.

Swimming in the pool of sorrow from which this book surfaced was exhausting. Whenever I thought of writing more, I felt tired and weary. Then a client would come into my office with a story of broken relationship, and I'd feel the urgency of this message build up within me again. I could relate to Jeremiah who tried to ignore the fire in his belly and couldn't: "But if I say, 'Forget it! No more God-messages from me!' The words are fire in my belly, a burning in my bones. I'm worn out trying to hold it in. I can't do it any longer!" (Jer 20:8).

The message of this book doesn't necessarily conform to the standard message of the Christian faith community, but I must put words to the fire that is in my belly. I expect that some will call me a heretic at worst, and misguided at best. I expect that others will share the sorrow that drives the writing of this book. I hope this book encourages some to minister from the sorrowful fire in their bellies, too.

THREE FOCUS QUESTIONS

According to statistics, most marriages in our faith community are in disarray, just as they are in the culture at large.[8] So, *how can intimate human relationships reflect intimate relationship with God?* From my perspective as a believer, this is an underlying theme of this book.

---

7. Allender and Longman, *Intimate Mystery*, 52.
8. Ontario Consultants.

From my vantage point as a Licensed Professional Counselor who specializes in the healing of childhood trauma, this book addresses another question. *How can I help people heal from old wounds and turn from harmful ways of being so that they are free to be in a covenant relationship with God and with a covenant companion?*

In my practice, I witness the aftermath of childhood wounds every day. Trauma, both overt and covert, sets people up to make poor choices. Few people seek help as soon as they need it, and in failing to obtain timely, wise counsel, they make more poor choices. I usually see these folks after their poor choices have resulted in horrendous pain to themselves and to others over a period of many years. Even (or especially) in the faith community, we often commit ourselves to an image of reality rather than to what is true. As I help people commit to truth at any cost, I find that marriages can heal only if both parties are willing to walk this path toward fundamental change.

I'm not only a therapist for traumatized individuals; I'm also a survivor of many kinds of childhood trauma, and a person who made poor relational choices in the aftermath of this abuse. I've had to ask another question, which I also address in this book: *How can a person heal from old wounds and then turn from harmful ways of being so that he or she is free to be in a covenant relationship with God and with a covenant companion?*

MY STORY

Perhaps you've seen the anti-tobacco advertisement with the singing cowboy who rides through the streets of New York City, mechanically intoning a cowpoke song through his tracheotomy voice box. He sings, "You don't always die from tobacco / Sometimes you just lose a lung / Oh, you don't always die from tobacco / Sometimes they just snip out your tongue / And you won't sing worth a heck / With a big hole in your neck / 'Cuz you don't always die from tobacco."[9] Sometimes you don't die from an unhealthy relationship choice, either; sometimes you just lose your faith, or your sense of self, or your dreams, or your principles. That's why I share my story in this book: I hope that some will learn from my poor choices and mistakes and avoid unnecessary pain.

---

9. Lyrics printed by permission from the American Legacy Foundation.

I also hope that sharing my story will bring the encouragement of solidarity to others who are in marriage crisis. You're not alone in your pain and in your feelings of failure. I hope that my process of coming to terms with my failure in my marriage will encourage you to do the same. I hope that what I learned from this failure qualifies me to speak with the kind of authority of someone who has escaped the fire and lived to tell of it. My message in a nutshell is this: don't do what I did, but if you already have, there is hope and healing.

I hope, too, that sharing my story will diminish the shame of those who are in or have been through the breakdown of a marriage. In the faith community, the mere mention of some subjects increases shame. Divorce is one of those subjects. As Atkinson says in *To Have and To Hold*, "there are some persons who having been through the trauma of a broken marriage now realize all the more clearly what marriage commitment means and who now—perhaps for the first time—want to call on God's grace for a new start, but find that the church is apparently unable to share with them at the crucial moment."[10] Sadly, the faith community adds the tragedy of rejection to the tragedy of a broken marriage.

Though my former husband and I eventually sought counseling together, we had nothing left in our marriage to salvage by the time we did. Both of us needed individual healing before we could do any meaningful marriage work, but Chip, a victim of subtle but insidious covert abuse, primarily in the form of emotional neglect, never committed wholeheartedly to a healing process, and our relationship became a casualty of the disparity that arises when only one partner seeks healing.[11] To be fair, I don't know if our marriage would've survived even if Chip had chosen to commit to his own healing—we had critical cracks in some of the most essential foundations of relationship.

As a person of faith and integrity, I had to wrestle through the teaching I'd received about divorce before I could ever seek one. Like many, I'd heard the verse "I [God] hate divorce" (Mal 2:16) so many times that I had little room to consider that God hates when we break our "faith-bond with [our] vowed companion," a phrase that comes from the same passage. No one had ever mentioned that part. No one had ever preached on grounds for *marriage*, only on grounds for *divorce*. This, as much as any other factor, set my husband and me up to continually

---

10. Atkinson, *To Have and to Hold*, 10.
11. Graber, *Ghosts in the Bedroom*, 26.

hurt one another for seventeen years, unaware all along that we never understood God's conditions for marriage. I hope that my failure as a covenant companion and my heart of repentance qualifies me to speak about the covenant of marriage from a unique perspective. Sometimes we learn best through our failures.

HOW *GROUNDS FOR MARRIAGE* IS ARRANGED

I approach the topic of grounds for marriage from three perspectives: Jesus-follower, therapist, and covenant-breaker. Each chapter is divided into three main sections, presented in an order that seemed to best address the content of each chapter. One section of each chapter presents a personal reflection, including stories of my personal journey of faith, before, during and after my marriage. Another section of each chapter presents a therapeutic reflection, which includes a review of relevant professional literature and anecdotes from my work as a therapist. Names of particular individuals and various details have been changed to protect confidentiality. And finally, each chapter presents a theological reflection, which includes a review of literature on the subject of the chapter. The review is relatively brief, so I encourage you to seek out the references provided and any others that will help you in your search for truth.

You may be more drawn to one section than to another, and you may choose to skip some sections. Although I've arranged this book in a sequence that seems logical to me, I hope that you'll read this book in whatever order is logical to you.

My training at seminary did a marvelous job of teaching me to read texts well. The "Theological Reflection" in each chapter seeks to read the text of *scripture* well and responsibly. (Not doing so has provided much pain for those in harmful marital unions.) Additionally, we need to read the texts of our *culture* well and responsibly. The "Therapeutic Reflection" in each chapter seeks to do this with a brief review of some of the most poignant literature and research on the subjects at hand. Finally, we need to read the text of the *soul* well and responsibly, an approach that is primarily presented in the "Personal Reflection" section of each chapter (although the "Therapeutic Reflection" sections, with their presentation of clients' stories, also exposes matters of the soul for careful reading and interpretation). This "text, culture, soul" model is a helpful grid to facilitate the understanding and interpretation of the "literature," or stories, of our lives. Unfortunately, these complex texts are not as plain and easy to interpret as some claim.

I approach the topic of marriage and divorce from the perspective of what covenant *is* (chapter 1) before addressing what it *isn't* (chapter 2). Many in the faith community try to determine criteria for healthy relationship by understanding grounds for divorce, which is a faulty starting point. Until we understand what comprises covenant, we cannot even begin to understand appropriate reasons to terminate one. I hope you'll find that focusing first on what makes a covenant work is much more hopeful than justifying its dissolution.

USING THIS BOOK

This book has been gestating for some time, and it needs to be birthed. However, I'm afraid about how the material might be misunderstood or misused. I'd be disheartened if I ever found out that someone had used this text to take vengeance on, or "deal treacherously with" his or her partner (Mal 2:16, NASB). If your marriage is in crisis but you haven't found compassion for your partner, even a partner who has deeply hurt you, I hope that you'll find it as you read this book.

Grounds for Marriage isn't intended to justify a disingenuous decision to divorce, although it may make some aware of previously unknown, legitimate, scriptural permission to seek to separate from their spouse. Even so, the purpose of *Grounds for Marriage* is intended to provide people with a higher view of marriage, not an easy reason to divorce.

Its purpose is fourfold. First, I hope that this book will lead people to a change of heart regarding how they've contributed to the failings in their marriages. If the reader's marriage is broken, *Grounds for Marriage* will lead him or her to walk *through* his or her pain, not around it, to find answers that can heal. This book isn't for those who want to take a short cut around sorrow and grief and soul-searching. At the same time, it won't encourage anyone to ignore the failings of a spouse. Covenant breakdown takes two, and we must be honest with ourselves and with our partners about the sources of harm so that we can inspire true change.

This material is meant to inform and encourage people to maintain both scriptural integrity and compassion as they navigate difficult intrapersonal, interpersonal, and theological terrain. *Grounds for Marriage* can help people in marriage crisis seek to make tough and painful choices about their covenant relationships while trying to be true to scriptural standards for covenant relationship.

Second, I hope this book will encourage readers to courageously study the scriptures for themselves, particularly regarding the covenant of marriage.

Third, I hope this book will help those who are seeking to be married to gauge their readiness for this privilege and responsibility.

Finally, I hope that this book will give clarity and practical suggestions to pastors, teachers, therapists, friends, and any others who are in positions to help those who are in covenant crisis. May this material foster compassion and understanding.

Part 1

Foundations—The Spirit of Ancient Past

1

Happily Ever After—A Match Made in Heaven?

A True Treaty

EVERYONE EXPECTS THAT "ONCE upon a time" will end with, "And they lived happily ever after." The good news is that fairy tale endings are possible under certain conditions. The less-than-good news is that we have to work hard to maintain these conditions, which requires being diligently intentional about practicing a high view of each other as creatures who bear the image of the creator. Happily, doing so creates the conditions that establish grounds for marriage, making beautiful and enduring relationship possible.

A THEOLOGICAL REFLECTION

A "Plain Reading" of Scripture with Regard to Relationship

Although many topics in the Bible require closer scrutiny than a plain reading, some topics are clear with a simple, cursory reading. For example, the Bible is unmistakable about how we're to treat one another. In the first several chapters of Genesis we learn about the basics of human harmony. The book, *All I Really Need to Know I Learned in Kindergarten*,[1] reminds us of the simple building blocks of human relationships, such as sharing, playing fair, being considerate, sincerely apologizing, living in wonder, and being responsible for oneself. Genesis is like that; if it were the only book in the canon, it would provide enough guidance to help us know how to relate to one another in ways that warm God's heart.

---

1. Fulghum, *All I Really Need to Know*.

Genesis describes how God created human beings in his likeness. Unlike any other creature, people are stamped with the imprint of their creator. Genesis 1:27 reads, "God created human beings / he created them godlike / Reflecting God's nature." There's something unique about human beings, says the writer of Genesis: we bear the insignia of the creator in a way that no other creature does, and this ought to leave us breathless with awe and reverence for one another. This is all we need to know and practice if we want to live in interpersonal peace and harmony.

Because of our responsibility to treat one another with dignity and respect, some scholars have suggested that we're all in covenant (an agreement between two people built on promise) with one another.[2] Based on how the scriptures describe our responsibility to one another and the corresponding rewards and consequences (note the Ten Commandments, for example), I have to agree. Simply being granted the privilege to breathe God's air as an image-bearer requires that I act in an honorable way toward other human beings, other image-bearers.

In *Weight of Glory*, C.S. Lewis wrote:

> It is a serious thing to live in a society of possible gods and goddesses, to remember that the dullest and most uninteresting person you talk to may one day be a creature which, if you saw it now, you would be strongly tempted to worship—or else a horror and a corruption such as you now meet, if at all, only in a nightmare. All day long we are, in some degree, helping each other to one or the other of these destinations. It is in the light of these overwhelming possibilities, it is with the awe and the circumspection proper to them, that we should conduct all our dealings with one another, all friendships, all loves, all play, all politics. There are no ordinary people.[3]

Can you imagine what the world would be like if we all were suddenly struck with the wonder of our neighbor's image-bearing dignity? If all of us were to live in awe of that, my job as a counselor would become obsolete. We wouldn't wound each other, or whatever offenses did occur could be rapidly and genuinely repaired without professional assistance. If only.

---

2. Atkinson, *To Have and To Hold*, 71.
3. Lewis, *Weight of Glory*, 45–6.

In addition to giving us the grounds for harmonious human relationships, Genesis also tells about the origin of conflict between individuals and between people and God when we fail to treat others with reverence. By the sixth chapter of the Bible, we read of such blatant disregard for others that, "God was sorry that he made the human race in the first place; it broke his heart" (6:5-7). God took a hard look at the state of affairs and saw that "the earth had become a sewer; there was violence everywhere. God took one look and saw how bad it was, everyone corrupt and corrupting—life itself corrupt to the core" (6:11-12). So God decided to clean house, sparing only Noah and his family, because "God liked what he saw in Noah . . . [He was] a good man, a man of integrity in his community" (6:8-10).

What would happen if each of us chose to be men and women of integrity in our communities? Noah proves to us that it's possible to live with integrity in a violent, corrupt society, and that people like him may prevent great destruction in our world. His treatment of his fellow image-bearers shows us what blessing can come from living with respect for God's creation.

The scriptures say that after destroying the land with a flood, God, through Noah, reinstated his relationship with those who bear his image. In God's blessing of Noah and his family, he reminded them of the sanctity of human life: "Whoever sheds human blood / by humans let his blood be shed / Because God made humans in his image / reflecting God's very nature" (9:6-7). Here, after God gave the human race a second chance, he reminded people of the reason we are to be so careful with human lives: we bear the image of the divine.

Unfortunately, it wasn't long before the human race again became corrupt, and God walked with another man of integrity, Abraham. The rest of Genesis tells narrative after narrative about the maltreatment of one person to another, with the hopeful ending that God is big enough to use our harm of others to turn evil on itself. After Joseph's brothers tried to eliminate him because of their father's favoritism, Joseph said, "Don't you see, you planned evil against me but God used those same plans for my good, as you see all around you right now—life for many people" (Gen 50:19-21).

While I'm grateful that God can use evil in the service of good, it's also clear that he's broken-hearted when he has to. He didn't create people to behave like rats, and when we do, it reflects badly on his image in us.

An Old Testament Hermeneutic of Human Relationships

A plain reading of the rest of scripture reinforces Genesis' message. *Exodus*, for example, tells the story of God's deliverance of his people when they're treated with indignity by the Egyptians. He promises to protect his people, and he establishes a written law to govern relationships. *Leviticus* describes what it looks like to live virtuously as people who represent God. *Numbers* tells of a community that honors God, living out justice and mercy. *Deuteronomy* reminds the people of Israel about their experience with God, including his covenant with them and their agreement to keep its conditions (reverence for God and one another) in exchange for God's provision and protection.

The history books (from *Joshua* to *Esther*) also reinforce the message of proper treatment of one human being to another by describing God's blessings when they honor his covenant and his judgments when they fail to do so. The wisdom literature (from *Job* through the *Song of Songs*, including *Proverbs*) also features powerful messages about human relationship.

In many places, Proverbs reads as simply as a primer on how to live well in relationship:

- "Good character is the best insurance / crooks get trapped in their sinful lust" (11:6).
- "Exploit or abuse your family, and end up with a fistful of air / common sense tells you it's a stupid way to live" (11:29).
- "Whitewashing bad people and throwing mud on good people / are equally abhorrent to God" (17:15).
- "Remove the wicked from leadership / and authority will be credible and God-honoring" (25:5).
- "You can't whitewash your sins and get by with it / you find mercy by admitting and leaving them" (28:13).
- "Speak up for the people who have no voice / for the rights of all the down-and-outers / Speak out for justice! / Stand up for the poor and destitute" (31:8–9).

Verses like these, and there are hundreds like them throughout scripture, give credence to the idea that we're all in an implied covenant with everyone else, simply by virtue of being human. Since this book is specifically about the particular covenant of marriage, let's note that these verses apply to marriage, as well. Proverbs 25:5 doesn't say, for example, "Remove the wicked from leadership (unless the leader is your spouse)." Proverbs 17:15 doesn't say, "Whitewashing bad people (unless it's your wife) and throwing mud on good people (unless it's your husband) are equally abhorrent to God." Proverbs 11:6 doesn't read, "Good character is the best insurance; crooks get trapped in their sinful lust, (but try to keep your loved ones from getting caught in their own poor choices)." These principles apply to all of us, no matter what type of relationship we have with each other.

The prophets (*Isaiah* through *Malachi*) speak for God, reminding the Israelites of the covenantal blessings for obedience to God and of the covenantal consequences for disobedience, as first laid out to Moses.[4] The gauge by which their hearts were tested was mostly how they treated one another, which was considered to be a reflection of their regard (or disregard) of God himself. When relational corruption, particularly sexual deviation, was rampant, the prophets warned of the curses that had been decreed in the original covenant. When the people lived out reverence and love for God, the prophets encouraged them with reminders of God's promised blessings for their faithfulness. The prophetic messages weren't new—they simply reinforced what was already spoken in the Pentateuch. Again, the message is that we express our wonder of God through our careful treatment of people.

Here are some messages regarding relationship as spoken by the prophets:

- "Say no to wrong / Learn to do good. / Work for justice. / Help the down-and-out. / Stand up for the homeless. / Go to bat for the defenselesss" (Isa 1:17).
- "This is God's Message: Attend to matters of justice. Set things right between people. Rescue victims from their exploiters. Don't take advantage of the homeless, the orphans, the widows. Stop the murdering!" (Jer 22:3).
- "Do what is fair and just to your neighbor / be compassionate and loyal in your love / And don't take yourself too seriously— / take God seriously" (Mic 6:8).

---

4. Fee and Stuart, *How to Read the Bible for All Its Worth*, 181–204.

- "Tell the truth, the whole truth, when you speak. Do the right thing by one another, both personally and in your courts. Don't cook up plans to take unfair advantage of others. Don't do or say what isn't so. I hate all that stuff. Keep your lives simple and honest" (Zech 8:15–17).

A New Testament Hermeneutic of Human Relationships

Like the prophetic writings, the New Testament reinforces the message of the Old regarding our obligation to think highly of one another. Remember these passages:

- "Do you want to stand out? Then step down. Be a servant. If you puff yourself up, you'll get the wind knocked out of you. But if you're content to simply be yourself, your life will count for plenty" (Matt 23:11–12).
- ". . . You shouldn't act as if everything is fine when one of your Christian companions is promiscuous or crooked, is flip with God or rude to friends, gets drunk or becomes greedy and predatory. You can't just go along with this, treating it as acceptable behavior. I'm not responsible for what the outsiders do, but don't we have some responsibility for those within our community of believers? God decides on the outsiders, but we need to decide when our brothers and sisters are out of line and, if necessary, clean house" (1 Cor 5:10–13).
- "Say nothing evil or hurtful / Snub evil and cultivate good / run after peace for all you're worth. / God looks on all this with approval / listening and responding well to what he's asked / But he turns his back on those who do evil things" (1 Pet 3:9–12).

It's important to remember that these passages are isolated from their contexts here, which can lead to faulty interpretation. However, a plain reading yields the unmistakable message repeated continuously throughout the Bible: our behavior toward one another, along with our requirement for respect from others, reveals our spiritual health. We would do well to examine our hearts to determine what our life conveys. For help with this, our family members are often the best sources of information. We tend to treat people we meet in public with more respect than we treat those in our own family, whom we tend to take for granted. So, if you really want to know how well you're loving *God*, ask your spouse, your children, your closest friends how you're treating *them*, and be open to an honest response.

A Plain Reading of Scripture with Regard to Marriage

When we talk about a plain reading of scripture with regard to marriage, we must first recognize that, because of the special nature of marriage as a reflection of the intimate union that we can have with God (Ephesians 5:22–23), the principles that govern non-marital relationships apply *even more so* to the marriage relationship. If you're to love your neighbor as yourself, you're to love your wife even more—as Christ loved the church. If you're to respect your neighbor, you're to respect your husband even more. If you're to hold your neighbor accountable for poor behavior, you're to hold your spouse even more accountable. If you're to be gentle with your neighbor, you're to be even gentler with your spouse. Depending on the circumstances, every interaction between two people needs to have some balance of strength and tenderness. As this is true in human relationships in general, it's even truer in marriage.

Let's take a look at the first couple in the scriptures.

The first human relationship in the scriptures is a covenantal union. God gives the lonely man, Adam, his counterpart, a special creation, Eve, to partner with him in the Garden of Eden. Adam is so relieved and overjoyed that he responds with the first poetry recorded in the Bible (Gen 2:23). Their relationship beautifully illustrates the "one-flesh" union of covenant partnership. Sadly, this first couple doesn't live happily ever after. In addition to providing the first example of intimate communion, they also provide the first example of human conflict. Their grasping to be like God leaves them not only knowing both good and evil but also feeling the curse of this knowledge. Adam resorts to ruling, and Eve resorts to controlling—a battle that's been raging ever since.

Fortunately, the battle of the sexes can be managed as long as we address it with the same dignity with which we're to treat all other relationships. A husband or wife who's dishonoring the other should be treated with the same balance of strength and tenderness with which we're to treat others. Not to require this runs counter to the biblical principles of integrity that we've already seen, and the church has often been guilty of allowing such dishonoring to continue—passively, through neglect of the less powerful partner in inequitable relationships, or actively, through false or inadequate teaching. Remember, intimate covenant relationships should be governed by even greater respect than any other human relationship because they reflect spiritual union with God.

Although loving your spouse falls generally under the category of "loving your neighbor," covenant companionship carries a much deeper spiritual meaning, rooted deeply within scripture. Marriage is one of those topics in the Bible that requires more than a plain reading to get a full picture of what scripture teaches. It's critical to understand the ancient Hebrew language and customs in order to interpret the scriptures responsibly, as we'll see in the next several chapters. A surface reading of scripture with regard to marriage misses much of the richness intended for this union. We need to dig deeper into the context of scripture for a better understanding of this most sacred of relationships.

The Meaning of the Marriage Covenant—Then and Now

A phenomenal resource with regard to the marriage covenant is *The Intimate Mystery*. In this book, Allender and Longman address the purpose of marriage, a concept that few contemplate before they enter this most sacred union. "The goal of marriage," Allender and Longman explain, "is to reveal God."[5] God is a relational being, and he's made his creatures relational beings, as well. God created male and female in his image, which means that men and women reveal something unique about God's character, and nowhere is this design clearer than in a marriage between a man and a woman. God himself is the perfect marriage of masculine and feminine—the complete expression of both genders together—and marriage is a reflection of God's being.

The passage in Genesis 2:24 provides the initial grounds for marriage: "Therefore a man leaves his father and mother and embraces his wife. They shall become one flesh." In order for intimacy to occur, both the man and the woman must leave their parents emotionally in order to be free to cleave to their new spouse with no emotional strings attached to their families of origin.

As Allender and Longman explain, "leaving [in the ancient Near East] was a division that implied a degree of privacy and primacy . . .

---

5. Allender and Longman, *Intimate Mystery*, 20.

[T]he relationship was to be given a primacy that supplanted all other commitments and loyalties—even to one's own parents."[6]

If a man or a woman isn't prepared to leave his or her parents emotionally, the couple doesn't have solid grounds for marriage. Allender and Longman say that "loyalty to a way of being that comes from a wounded past"[7] is the most difficult loyalty to discern, and it's the most difficult attachment to walk away from. Such *past baggage* is one of the three potholes, along with *contempt for differences* and *failure to grow*, that Allender and Longman peg for marital discord. We must forsake the baggage of our families of origin, forging a new way of being as a couple if we want to honor God's purpose for covenant companionship.

God also reveals himself through his covenant with Israel, a concept for chapter 3. Suffice it to say for now that God desires intimacy with his people, but that he's not willing to suffer divided loyalties forever. To be intimate with God, we must leave our idols and cleave to him with our whole hearts. When we're unfaithful, God requires confession and repentance as conditions for repair and reconciliation of relationship. Otherwise, we must accept that our relationship with God will be obstructed to the degree that our loyalty is divided. If we want deep intimacy, we must lay down whatever ideas, attitudes, beliefs, people, or things are more important to us than he is. There are always consequences to broken covenant. Fortunately, there's a way to repair our broken promises.

The Torah only indirectly addresses specific grounds for marriage. In the Jewish tradition, the most significant reason for marriage is to "be fruitful and multiply" (referred to as the "cultural mandate"), one of the 613 commands that the Jews believed to be given by God in the Torah. This concept was so deeply embedded in the covenant of marriage that a couple who didn't bear children within ten years of their marriage was expected to divorce and remarry someone with whom they might be able to have children.[8] Although infertility is never scripturally sanctioned as grounds for divorce, the Jews treated it as such.

While covenant partnership is certainly the proper context for bearing and rearing children, God created the union between a man and a woman because, unlike the animals, Adam had no mate. "It's not good

---

6. Ibid., 37.
7. Ibid., 52.
8. Instone-Brewer, *Divorce and Remarriage in the Bible*, 92.

for the Man to be alone," God said. "I'll make him a helper, a companion" (Gen 2:18).

So marriage was created to provide companionship for life and to create a context to rear children who bear the likeness of their parents and the image of God. How the woman and the man are to relate to one another in the context of their marriage may be illusive to those who forget that the scriptures are full of injunctions regarding how we're to minister to one another as human beings. While the Torah is surprisingly quiet on how a married couple ought to treat one another, it is deafeningly unyielding on how people in general, no matter what their relationship, ought to regard one another.

Other than providing a specific context for emotional and sexual intimacy (Gen 2:18 refers to companionship), and for children to grow in the knowledge of their creator (Mal 2:15), grounds for marriage are no different than for any other relationship: reverence and awe for another human being made in the image of God. When *both* spouses regard one another with dignity, intimate companionship will inevitably follow, and *together* the two will, through God's design, reveal both the strength and tenderness of the creator to their children.

A PERSONAL REFLECTION

Several years ago, I attended a two-day seminar in Vancouver, B.C. On the morning of the second day, I stood on the balcony outside my hotel room, several floors above street level, watching the city awaken. One woman in particular caught my attention when she disembarked from a bus that had pulled up in front of my hotel. The woman was blind and was accompanied by a seeing-eye dog. As I watched, she walked to the nearest intersection, pressed the "walk" signal on the light post, crossed to the other side when the signal changed, turned right when she made it to the sidewalk on the other side, and completed the twenty yard trek to another bus stop. There she waited several minutes until the next bus she needed arrived.

I was amazed. What had it taken for this non-seeing woman and her dog to learn to function so deftly in a seeing world? I admired her courage and tenacity. Everyone around her equally amazed me. She was the picture of vulnerability, and any one could have easily taken advantage of her handicap. But no one tried to take her purse, no one tried to interfere with her progress, and no one tried to trick her or her dog.

Instead, they treated her with respect and dignity. Without even thinking about it, the people of Vancouver reflected the tender care of God for his creatures when they cared so well for a blind woman amongst them. It was a beautiful sight.

I'll never forget the day when my husband, Chip, reflected God's care to me in an especially beautiful way. We'd been trying to have children for eight years to no avail. I'd assumed that having children would come as easily and as naturally as all of my other endeavors, as naturally as it seemed to come to our friends. I'd never even considered the possibility of failing, or I might not have tried to conceive. The word *infertility* was just a word, and the experience was beyond my imagination.

However, after several months of failing to conceive, it was clear that I wasn't in control. Our friends were having children all around us, even those who were trying to prevent pregnancy, and I remained barren. It seemed like a cruel joke. After a year, Chip and I began the shameful and lengthy process of trying to identify the problem. The testing became increasingly invasive and embarrassing, and no one was able to figure out what the problem was.

Every month when I began my menstrual cycle, I experienced a new cycle of grief. As months turned into years, my hope turned to despair. The longer I went without conceiving, the stronger my desire became to have a child. I'd never noticed how babies were used as marketing ploys, but suddenly it seemed like baby advertisements were all over the place. I'd never noticed pregnant women before, but they seemed to be everywhere. It was depressing to attend our small group at church where it felt like someone was announcing a new pregnancy, a new birth, or a new baby shower every week.

After a couple years, Chip and I began to consider fertility treatments. I began taking Clomid, a drug used to stimulate the ovaries to produce multiple eggs. The medication made me so edgy that I had to discontinue using it for my sanity's sake. Still, every month I would allow my hopes to rise, only to be disappointed each time I was found not to be pregnant. The grieving process had no end—it was like someone died every month.

Years passed, and we continued to seek more sophisticated fertility treatments, all to no avail. The shame I felt was immense. I pled with God for a child, but the heavens were silent. I knew that God could intervene, and it didn't make sense to me why he didn't. Perhaps he withheld children from us because he knew something dreadful that we didn't know. Perhaps he knew that I'd be a bad parent, and wanted to spare any children the damage I'd inflict on them. Or maybe this was true of Chip? But other people, people who were clearly unfit to rear children, such as addicts and teenagers, were getting pregnant, and God didn't seem to be preventing that. I couldn't make sense of a God who could change things and didn't, and it bothered me that I was having such questions— I thought I'd resolved my questions about God's trustworthiness long before during the process of coming to terms with various abuses in my childhood. But suddenly, God seemed like the abuser again.

I began to hate going to church . . . all I did was cry there. God's presence was especially real to me through prayer and music, and I couldn't escape my emotions at church. Every week, I found myself grieving. People often made insensitive comments due to their own ignorance, and every comment cut to the core of my soul.

During one intense moment of anguish, I asked Chip, "Where's God in this? He's completely absent, and I feel like he's abandoned us."

Chip drew me into his arms and I wept bitter tears against his chest for several minutes. He was silent for a while as he held me, but then he spoke. "Do you feel my arms around you?" Chip asked. I nodded. "These are the arms of God."

It was a beautiful moment. With those words Chip captured the essence of what it means to bear the image of God. As image-bearers we can minister the presence of God to other image-bearers, and when we do, we live out our lofty calling. When we treat others with high regard, we show our wonder toward one another and we reflect on a physical level the relationship we can have with God on a spiritual level.

A THERAPEUTIC REFLECTION

As we work with clients, therapists have the same privilege. Often, the therapeutic relationship is the first one in which an individual experiences what it feels like to be treated with dignity. In this way, therapists can image to the world relationship with God.

Psychology pioneer Carl Rogers (1902–1987) modeled this high regard of people in his client-centered approach to counseling. The concept of "mirroring" is one of his most significant contributions to the therapeutic relationship. Mirroring refers to the dialogic practice of reflecting back to the speaker the words that the receiver has heard.

Without adding any commentary or opinion, the listener simply uses the words of the speaker to demonstrate attentive listening. In this way the receiver images, or reflects, the message of his or her partner, sending a clear message of respect and care, a feature of relating that keeps covenants strong. As I work with clients, I incorporate this kind of dialogue in counseling sessions, modeling for them the kind of communication that helps maintains a healthy covenantal bond.

In his best-selling book, *Getting the Love You Want*, Hendrix takes this concept into the world of marriage therapy to help couples communicate effectively by listening accurately, understanding and validating their partner's point of view, and expressing empathy for their partner's feelings. The "Couple's Dialogue"[9] is an exercise in which partners mirror or reflect back to each other what they hear the other saying, using the following steps:

First, the couple chooses who will be the sender and who will be the receiver. Second, the sender describes what she's thinking or feeling. The receiver then mirrors, repeats back, what he hears his partner express, using as many of the words of his partner as possible. Then the receiver asks if he understands accurately, and if the sender affirms that he does, the receiver asks if there's more. This process continues until the sender feels the receiver has heard and understood everything communicated. Third, the receiver summarizes the whole message. Fourth, the receiver validates the sender's message, affirming that the sender has made sense to the receiver. Fifth, the receiver then expresses empathy for the feelings of the sender. Sixth, when the receiver has completed mirroring, validating, and showing empathy, he asks permission to respond. Then the individuals switch roles and the receiver becomes the sender. During this process, the receiver may ask clarifying questions, but shouldn't analyze the partner or make interpretations or express frustrations or criticisms.

When I use this exercise in my work with clients, I add a step between steps five and six. I encourage the receiver to ask what the partner needs from him or her regarding the topic of discussion. This creates a spirit of teamwork and provides a context of healing for old wounds re-injured or new ones inflicted. It also communicates that the receiver thinks highly of the speaker, and wishes to respect his or her needs and interests.

9. Hendrix, *Getting the Love You Want*, 261–64.

I also suggest that the couple take a substantial break before switching roles so as to: 1) keep the conversation slow enough to increase the likelihood of empathic connection; and 2) ensure that both partners have the opportunity to feel completely heard and understood.

(See Appendix A for a reproducible worksheet to help couples learn the skill of active listening.)

SNEAK PREVIEW OF THE NEXT CHAPTER

Committing to do no harm as we seek to understand people and scripture provides a safe and sound foundation for understanding grounds for healthy relationships, particularly grounds for marriage. Now that we've established what covenant *is*, chapter 2 will explore what covenant *isn't*.

2

Happily Never After—Mates By Mistake?

A False Treaty

A THERAPEUTIC ALLIANCE IS a special kind of covenant. In the first few sessions, my clients and I establish agreements for our work together. We discuss my theoretical framework; we talk about what confidentiality means; we establish therapeutic goals and a treatment plan; we talk about how to manage our session time; we establish financial agreements; we discuss professional practices. We also talk about what will happen if either of us fails to keep our agreements—our covenant—for the relationship.

These agreements include stipulations to guard the safety of the relationship. I agree to treat my clients professionally and ethically, to honor their internal and external boundaries, and not to abandon them, but provide them with credible referrals if, for whatever reason, I leave the practice before they're finished with treatment. If I fail to follow through on the terms of our contract (covenant), I could suffer legal consequences in some circumstances (e.g., if I am found to be practicing unethically or unprofessionally).

In turn, my clients agree not to verbally abuse me, not to threaten me, and not to attempt suicide in my presence. If my clients engage in this kind of behavior, they know that the therapeutic relationship will likely be terminated. Establishing the parameters of the therapeutic relationship sometimes takes several sessions, but it's critical to lay the foundation so that each party knows and agrees to what's expected from both sides. The "Professional Disclosure/Informed Consent" document, signed by all parties, stipulates the grounds for our covenant and the consequences for breaking it.

A THERAPEUTIC REFLECTION: COVENANT VS. BETRAYAL BOND

Establishing a marriage covenant occurs in a similar fashion, and my work with couples in crisis has led me to consider the idea that God isn't the author of every marriage. This is obvious to some denominations of the faith community, but in others such an idea is heretical. According to the scriptures, marriage was designed by God to be a union between two people who are to protect and provide for one another in a way that physically mirrors the spiritual relationship that God desires to have with human beings. However, I see many couples who, instead of enjoying a marriage covenant that reflects their relationship with God, have entered into a bond that re-enacts their childhood trauma.

Of the thirty clients I see each week, about twenty of them are in marriages that have all the features of a betrayal bond, sometimes called a trauma bond, defined as a "highly addictive attachment to the people who have hurt you."[1] The motivations that drive these bonds are usually outside of our conscious awareness, so we can come to recognize them only if we're willing to enter the pain of our past.

We tend to marry people at our same level of dysfunction,[2] so it's likely that if you take unresolved wounds with you into your adult life, you'll marry someone who's just as hurt and confused as you. In order to resolve our past wounds, we get ourselves into familiar-feeling situations, hoping that we can get them to resolve differently. Mental health professionals call this a "repetition compulsion."[3]

Unfortunately, because of this compulsion, many people enter into a false marriage covenant, forged by an unconscious motivation to re-enact their childhood experiences. A false covenant is an agreement based on false pretenses, a kind of union I often see. Many people in our culture converge two traumatic histories when pairs of broken people unwittingly find mates that can help them re-create the familiar features of their chaotic histories, hoping to resolve past hurts. As someone has said, however, doing the same thing over and over again expecting different results is the definition of insanity. To be sure, such a union is crazy-making.

---

1. Carnes, *Betrayal Bond*, xvi.
2. Graber, *Ghosts in the Bedroom*, 25.
3. Carnes, *Betrayal Bond*, 24.

Betrayal bonds are not legitimate grounds for marriage. I believe that marriages forged in this kind of chaos are man-made, not God-ordained, although some could become workable unions. If we believe that all marriages are made in heaven and are God's unchangeable will, we set people up for tremendous disillusionment about God's trustworthiness. If we acknowledge, however, that people can make poor choices and mistakes in every area of their lives, including marriage choices, we can allow the God of all compassion and understanding to forgive us and to restore our broken lives. I'm not sure how large sectors of the Christian faith community came to dogmatically teach that a poor marital choice is the only mistake that must be corrected within the relationship or not at all, regardless of the impossibility of success in some situations. Sometimes such an approach spells a death sentence, literally, for those who accept this idea, and for their children who become the innocent casualties in these unions.

Let me be clear. Dissolving a marriage covenant, whether it's a false covenant or a true one, isn't something to do lightly, and I've never seen anyone do so flippantly. In my experience, people don't rush into separation or divorce; they resist it, so as not to lose the approval of those who shun people with marriage problems. The only thing people resist more than dissolving their betrayal bonds is getting help with resolving their conflicts before they have no other choice but to end their destructive union.

The couples I work with often enter counseling after they've avoided looking honestly at their marriages far too long, doing horrible damage instead of seeking help before there is nothing left to salvage. I suspect that many marriages could be mended if the partners would humble themselves and get counsel early and often. Having worked with couples early in their relationships and with those who've waited years to deal with the pain they've built up, I much prefer working with those who seek help early. It's painful to watch couples come limping into session, having emotionally bludgeoned one another during the week.

I don't mean to suggest that we should evaluate our marriage choices lightly or that we should automatically choose to divorce if we discover that we've bound ourselves to trauma instead of a God-honoring covenant in our marriage. Reconciliation is always the preferable outcome of an honest look at a trauma bond, marriage or otherwise, and some are courageous enough to break the traumatic features of the bond so that they can discover whether or not they're able to enter into a true covenant together.

Emma and Terry

Emma and Terry's story illustrates the hard work of identifying the origins and outcomes of one's betrayal bonds. Emma had been reared by a controlling mother and a passive father who didn't require that his spouse honor her covenant commitments; he merely removed the kids from their mother's presence when she drank herself into a rage, depression, or frenzy. Emma learned early in her life that she'd have to protect herself and that she needed to control her world. Although she longed for the affection and nurture of her mother, she learned to put her needs aside, in deference to her mother's.

Emma decided that if she was a good little girl, she could prevent her parents from arguing and her mother from drinking. Emma became the peacemaker between her mom and dad, even when it was revealed that her mom had broken her covenant in another way—by having an affair.

When her mom's unfaithfulness was discovered, Emma became her mom's confidante. As an adolescent, she heard all about her mom's sexual dissatisfaction with her father and how exciting it was for her mom to be with another man. Emma watched her mom dress seductively to go jogging and learned that such behavior could win her the attention of men.

But Emma had first learned of her feminine power long before. When she was six years old, a fifteen-year-old neighbor enticed her into the family camper with the promise of playing a game. Instead, he molested her. Emma never told anyone her secret because she was sure that she was somehow responsible for the event, and she knew that she'd get in trouble if anyone ever found out. So she carried the burden alone.

Although Emma had been taught that sex outside of marriage was wrong, her mother had modeled for her a way to get the male attention that she'd longed for all of her life, and she entered into a sexual relationship with a friend when she was eighteen years old. This boy, Terry, was a couple years younger than she, but Emma enjoyed his company and his worship of her. She was also compelled by the chance to fix Terry, who seemed immature, impressionable, and helpless. Emma's mother expressed her disgust for the young man whose body was undeveloped—she was convinced that his body would never fill out into a manly form—and she told Emma that the thought of the two of them being sexually involved nauseated her. However, when they were caught having sex a couple of years into their relationship, Emma's parents insisted they get married.

So they did. Emma wedded her project. Terry could provide for her a golden opportunity to fix an impossible situation, which would redeem her previous failure to fix the impossible situation of her family of origin. Instead of making an exclusive commitment to Terry for the rest of her life, she was still highly addictively attached to the people who had hurt her, so she was unconsciously determined to make her marriage a place to assuage all of her pain and shame.

Terry, on the other hand, wedded his savior. Terry was relieved to have found someone so competent and wise and controlling as Emma. His own family of origin was chaotic, with a violent father whose wartime experience had left him mean-spirited and unpredictable. Terry's mother was ineffectual against such rage, and Terry desperately wanted someone to make his world orderly. Emma was his ticket to a stable life.

Six months into their marriage, at the age of nineteen, Terry suffered an accident that left him physically disabled. Emma was angry with God, but she redoubled her efforts to fix Terry, prodding him to do his physical therapy exercises and to get back on his feet. Terry made significant progress with Emma's strong leadership, but his body still carried permanent damage.

Emma had become as disgusted with Terry's body as her mom had been, but she forced herself to engage in sexual activity with him because she desperately wanted a child. Finally, after a struggle with infertility, Emma conceived and bore a son, who became the first bearer of the family dysfunction to the next generation.

Emma immediately bonded with her son in an emotionally incestuous manner, which likely contributed to his gender confusion. Of course, it didn't help that one of his uncles also struggled with gender confusion and another with cross-dressing.

All of these issues were covered up by chronic spiritualizing. When Emma began seeing me for therapy, it was clear that she was resistant to looking honestly at the dysfunctional patterns in her family system.

I began to notice a pattern in our sessions: Emma came to sessions ready to defend her breaches of the covenant, including several extramarital affairs, and her belief system, which I believe was motivated more by fear than by devotion. She was terrified that if she admitted her mistakes that God would punish her.

After each session, I wondered why Emma came. She didn't challenge her preconceived notions, and she was committed to keeping up an image at all costs rather than facing the truth. Although she did attend my sexual abuse survivor's group based on Allender's book, *The Wounded Heart*, and although she did make some progress in combating her spiritually-defended black-and-white thinking, she eventually dropped out of therapy when I suggested that we address the patterns that had begun to emerge in our sessions.

There were times when I caught a glimpse of Emma's sweet, tender heart, and I hope that she'll decide that personal integrity, defined well by Larry Crabb as "a commitment to never pretend about anything,"[4] is more important than acquiring the approval of her parents. When push came to shove, Emma needed to continue to control her world, so she couldn't embrace a way of thinking that she hadn't considered before. As far as I know, Emma and Terry are currently trying to conceive another child. My concern is that Emma won't return to therapy until life has squeezed her so hard that she can't breathe—after many years have passed, and after she has inflicted much pain on her husband and on her innocent child.

I got to know Terry when his counselor and I conducted conjoint counseling sessions with the couple. Terry contributed to the mess of his relationship with Emma, including his avoidance of addressing, in any meaningful way, Emma's multiple affairs. As Terry struggled to take responsibility for his own life, he continued to allow Emma to mother him, which he both resented and appreciated. He, too, had attached to his trauma, and he, too, is responsible for the damage that his child will suffer for not resolving the pain that compels him to remain in this betrayal bond.

As far as I know, Emma and Terry maintain their trauma bond to this day, thinking it's a true covenant, though it has none of the features of healthy relationship as described in chapter 1. As is true of betrayal bonds, the power of Emma and Terry's is as strong as the trauma that created it. Breaking such bonds is difficult because it requires us to deal with the original wounds that bound us to those who betrayed us.

---

4. Crabb, *Inside Out*, 192.

A PERSONAL REFLECTION

My own marriage represented a betrayal bond rather than a true covenant, as well, and the pain of trauma re-enactment began to catch up with me six years after Chip and I were married. At age twenty-six, I finally humbled myself and sought help with a counselor, John King. A few weeks into the relationship, John recommended that I read *Inside Out*, by Larry Crabb, and it opened my heart to understand the ways that I'd been trying to make life work on my own terms. I became convicted of the hardness of heart that was contributing to the breakdown of my six-year marriage.

The failure of my marriage had worn me down. I wanted to be kind to my husband, like I was to everyone else, but it seemed I couldn't sustain my kindness for long, and I had come to hate myself for my failure. My strategies to make life work were failing me, so I was ripe to understand why, even if it meant that I had to acknowledge that my heart was hard. I was relieved to discover as I read *Inside Out* that it's possible to change; I only needed to be willing to face the truth, whatever the truth may be. When I finished reading *Inside Out*, John suggested that I read *The Wounded Heart*, by Dan Allender, which presented God to me in a way that I'd never seen him before: I encountered a suffering God, one who could empathize with the pain in my heart because, in his incarnation, he'd experienced the pain of the human condition.

By the time I'd finished reading these books, I'd encountered a God whose love I couldn't resist. My heart was broken and soft. For the first time since I was a child, I felt alive. My heart was changed.

If relationship with God had erased all the wounds and the wrong strategies I'd developed to save myself from more pain, my marriage might have been happy from that point on, but a changed heart doesn't alter every unhealthy psycho-spiritual pattern instantaneously. Also, recovering from marriage breakdown takes two, and my husband had his own healing process to go through. Though Chip continued to avoid facing the problems, I continued to try to *make* our relationship work, like a child who tries to put a square block in a round hole; together, we continued to bump along in (almost) the same manner we always had. Though I had a new bent—an inclination toward honesty and awareness—I still had old habits. I was inclined toward self-protection, manifested, for example, as over-functioning. Chip, too, had self-protective habits, including passivity and avoidance, and our marriage continued to suffer from the clash of our destructive styles of relating.

It took almost ten more years before I began to evaluate my marriage even more honestly. The frustration that accumulated during this time finally prepared me to face the truth, at any cost. In *The Road Less Traveled*, M. Scott Peck says that mental health is "an ongoing process of dedication to reality at all costs,"[5] and, as I tested this axiom, I found it to be true.

My pursuit of reality at any cost came at a high price, though. The first price I paid was with my own pride. I had to face the fact that I was a significant contributor to our marriage becoming a broken covenant. My greatest fear since childhood was failure, so I'd avoided any task in which I wasn't ensured success. My marriage, however, was a glaring exception to that commitment never to fail, and I had to face the fact that I couldn't make our marriage work on my own. Chip and I had managed to keep our marital difficulties mostly private, so when I rigorously evaluated the relationship, I committed to no longer hiding the fact that we were in crisis. Although I only shared details about our issues with a few very close friends and with my therapist, I committed to no longer present an image that wasn't true.

My commitment to truth led me to face some ugly things about myself. I came to realize over time and through various events that I had chosen, unconsciously, to marry Chip as a way to re-create, and hopefully resolve, my childhood pain. I had to admit that, as self-aware as I thought I was, I'd been compelled by an unconscious motivation to make the pain go away, and in my compulsion, I'd entered a betrayal bond, not a true covenant. In the process I'd harmed an innocent victim, my husband.

It was a horrible reality to face, but I could no longer deny the truth. After I made this connection, I experienced both relief (due to finally understanding something that hadn't made sense for a long time) and dread (due to the implications of the truth). Eventually, I described this reality to Chip in counseling by sharing a letter that I'd written to him. The beginning of the letter describes this betrayal bond:

---

5. Peck, *Road Less Traveled*, 50.

Dear Chip,

I hardly know how to express what I need to confess to you. I just realized what I have to say last night when preparing to do my counseling homework assignment, which was this letter, expressing my needs and longings. Writing this letter put several loose ends together for me.

After I jotted down some notes, I began. "Dear Chip, my childhood buddy," I wrote. But I couldn't go on. There was something about that phrase that didn't seem quite right, and my stomach churned within me. Certainly we met when we were young, and I've often said that we married as kids. This is partially true, but the phrase "childhood buddy" seemed just a bit too young to truly describe our reality at eighteen and nineteen. Then I realized that my childhood buddy was my brother *Davie*, and I knew why my stomach was churning. When I met you, I experienced you as lost, dazed, dreamy, insecure, childlike, sexy, wiry. I experienced you as Davie; I'd unconsciously found a "brother" to revoke his abandonment of me when I stopped the sexual abuse. Who you *really* were, neither one of us knew, but that didn't matter to me. I'd found a way to both rescue my brother (for whom I've always felt compassion, with his unfortunate hand of cards) and to get him to love me. If I could rescue you, and if you could love me, you'd fill my brother-hole. My heart sank when I realized this last night, and I wanted to throw up. I hadn't fallen in love with you, Chip. I'd fallen in love with Davie. I've known for a long time that I've objectified you in demanding that you heal my father wounds, but I hadn't realized that I've demanded that you heal my brother wounds, as well.

So, I have to confess, and it gives me much sorrow to do so, that on October 22, 1988, I didn't marry *you*. I married someone whom I hoped would be a brother surrogate. I didn't marry a unique, young, male image-bearer of God whose life was sacred ground; I married, in my subconscious, a young man who, to me, was an image-bearer of my brother whom I idolized. I didn't fall in love and establish a true covenant with you; I fell into a classic trauma bond, "a highly addictive attachment to the people who have hurt you," as described in *The Betrayal Bond* by Patrick Carnes.

Several details of late also point to this sorrowful reality. Remember my interaction with Pierre [graduate school professor]? I was concerned that Pierre's playful "smart ass" comment about me after I'd left the room might have meant that he had engaged in a power play . . . and won. I was concerned about losing my "playmate" over a power struggle. The feeling of being played by an authority figure to both engage and exploit me was a familiar one [a throwback to sexual abuse scenarios orchestrated by Davie], and the interaction with Pierre triggered an old reaction in me, despite Pierre's lack of malice in his good-humored comment. I had to acknowledge that I was still hanging on to one last hope that Davie would connect with his harm of me and initiate reconciliation in our relationship. I knew that I'd lost my childhood playmate when I was thirteen years old, but I hadn't let him go emotionally. Unconsciously, I've been living in fear of losing Davie completely, and now it's painfully clear to me. My emotional attachment to Davie hasn't been fair to you; I've required that you take his place, which has prevented me from simply letting you be who you are. I've had you playing a role in my story, a role you should never have had to play.

Another piece that completes this picture is the dream I had this past Monday night. In my dream, a boy with a long face (like you) relentlessly pursued me, sexually. I had a sense that I was already "spoken for," so I resisted this guy, even though I was attracted to him sexually. That I was already attached, to whom was not clear, made the "forbidden fruit" seem sweeter. Then when this long-faced guy pursued me for the sole purpose of pleasuring *me*, I could resist him no longer. When I woke up, I broke into spontaneous sobbing. The seemingly incongruent phrase that kept coursing through my mind was, "I don't want to lose my childhood buddy. I don't want to lose my childhood buddy. . . ." I've never cried like that after a dream.

I wondered whether this childhood buddy, this guy to whom I was attached, might have been you, but somehow that didn't seem accurate because it felt like you were the one *pursuing* me, and that I was already attached to *someone else*. Something didn't add up. Then, after writing that original opening line to this letter ("Dear Chip, my childhood buddy"), I realized that my prior attachment was to Davie, and that my attraction to you has really been an attempt to get Davie, my childhood playmate, to whom I've been trauma bound through betrayal, to love me again. I've been unconsciously demanding that you take Davie's place. I also realized that if I wanted to have a (sexual) relationship with this long-faced young man who wanted to give me pleasure (the only guy who ever pleasured me, like this guy did), I'd have to lose my childhood buddy . . . I'd have to let Davie go if this new young man was going to have the chance to pursue me.

I don't know if you feel the implications of this. I don't know if you've connected with what it feels like to be objectified, used, exploited, consumed, and unappreciated for your own uniqueness, but I know exactly what that feels like, because it's the most painful part of my history. My whole childhood was about being used to satisfy this or that need of someone else. I was never Jade . . . no one ever really knew who Jade was, because she didn't matter. She was always enlisted in the service of someone else—to make him or her look good or feel good. I wasn't a person; I was an object. And when I was old enough to do the same thing, I did, and you became the biggest casualty in my desperate quest to regain my brother's love.

Chip, I'm so sorry for what I've done to you, and I don't know what to do with this new understanding. There's no way to go back and change how I've hurt you, and there's no way to make it up to you. I can only say that I sorrow deeply over having used and exploited you in this way. It was unfair, unkind, and cruel. I've stomped around on the holy ground of your soul for half your life, with little regard for the sacred place on which I've trampled with such irreverence. . . .

It was important to share this reality with Chip so that he could make a choice about whether or not to remain in relationship with me. I had to confess my failure to him, to sincerely apologize for it, and to ask for his forgiveness. If he didn't want to be with me after such a confession, I couldn't blame him, and I was willing to accept that consequence.

Acknowledging my failure of Chip opened me up to clearly name his failure of me, as well. I had to face that Chip had similarly dishonored me, in a re-enactment of his own childhood wounds. Trauma bonds tend to go both ways, and sadly, severing them sometimes requires untying the marriage knot.

Some argue that a marriage based on false pretenses, whether conscious or unconscious, isn't really a marriage at all. In the Catholic tradition, for example, false pretenses would be appropriate grounds for annulment, due to a lack of the union's validity.[6] Although I wouldn't take this stance, I would say that my marriage to Chip possessed the "external framework" of a covenant and lacked the "internal meaning" of one. This distinction "enables us to distinguish between good marriages (in which the external is the framework for the internal) and bad marriages (in which the former is but a hollow shell); and of course many gradations in between. . . . It is clearer and more in keeping with

---

6. Atkinson, *To Have and To Hold*, 162–71.

the meaning of covenant to hold that bad marriages are still marriages until dissolved by divorce, rather than suggest that they have never been marriages at all."[7]

As Atkinson suggests, some bad marriages, marriages made "by mistake," may be able to grow into good ones, as long as both parties are willing and able to do so.[8] In my case, Chip was unwilling to wholeheartedly commit to a healing process, either individually or together. There were a couple half-hearted attempts to "figure things out," but a meeting of our hearts didn't come to pass, and our eventual divorce simply made official what was already true in our relationship. And as I mentioned earlier, had we simultaneously engaged in individual and relational healing, there were foundational cracks in our union that I believe would have proven insurmountable anyway.

This is not to say that our bad marriage didn't have its good moments. It did. But covenant is a matter of the heart, and in our marriage, the heart had stopped beating, and the life-support of the written document had become a mere formality to an otherwise flat-lined relationship.

A THEOLOGICAL REFLECTION

In the scriptures, the theme of covenant runs from Genesis to Revelation. Although the word תְּיִרְבּ (*berit*—covenant) is of uncertain derivation, and although its first explicit mention is in Genesis 6:18 regarding a commitment between God and Noah, the concept of covenant (a treaty) is as old as Adam and Eve. In the beginning, God initiated a treaty with the first couple, and established the basis for unobstructed relationship with Adam: "You can eat from any tree in the garden, except from the Tree-of-Knowledge-of-Good-and-Evil. Don't eat from it. The moment you eat from that tree, you're dead!" (Gen 2:16–17). From the very beginning, fellowship with God was conditional. We can't have relationship and violate it, too. God requires that we respect his conditions if we want to be in unobstructed communion with him.

Notice that I didn't say that God's *love* is conditional, only that *relationship* with him is. Our communion with God will be as intimate as our devotion to him. When we allow other gods—people, ideas, things,

---

7. Ibid., 169–70.
8. Ibid., 170.

attitudes, or whatever—to come before him in our hearts, our divided loyalty prevents us from having full fellowship with him.

After Adam's children had broken fellowship with God repeatedly and in despicable ways, God regretted creating humankind, and he turned his attention to the only upright man he could find: Noah. God covenanted with Noah (Gen 6:18), telling him to build an ark or be destroyed with the rest of the land's inhabitants, who had filled the land with violence. Noah had to obey this command in order to receive the covenant blessing.

Abram was the next recipient of God's covenant blessing, as described in Genesis 15 and 17. In keeping with covenant, both parties assumed responsibilities: God committed to give Abram and his descendents the land of Canaan and to be their personal God. In exchange, Abram was to "live a blameless life" (Gen 17:1, NLT), indicating the essence of any covenant relationship with God: one who knows him is expected to live with integrity.

The next covenant God established with mankind was at Mt. Sinai, when he covenanted with the nation of Israel through Moses. In this covenant, the nation of Israel entered a state of extraordinary privilege: representation of God to the world. In *Old Testament Roots*, Cate explains the significance of the Sinai covenant terms based on other ancient Near-Eastern cultures. The covenant God established with Israel closely resembles an ancient suzerainty treaty, an agreement between a great king and his vassal. Such treaties were made binding by an oath between the two parties.

At least seven features were common to these treaties: the identification of the great king, a detailed presentation of the historical background of the two parties, a prohibition against the vassal's entering into any foreign alliances, a statement of the stipulations and obligations of the covenant, a stipulation concerning where to keep the treaty document and when it should be publicly read, a designation of witnesses, and a list of blessings and curses.[9] We can easily identify these features in God's covenant with Israel at Sinai; "The covenant sealed the fact that they had been chosen by God . . . as his bride."[10] If Israel agreed to the covenant, she could acknowledge no other master. Her freedom and strength lay in her wholehearted commitment to God alone.

9. Cate, *Old Testament Roots*, 117–22.
10. Ibid., 122.

The Ten Commandments, also called the Decalogue or the Ten Words (Exod 20:2–17), and the detailed civil law code that followed (called the Book of the Covenant in Exod 24:7), regulated the personal, social, civil, and religious obligations of God's earthly representatives (Exod 20:2–7; 21:1–23:19). The Decalogue wasn't the first time God required social order. As we discovered in the previous chapter, from the beginning, human beings were expected to treat one another as image-bearers of God. The Sinai covenant, however, established God as the head of the nation of Israel, making it a theocratic state: "in ancient Israel the status of the Ten Commandments was approximately that of the code of criminal law in a modern nation-state. To break one of those laws was to commit a crime against God, the head of the state. Yet the laws had a positive purpose. They set down a way of life that would result in a full and rich communion with God and community with others."[11]

As was typical of ancient covenants, the Sinai covenant stipulated blessings for obeying the covenant conditions and curses for breaking them (Deut 27–33). When Israel gave her oath to abide by these conditions, she sealed the promise of the covenant (Exod 24:1–8), agreeing to serve the Ruler who'd delivered her from slavery in Egypt. This passage in Leviticus is one of many that lay out the conditions of the covenant:

> "If you live by my decrees and obediently keep my commandments . . . you'll have more than enough to eat and will live safe and secure in your land. . . . But if you refuse to obey me and won't observe my commandments despising my decrees and holding my laws in contempt by your disobedience, making a shambles of my covenant, I'll step in and pour on the trouble. . . . And if none of this works in getting your attention, I'll discipline you. . . . I'll break your strong pride. . . . On the other hand, if they confess their sins and the sins of their ancestors, their treacherous betrayal, the defiance that set off my defiance that sent them off into enemy lands; if by some chance they soften their hard hearts and make amends for their sin, I'll remember my covenant."
> (Lev 26:3, 5, 14, 18, 40–42)

Each generation had to renew the original Sinai commitment (e.g., Exod 24, Deut 29, and Josh 24), choosing anew whom it would serve. God knew that Israel would break the covenant, and he reminded them of what would happen when they did: "They will abandon me and

---

11. Elwell and Comfort, "Covenant," 325.

violate my Covenant that I've made with them. I'll get angry, oh so angry! I'll walk off and leave them on their own, won't so much as look back at them. Then many calamities and disasters will devastate them because they are defenseless. They'll say, 'Isn't it because our God wasn't here that all this evil has come upon us?' But I'll stay out of their lives, keep looking the other way because of all their evil; they took up with other gods" (Deut 31:17–20).

Even today, Jewish boys and girls have the opportunity to make this personal choice when they're twelve years old, becoming *bar* or *bat mitzvah* (literally, "son or daughter of the commandment"), accepting responsibility to live out the stipulations of the ancient Mosaic code.

It would be easy to wrongly infer, as many have, that following the law was all that was needed for relationship with God. But God reminds his people over and over again that he wants our hearts, not just our moral behavior. Covenant with God must be established in our hearts first; our blameless behavior, as evidenced in our relationships with people, will follow (John 13:35; 1 John 3).

Jesus provided a concise summary of the covenant law when he said that the greatest commandments were to love God and to love others as well as we love ourselves (Matt 22:37–38). As in marriage, love is a matter of the heart, not merely a matter of behavior. This is how the Pharisees had gotten so far off track. They had a detailed system of do's and don'ts over and above the Law of Moses. They were so concerned with *appeasing* God that they had no idea how to *please* him. Their hearts were more committed to the idol of their own righteousness than to practicing justice, loving mercy, and walking humbly with God (Mic 6:8).

Covenant in Malachi

The prophecy of Malachi describes the repercussions of when we break our covenant commitment to God by offering mere behavior and empty performance, and makes a direct comparison between Israel's covenant with God and covenant companionships between human partners.

Malachi's prophecy comes into Israel's history during the post-exilic period, after the temple had been rebuilt, the sacrificial system had been re-established, and the city of Jerusalem had returned to normalcy. Already, disillusionment had set in, including lethargy, laxity, and leniency in spiritual matters.[12] The various abuses that result from this atrophied state of affairs and a reminder of the curses they'd experience if they didn't repent of their unfaithfulness[13] are the subject of Malachi's prophecy.

The book is laid out as a series of six disputes in which God describes his character, challenges the abuses of the priests and of the people, and lays out his judgment.[14] God presents his first dispute by reminding the people that he's held up his end of the bargain (covenant): "I have loved you," he says (Mal 1:2–5, NIV). The people question how God has loved them, and he presents his evidence: he protected Israel by destroying her enemies, again and again. The Edomites, the offspring of Esau, had been a particularly bothersome foe of Israel's (see the book of Obadiah), and their destruction was evidence of God's love for his covenant companion.

Later in the prophecy, God refers to his ancient promise to give life and peace (2:6) and to bless the land (3:11), if Israel kept the covenant conditions. God's heart still longed to bless his people as he'd promised, if they'd only keep their end of the deal.

The Lord narrows his focus in his second dispute, zooming in from looking at the whole nation to specifically scrutinizing the priests, who placed a low priority on the worship of God (1:6–2:9). Instead of bringing sacrifices of the highest quality, they offered animals that were blind, sick, and crippled. They wouldn't think of giving such shoddy gifts to others they considered important, God observes to them, so he concludes that they must think very little of him. He demands that the priests get on their knees and beg for God's grace, because their half-hearted worship was getting everyone in trouble. God wasn't impressed with the way the priests were treating relationship with him as merely a game or a big show. (Does this sound like some marriages you're familiar with?) He wanted nothing to do with such hypocrisy, particularly when people of other nations were bringing their best to him (1:11).

God reminds the Israelites of his position as the covenant king and of his intentions to make good on his threats to allow the covenant curses to fall upon them (2:1–2). He's careful to acknowledge that his curses are intended to wake them up, to prod them to renew their covenant

---

12. Barker and Kohlenberger, *NIV Bible Commentary*, 1:1542.
13. Fee and Stuart, *How to Read the Bible for All Its Worth*, 181–204.
14. Dillard and Longman, "Malachi," 437–42.

with him (2:4), to restore a sense of reverent awe and a commitment to teach truth, so that the spiritual leaders will lead the people on a truthful spiritual journey (2:5–6).

The priests' false teaching had caused many to stumble and had "messed up many lives" when the people should've been able to "look up to the priests for guidance" as messengers of God himself (2:7). For this, God promises to punish Israel severely (2:1–5):

> "And now this indictment, you priests! If you refuse to obediently listen, and if you refuse to honor me, God-of-the-Angel-Armies, in worship, then I'll put you under a curse. I'll exchange your blessings for curses. In fact, the curses are already at work because you're not serious about honoring me. Yes, and the curse will extend to your children. I'm going to plaster your faces with rotting garbage, garbage thrown out from your feasts. That's what you have to look forward to. Maybe that will wake you up. Maybe then you'll realize that I'm indicting you in order to put new life into my covenant with the priests of Levi."

The third dispute concerns the practice of marrying foreign women, a practice that was expressly forbidden in the Law, and had been addressed by many of the other prophets. Apparently, the Israelites were divorcing their native-born wives in order to take up with foreign wives who worshipped idols,[15] which was another indication that Israel's heart was hardened against God.

This is the context of the verse often quoted with regard to divorce, the most difficult verse in the book, grammatically.[16] It was bad enough that the men of Israel were divorcing their wives to take up with possibly younger,[17] foreign women, but they were adding insult to injury by coming to the temple and whining that they weren't getting what they wanted from God. God explains that he couldn't bless them when they took their marriage vows to their covenant companions lightly, sending their wives packing simply because they wanted to be with someone else. God called this cheating on their spouses, and he condemned them for it (2:15).

God hates when people break their vows, their promises to love their spouse and to rear children who know and love God. He hates the

---

15. Ibid., 441.
16. Barker and Kohlenberger, *NIV Bible Commentary*, 1:1546.
17. Ibid.

hardness of heart that leads people to do violence to the tender heart of the one they're supposed to cherish, the one to whom they promised to give undivided loyalty, and he hates that people get hurt by those whose hearts are hard. "Don't cheat," God says (2:16).

The next dispute concerns the false accusations of Israel against God: they've accused God of ignoring evil (2:17). In response, God promises to send his messenger to clean house, bringing judgment against the priests, so that Jerusalem can be fit and pleasing to God, as it had been years before (3:4–5).

The fifth dispute concerns repentance. God hasn't changed, but Israel must change and repent if she is to be restored to relationship with God. What would repentance look like? Bringing the full tithe—not robbing God of his rightful due. In exchange, God says that he'll renew his promise to protect Israel from her enemies and from plunderers who would rob her of her agricultural bounty.

In the final dispute, God accuses Israel of verbal abuse and slander. They have said that serving God doesn't pay off, that rule-breakers get ahead and that God-fearers get no perks. In response, God promises to give special treatment, the same kind of consideration that a parent gives a respectful child. He reminds the people of the Mosaic covenant and promises to send another prophet who will clear the way for justice to be served. Finally, the prophecy ends with a final condition: If parents refuse to look after their children, and children don't respect their parents, "I'll come and put the land under a curse" (4:5).

Contrary to the understanding of many, the subject of divorce is only one of the issues addressed in the prophecy of Malachi, and it's presented within a specific context. The larger context is covenant between God and the nation of Israel, not between human beings and their spouses. The way the men of Judah were treating their wives was merely one piece of evidence that their hearts had turned away from God and had become hardened to him. God's call was for their hearts to be softened and turned back toward him. Then they would cherish their wives with their whole hearts as they had promised, and they wouldn't even consider divorcing their wives in order to marry foreign women. God hates such divided loyalty.

The Greater Social Context

In poor hermeneutical fashion, we often superimpose our own cultural mores about divorce over Malachi 2:16. As we noticed in the Introduction, some who appeal to a plain reading of scripture insist that, because of this verse, divorce (and divorcees) should be avoided at all costs, without truly counting the cost of such a stance.

When we allow this scripture, and other scriptures that address divorce, to remain in their social, literary, and canonical contexts, however, a very different picture emerges. Examining the grammatical-historical-canonical context of covenant in the scriptures, including the nature of treaties in the ancient near East, helps us better understand and reconcile difficult passages such as Hosea 2:1–2 and Jeremiah 3:6–11 (both of which refer to God's divorce from Israel) with God's statement, "I hate divorce" (Mal 2:16). David Instone-Brewer has done a tremendous job of researching the social contexts of the passages on divorce that cause the most difficulty, and I strongly recommend his works on the subject.[18] Let me summarize Instone-Brewer's research findings here.

In the ancient Near East, the social context of the Bible, the word covenant (*berit*) referred to a conditional agreement between two parties that was mutually binding. Covenants were implemented by a document or by a ceremony, and they could be made, kept, and broken. The sanctions to which both parties agreed came into force when a stipulation of the covenant was broken.

Marriage was considered a covenant because, like all other types of contracts, it was a conditional agreement between two parties that contained stipulations to keep and penalties for either party who didn't keep these stipulations. In forming the agreement, the groom paid the bride's father a *bride-price* (*mohar*), which represented many months worth of wages. This expense prevented people from entering into marriages lightly. In addition, the bride's father paid the bride a *dowry* (*nedunyah*), which was equivalent to the daughter's share of the estate, and was held in trust for her by her husband. The dowry gave personal security to the bride, who would keep it to live on if her husband died or divorced her, as long as she was the innocent party in the divorce. If the wife divorced her husband without cause, however, she lost her right to some or all of her dowry.

---

18. Instone-Brewer, *Divorce and Remarriage in the Bible*; *Divorce and Remarriage in the Church*; and *Divorce and Remarriage in the 1st and 21st Centuries*.

Like the bride's father, the groom gave the bride gifts, often of clothing and jewelry. All of these payments were intended to give security to the marriage.

The rights and responsibilities of an ancient Near Eastern marriage were rarely written down, but they were uniform for every marriage. A husband was expected to provide food, clothing, and love for his wife. Exodus 21:10–11 describes the minimum provisions that a slave-wife was to receive from her master-husband if he took her as a second wife. This case law provided the rabbis with the following principle: if a slave wife had the right to divorce her husband if he neglected to provide food, clothing, and love, a free wife would certainly have these rights, as well. Furthermore, if a wife had these rights, then a husband was also entitled to divorce his wife if she neglected him by not preparing the food and cloth for the family's use or by not reciprocating her husband's love. Sexual faithfulness was understood as an unwritten stipulation and carried stiff penalties for violation. These four obligations comprised the marriage vows exchanged by ancient Jewish couples.

Several passages speak about divorce without commenting on whether divorce itself is desirable or not (e.g., Exod 21:10–11, Deut 24:1). However, the Pentateuch records very little about the details of divorce, only addressing those situations where the Israelites were distinct from their neighbors. One of the requirements for divorce within the Israelite community was the divorce certificate, which provided a clean and proper end to a broken marriage. The purpose of this document was to give proof of the divorce so that an abandoned woman had the right to remarry.

Like Malachi, the prophecy of Hosea condemns the breaking of marriage vows, and results in a divorce between *YHWH* and Israel. "She's no longer my wife. I'm no longer her husband" (Hos 2:1–2), says *YHWH* to Israel in the words of an ancient Near Eastern divorce formula. Although God is the one who initiated the divorce, he's actually the injured party who was forced into it. He suffers the divorce because Israel had broken every one of her marriage vows, including preparing the gifts that Husband-God had provided (food, clothing, and wine) as offerings to Baal, instead of as offerings to Adonai (Hos 2:8).

Jeremiah further develops the marriage-divorce metaphor, this time addressing Judah, who has followed the same path of spiritual adultery as Israel. Judah is warned that she may suffer the same fate as Israel, who had been sent away with a divorce certificate (Jer 3:6–11). Ezekiel also expands the metaphor about Judah as an unfaithful wife in chapters 16 and 23, where she again stands accused of offering the lavishly-bestowed gifts of her husband, YHWH, to Baal, in addition to seducing other lovers with the garments she had prepared for herself, using the cloth that YHWH provided for her.

Isaiah also refers to Israel's unfaithfulness and to a divorce certificate that Israel cannot produce, perhaps arguing that God has not divorced Judah but has put her away (separated from her) because of her sins (Isa 50:1). Although the word here, *shalach*, is normally a technical term for divorce, Isaiah seems to be saying that although God has sent Judah away, this is not a legal divorce because he has not given her a divorce certificate, and he intends to seek reconciliation.

Together, these prophets develop a picture of God that begins with the covenant at Sinai, concluding that YHWH had a real marriage contract with Israel and Judah, and that YHWH was a divorcee, not by his own choosing, but because his bride had broken her marriage vows. God's relationship with Israel was a marriage contract, with stipulations (to feed, clothe, and share mutual love), promises (a happy life together), and penalties (including divorce) for breaking the stipulations. Israel continued to break these stipulations, and God gave her many opportunities to repent. Eventually, however, God had had enough, and he finally divorced her. The marriage was already broken and dead, and God simply carried out the legalities of divorce to recognize that fact.

Malachi applied God's anger and hurt regarding these broken vows to all marriages, not just to God's marriage with Israel. Although more traditional interpretations of Malachi 2:16 suggest that God is against divorce of any kind, the context shows that this is not so. Instead, these verses constantly reiterate that the real issue is faithfulness to the terms of a covenant. Criticism is not directed at the person who carries out the divorce but at the person who causes the divorce by not being faithful to the marriage covenant. God hates the breaking of marriage vows that results in divorce, knowing the pain that comes from spousal neglect and broken promises. Sometimes it's more painful to remain in the marriage, suffering continual physical or emotional abuse or neglect, which can bring the whole marriage covenant into disrepute.

Statute Law vs. Case Law

Though the Torah rarely specifically addresses human marriage covenant, it does so most often within the context of case law (e.g., Deut 21–25). The Hebrew legal system, like our own legal system, was divided into two parts: statute law and case law. Statutes summarize a whole subject of law, such as theft. Case law, in which the principles are more important than the details, is a collection of judicial decisions made in the context of actual situations, the rulings of which establish a precedent for similar cases. In ancient Hebrew culture, the rabbis were responsible for interpreting the statute laws as various cases arose, and their rulings then became the basis upon which they would make future rulings in similar cases.

Regarding the subject of divorce, statute law initially stipulated one ground for divorce: sexual impropriety. Case law, from Exodus 21:10–11, established a precedent for three additional grounds for divorce, as noted earlier. When it became clear that spouses were treating their partners without dignity, Moses permitted divorce for *hardness* (or stubbornness) *of heart*. Based on this subjective stipulation for divorce, every case needed to be tried separately.

Because oral tradition requires brevity, and because there were already principles established concerning human relationships, the scriptures make no attempt to address every way in which hardness of heart may manifest itself in marriage. Based on these already established principles, and on the four specific and undisputed grounds for divorce, judges could rule on each marital breakdown. When the judges did grant a divorce, they were merely legally recognizing what had already happened: broken covenant in which at least one of the parties had stubbornly refused to repent and to honor *all* the vows of the union.

Judaism failed to address some gross neglect of the marriage covenant. For example, polygamy, which God clearly condemns, was widely practiced in ancient times, mostly among the wealthy—a reality that Jesus addressed. The Pharisees habitually strained out gnats (such as allowing a husband to divorce his wife if she burnt his food) but swallowed camels (such as using God's name for disingenuous profit), and Jesus was not impressed with their pattern of majoring on minor issues and minoring on major ones. Because of their inconsistency and hypocrisy, Jesus reminded the religious leaders that Moses allowed divorce for hardness of heart, although it wasn't so from the beginning.

During the 400-year intertestamental period, changes in divorce law resulted in more rights for women but also greater instability in marriage. Divorce became more equitable, so that it wasn't as cruel to women, but it also became more common. These changes formed the backdrop for the debate in Judaism concerning the grounds for divorce, which was eventually presented for comment to Jesus.

Jesus on Marriage and Divorce—A Not-So-Plain Reading

The church's misunderstanding of Jesus' teaching regarding divorce is understandable given its lack of knowledge of first century CE language and culture. Applying sound hermeneutics to the passages in which the Pharisees question Jesus regarding divorce is no easy task, but it's a particularly important one, considering the number of couples who find their marriages to be full of pain but who want to honor the scriptures in the relational choices they make.

As we approach these difficult passages, we need to consider the greater context. When probed about the Law regarding a variety of topics, Jesus addressed each issue with a deep respect for the ancient scriptures. He not only supported the letter of the Law, but the spirit of the Law, too. He drew attention to the "why" of the laws, the principles behind them, not just to the literal words. It's our attitudes that determine whether or not we're following the spirit of the law, and this was Jesus' major criticism of the religious leaders. The Old Testament wasn't the problem; it was how people interpreted it. Their hermeneutics were problematic, leading to graceless, legalistic practice.

Based on Jesus' example and teaching, we, too, need to honor the spirit of the law as we apply the principles of the Torah to our culture and era.

What isn't so clear from a plain reading of the scriptures is that when the Pharisees approached Jesus to question him about divorce, they were referring to a particular type of divorce that was the common subject of debate during that time period. Prior to Jesus' era, divorce was accepted on certain grounds, mentioned above. During Jesus' lifetime, however, the idea of groundless divorce—divorce for any reason—grew in popularity.

The Jewish community was divided on the validity of this kind of divorce between those who studied in the school of Hillel and those who studied in the school of Shammai. The debate centered around Deut 24:1

where the wording isn't entirely clear regarding the meaning of the phrase 'ervat davar, often translated "cause of sexual immorality." The Hillelites interpreted 'ervat davar to mean that divorce could be sought for any cause, while the Shammaites argued from this phrase that adultery was the only reason people were permitted to divorce. Consequently, most people seeking to divorce requested Hillelite judges to rule in their case because the Hillelites and the Shammaites mutually recognized each other's rulings, even if they disagreed with how they arrived at them. By the time Jesus came on the scene, the "any cause" divorce was the most common type, but it was still a subject of debate.

When the Pharisees approached Jesus about divorce, it was the "any cause" kind of divorce that they had in mind. No one questioned whether it was lawful to divorce—everyone accepted that it was, and that the scriptures provided for this in cases of neglect of the three marital obligations and in cases of adultery. The accounts do not explain this cultural context because any first century reader would have been familiar with the debate between the Hillelites and the Shammaites.

What becomes clear when we understand this context is that Jesus rejected an "any cause" divorce as valid, and that he was much more interested in grounds for marriage. He turns the question around to address first the practice of polygamy, which he condemns based on the idea of Genesis 2:24, referring to two becoming one flesh.

Jesus then addresses and supports the reason why God permitted divorce in the first place: hardheartedness—a stubborn refusal to soften one's heart and to stop breaking marriage vows. Moses allowed divorce for this reason, and Jesus affirms such dissolution of a marriage in his teaching.

Finally, Jesus addresses the mandate to "be fruitful and multiply" which the Jews had interpreted to mean that marriage and family was compulsory. Jesus explained that marriage is optional—an idea that was completely foreign to Jewish culture.

Divorce on the grounds of neglect and abuse wasn't foreign to Jewish culture, however, and was widely agreed to be valid. Even the Hillelites and the Shammaites agreed that neglect provided valid grounds for divorce; they only disagreed on what exactly constituted neglect.

We have no record of Jesus disagreeing with these grounds for divorce. If he did disagree, it's strange that at least one of the Gospel writers wouldn't have said so due to Jesus' countercultural and controversial life.

If there were some way in which Jesus disagreed with the religious authorities, they would likely have recorded it. There are several issues that Jesus doesn't address because no one specifically asked. For example, Jesus never spoke to the question of what to do if your spouse physically or emotionally abuses your child. Or what to do if your spouse murders someone in a bar fight, or if you come to realize that you made your wedding vows under false pretenses. Or what to do if.... There is no end to the hypothetical situations we could consider, and there would be no end to the debate, either. Such situations would be addressed on a case-by-case basis, and would bring case-specific ruling. By implication, we, too, need to follow general principles in scripture about how human beings should treat one another and seek to uphold the spirit of the law in specific situations.

Paul on Marriage and Divorce—A Not-So-Plain Reading

Paul takes up the subject of marriage and divorce, as well, but addresses different concerns, because he was asked different questions. It's critical to remember hermeneutical guidelines when approaching New Testament scriptures that address marriage in the context of particular cases. When Paul addresses the concepts of marriage and divorce, he does so when the occasion calls for it. When specific churches pose specific questions about specific situations, they ask Paul to address these situations. From these situations, we may extract principles to help us address similar situations today, as long as we understand the context and the culture that is embedded in the texts, and as long as we avoid superimposing our own cultural or personal biases into the texts. Our trouble most often occurs when we try to squeeze every marital issue into a few scriptures that were never meant to address the kinds of relational harm that are addressed elsewhere in the scriptures. Remember, a text cannot mean what it never meant, so it's important to keep in mind that when the Corinthian church asked Paul some direct questions about marriage and divorce, he answered them within their context.

Their first concern was about whether marriage was compulsory, as was the Jewish and Roman custom. When Paul suggested waiting to get married until the present distress was over (1 Cor 7:26), he was likely referring to the famine of that time period, a difficult situation in which to support a family. He wasn't suggesting that all people of all situations, times, and cultures should refrain from marriage if at all possible. His remarks were delivered to a specific people during a specific time for a specific occasion. (Remember the hermeneutical principles from the Introduction.)

Paul's remarks about refraining from sex with one's spouse were also delivered to a specific people during a specific time for a specific occasion. Some of the Corinthian believers thought that refraining from sex was a mark of holiness and wanted Paul to uphold that. Paul assures them that depriving one another sexually wouldn't result in superior spirituality, and he affirms that an exclusive covenant is the proper context for sexual union. He's not saying that a man can demand that his wife fulfill his sexual needs when he's deprived her of her emotional needs, although this is sometimes how this scripture is used. Remember, scripture cannot say what it never meant, so we need to read this passage in its proper context. This passage is about whether or not refraining from sex with one's spouse is more righteous than engaging in it.[19] Paul says that it isn't.

In his correspondence with the Corinthians, Paul also addresses the problem of how easy it was to obtain a divorce under Roman law, which operated similarly to the "any cause" divorce that Jesus addressed. In Rome, all you had to do was walk out of the house (if your partner owned it) or demand that your partner leave the house (if you owned it), and you were considered to be divorced and free to remarry. Paul rejects the validity of this kind of divorce-by-separation and tells the Corinthians not to recognize it because it's groundless. In fact, he addresses those who had already used this method and tells them to return to their spouses or to remain unmarried (1 Cor 7:11). Without a formal divorce decree, a couple is still legally married, therefore not permitted to remarry.

In Ephesians 5, Paul provides concise and clear grounds for marriage: just as the church is the spiritual bride for whom the spiritual husband, Christ, provides food, clothing, and love, so a physical marriage is to reflect this spiritual union. Paul couches all of this teaching in the larger context of all human relationships. "Out of respect for Christ," Paul says, be courteously reverent to one another" (Eph 5:21). Such courtesy and reverence are the basic, fundamental grounds for all human relationships, and for marriage in particular. If we all practiced such high regard of one another, as we promised to do when we said

---

19. Elwell and Comfort, "Sex, Sexuality," 1181.

our marriage vows, we wouldn't need to talk about grounds for divorce. After all, talking about grounds for marriage is a much more pleasant conversation.

In effect, both Jesus and Paul deliver the same message to two different cultures: 1) believers should keep their marriage vows to provide for one another, and 2) groundless divorce is invalid. These are common threads of marriage covenant across time and culture.

Common Objections

So, what are we supposed to do if one or both partners fail to keep their marriage vows—the covenant they made before God? Doesn't the Bible say that we shouldn't separate what God has joined together? And doesn't Jesus say that remarriage after divorce is adultery? Isn't marriage a sacrament? And don't the scriptures say that only death can end marriage?

These questions are common ones; they, and many other marriage questions come from passages that have been lifted from their contexts. First of all, the scriptures don't say that no one *can* separate the two partners of a marriage, but that it is *undesirable* to do so (Matt 19:6). I don't think anyone would dispute that separation or divorce is dreadful, even when the marriage is neglectful or abusive. However, God doesn't sanction all unions. David's marriage to Bathsheba, for example, wasn't a marriage made in heaven. In reality, some people create marriage bonds that have nothing to do with a desire for the best of their partner, and they make vows that they cannot, or are unwilling to, keep. The same happens with business covenants, and no one questions the wisdom of canceling such contracts when they spell doom for any of the parties who agreed to the treaty.

Second, when Jesus says that remarriage after a divorce is adultery, he's addressing a certain kind of divorce, namely the "any cause" divorce that he pronounced invalid. If two people aren't really divorced, they're not really free to remarry, because remarriage would create a polygamous and adulterous union. Jesus doesn't address whether remarriage after a valid divorce is permissible because the whole point of providing a certificate of divorce for a wife was so that she had proof that she *could* remarry. Everyone expected that divorcees would (and should) remarry (those who didn't were often met with judgment and suspicion), and as far as we know, Jesus never opposed this. No one questioned this in the first century, including Paul, who told victims of divorce-by-separation that they were no longer enslaved, which would've reminded them of the promise of their divorce certificate that they could marry any man they wished.

Next, the one-flesh privilege of marriage isn't the only one-flesh possibility. Paul refers to the problem of entering into a one-flesh union with a prostitute (1 Cor 6:15–20). This doesn't mean that having sex with a prostitute leaves the individuals married. The one-flesh union between covenant partners is what God designed, but it's possible for human beings to violate that design. So the act of sex doesn't, in and of itself, create a covenantal bond between individuals, although it is a most sacred intimate experience that covenant companions can share.

Fourth, the idea that marriage is a sacrament arose in medieval times. In Ephesians 5:32, Paul refers to marriage as a *mystery* (*musterion*), meaning *a secret hidden in holiness*, and was later translated with the Latin word, *sacrament*, (*sacramentum*) meaning *an unchangeable sacred reality*. Of course, we ought to enter into marriage unions with this kind of reverence, but we shouldn't presume that the scriptures say every marriage has some kind of permanent form in the heavens, particularly if the couple treats their union in a habitually unsacred way.

Fifth, the scriptures that address the fact that death can end marriage (1 Cor 7, Rom 7) are not talking about divorce and remarriage. 1 Corinthians 7 refers to people who've lost their spouses to death and about the widow's freedom from the law of levirate marriage (Deut 25:5–10), marriage to a deceased husband's brother. To mention divorce in this context would be out of place, a hermeneutical error. In Romans 7, Paul makes an analogy for believers: just as death frees a woman from her spouse, so does Jesus' death free us from the law so that we can marry Messiah. The passage says much about relationship with Messiah, but it wasn't intended to teach about divorce and remarriage any more than the parable of the sower was intended to teach about farming.

Many believe that the description of love in 1 Corinthians 13 is the answer for anyone in a difficult marriage. (Keep in mind that Paul writes this passage to the believers in Corinth who had difficulty loving one another through the clash of Jewish and Gentile belief systems they encountered as they tried to create a new community of faith together.) In reality, the passage describes the qualities of love (which takes only one person), not the qualities of mutual relationship (which takes two). For example, God loves every person who has ever lived with the kind of love described in 1 Corinthians 13. However, he doesn't have a mutual relationship with every person who has ever lived. Again, love is unconditional; relationship is not. Relational harmony is based on both parties keeping the terms of the covenant.

Finally, for those who fear that if the marriage covenant is conditional then the promises God has made to individuals are also conditional, understand that the metaphor of the marriage covenant breaks down when we try to apply the metaphor of God's *corporate* relationship with the nation of Israel to his *individual* relationships with people. For example, when God originally covenanted with Israel, his side of the bargain was to protect her from her enemies (as long as she was faithful to him), and at various times throughout Israel's history, he did so, although not always immediately, and not without Israelite bloodshed. It would be easy, but hermeneutically unsound, to interpret such passages to mean that God works the same way with individuals. Consider that at the very moment that God was fulfilling his covenant promises by rescuing the nation from her enemies, individual Israelites were experiencing the very predictable pain of the human condition: disease, death, relational breakdown, crime, etc. If those individuals had accused God of not rescuing them from the pain of the human condition as he had promised, they would have been accusing him of reneging on a promise that he'd never made. In fact, what God *did* promise originally to the first individual, Adam, was that breaking the one rule he gave would result in a broken (but reparable) relationship with him and in a curse upon all of creation. We shouldn't be surprised, then, when we experience the pain of a fallen world—a pain that God promised, and that humankind could have originally avoided. When we as individuals expect God to save us from the pain of living in this fallen, cursed world, we set him up to do something he never promised to do. He's promised to be *with us* in it—which is more costly for him—not to remove us from it. The promise that God made to the nation of Israel to save her from her enemies doesn't apply to individual salvation of any kind, and the covenant of the heart that he makes with individuals doesn't include rescuing individuals from the pain of the human condition.

In the end, the Old and New Testaments conclude the same thing: God allows the victim of abuse, neglect, or unfaithfulness to divorce his or her spouse. Rarely is a broken marriage the fault of only one of the partners, as by the time most marriages end in divorce, both have incessantly broken their vows to love and support each other. Even so, our legal system, like the Jewish and Roman legal systems, doesn't require the seeker of a divorce to site grounds for it. However, just because grounds aren't cited in a particular case doesn't mean that valid grounds for divorce are unnecessary. Even Joseph was going to divorce Mary with the "any cause" divorce to spare her the shame of what he believed was her unfaithfulness. Whether our legal system acknowledges appropriate grounds for divorce or not, we must be careful to endorse divorce that results from broken vows or from faulty foundations for the marriage.

When the Vow Breaks

Our vows today—to love, honor, and cherish—have evolved from the love, clothe, and feed vows of ancient history and Exodus 21. When we fail to keep these promises to each other, the marriage relationship breaks down. God knows what it feels like to have a spouse who loves him only half heartedly, and with a hard, stubborn heart. In such cases, he allows for the victim to seek the dissolution of a broken marriage, just as he did in the time of Moses.

For a more complete discussion of these issues, I recommend Dr. David Instone-Brewer's books, *Divorce and Remarriage in the Church*, and *Divorce and Remarriage in the Bible*. *Grace and Divorce*, by Dr. Les Carter, also treats these subjects with sensitivity and reverence for the scriptures and for human beings.

SNEAK PREVIEW OF THE NEXT CHAPTER

In the community of faith, we sometimes refer to God as the Lover of our Souls—a heartwarming concept. In the next chapter, we'll trace through the scriptures the intimate relationship between God and his human creatures, observing how intimacy with him provides a model for the intimacy that we can have with a covenant companion. Using the hermeneutical guidelines established in the Introduction, we'll come to esteem our relationship with God even more highly and enter it more intimately. A love like God's is easy to exploit even when we allow ourselves to feel what it costs God to offer such depth of relationship. Similarly, feeling the harm we inflict on others when we fail to love well provides the motivation to remain undivided in our loyalty to our Loved One and to our loved ones.

3

God's Love Languages

THE NOTION THAT GOD created the universe, set it spinning, and then removed himself from involvement with it is completely foreign to the scriptures. There we find a God who created a world with a unique opportunity for relationship, communion, friendship and intimacy with him. The God of the Bible so longs for relationship with his creatures that he is willing to sacrifice himself to increase the likelihood of its occurrence. In 1 Peter 1:18–20, the apostle Peter indicates that God planned to sacrifice himself to redeem the world before he even created it. The vocabulary used of God, the lover of his people, includes words like *passion, pursuit, covenant, intimacy,* and *loyalty*. This is the vocabulary of lovers, of a bridegroom and his bride.

Sadly, words like *adultery, seduction, prostitution, unfaithfulness, uncleanness,* and *jealousy* have also entered (and marred) this relationship. God's bride is more often adulterous than she is faithful. Consequently, the ugliest word that enters the story of God's relationship with his bride is *divorce*. God hates divorce because it disrupts a union that symbolizes his relationship with his people (Eph 5:21–32). While he allowed it because of the hardness of human hearts, God does whatever is within his power to avoid such a fate with his bride. As we've seen, however, relationship with God isn't unconditional. Covenant isn't all blessing; without faithfulness, God's marital vows call for consequences.

It's fascinating to trace God's intimate relationship with people as described in the Bible. The scriptures employ a myriad of images to help us understand the nature of God's involvement with humankind, one of the most intriguing of which is the picture of God as husband and lover of his people. Neher explains that the marriage metaphor represents the history of the covenant. Every stage in Israel's history corresponds to a stage in the marriage between *YHWH* and Israel.[1] In order to explore the metaphor of God as Lover, we must understand the "love languages" he uses. If God has read Gary Chapman's book,[2] he might identify "words of appreciation" as one of his primary love languages. Let's look at the Hebrew words for *know, choose, acquire,* and *love.* They give us insight into his loving heart and into covenant with him.

A THEOLOGICAL REFLECTION

The Words of Covenant

Intimacy is about knowing and being known. The most common Hebrew word for *know* is ידע (*yada*). This term is used more than one thousand times in the Bible[3] and is translated in many different ways, including *know, acknowledge, understand, teach, realize, make known,* and *make love. Yada* commonly refers to gaining all kinds of knowledge through the senses, such as information and skills, but it also refers to acquaintance with someone, and even to sexual intercourse.[4] Knowing involves the whole being, including the heart, soul, and mind.[5] In ancient Hebrew, there's no word for *brain*; the *heart* is the seat of the intellect, and it's never separated from the will or the emotions.[6] This linguistic history is why the King James Version of the passage in Genesis 4:1, for example, refers to sexual intercourse as *knowledge*: "Adam *knew* his wife, and she conceived and bore Cain" (italics mine). This refers to the most intimate knowledge that a man and woman can have of each other.

This knowledge is the kind that God wants with his human creation. To "know" God is to have an intimate, experiential knowledge of Him.[7] He didn't want the Garden couple to simply know *about* him. He wanted them to be in passionate relationship with him, with their whole beings. This is the kind of relationship he has made possible with all people. As a lover, he wants our hearts. Anything less is *spiritual adultery*

1. Neher, "Le symbolisme conjugal," 30–49.
2. Chapman, *Five Love Languages.*
3. Vine, Unger, and White, *Vine's Complete Expository Dictionary.*
4. Richards, "Knowledge," 382.
5. Elwell and Comfort, "Knowledge," 789.
6. Smith, *Old Testament Theology*, 102.
7. Vine, Unger, and White, *Vine's Complete Expository Dictionary.*

because any kind of divided loyalty in an exclusive covenant relationship demonstrates unfaithfulness to the union.

Knowledge of God carries an added component: responsibility. To "know God" means not only to have an intellectual understanding of who he is, but "to be related to him personally and emotionally, and to be obedient to his covenant and commandments."[8] Not to know him, then, doesn't necessarily indicate ignorance of him; sometimes it means an unwillingness to obey. Therefore, rebellion is also *adultery*, another evidence of a broken faith-bond.

While the book of *Genesis* records the beginnings of God's relationship with all people, it also tracks his *choice* of a few specific individuals, such as Abraham, Isaac, Jacob, and Moses. "Being 'chosen' by God brings people into an intimate relationship with Him."[9]

Exodus then tracks God's choice of a nation: Israel. It's important to note that when the word בחר (*bachar—choose*) is used of God, it stresses that his choices are internally motivated.[10] They don't depend on the qualities of the object of his choice. For example, when God chose Israel to be his special people, his bride, it wasn't because Israel *deserved* such an honor. The passage in Deuteronomy 7:7–9 says, "God wasn't attracted to you and didn't choose you because you were big and important—the fact is, there was almost nothing to you. He did it out of sheer love, keeping the promise he made to your ancestors. God stepped in and mightily brought you back out of the world of slavery, freed you from the iron grip of Pharoah king of Egypt." In Deuteronomy 9:4–6, the author adds that, despite Israel's lack of righteousness and integrity, God, the loving husband, still chose to lead her to the land he promised.

The concept of God's choice cannot be understood in terms of a single word, however. The words *yada* (*know*, described above), and לקח (*laqach—to take*, described next) round out this idea. In addition, the idea of God's choosing underlies many Biblical words and phrases, such as "people of God" (Deut 27:9), "special treasure" (Exod 19:5), and "holy nation" (Exod 19:6), concepts we'll explore as we trace the theme of God as Lover.

The verb *take* (*laqach*) is important to this subject because of its direct link to marriage. "In all the Hebrew scriptures, there is no

---

8. Smith, *Old Testament Theology*, 102.
9. Vine, Unger, and White, *Vine's Complete Expository Dictionary*.
10. Richards, "Choose," 160.

single word for the estate of marriage or to express the abstract idea of *wedlock*,[11] although the relationship of marriage was established by God from the beginning. Most often in ancient Hebrew culture, marriages were arranged; the father of a young man of marriageable age would *take* a woman for his son, such as when Abraham sent a servant to *take/get* a wife for Isaac (Gen 24:4). The father would then pay a price to acquire the woman and seal the covenant with gifts, establishing his authority, as head of his clan, over the bride.[12] This act would also initiate the betrothal period, during which time the young man would prepare a place in his father's house for his bride, while the bride prepared herself for married life.[13] After this period, the son would officially *take* the woman to live with him, and they would be husband and wife. As we'll see, this is precisely what God does as Lover of his people.

The last term we'll discuss before tracing the theme of God as Lover through the Bible is the word חסד (*checed*), translated most often as *love*. This term is to be distinguished from the more common Hebrew word for *love*, בהא (*ahab*), which can be used for *love* or *like*, depending on the object of affection and depending on the intensity of the subject's feeling for the object.[14] *Checed*, on the other hand, refers to a "higher form of love, involving loyalty, steadfastness, and kindness."[15] Most occurrences of this word feature God as agent, although in a few (possibly redacted) cases, humans are said to possess it.[16]

The passage in Hosea 2:19-20 (NLT) most clearly connects the ideas associated with *checed* to the theme of God as Lover. Through this prophet, God said to Israel, "I'll marry you for good—forever! / I'll marry you true and proper, in love and tenderness [*checed*]. / Yes, I'll marry you and neither leave you nor let you go. / You'll know [*yada*] me, God, for who I really am."

According to the philosopher Rosenzweig, God's revealed love is the basis for our knowledge of him. "The revelation, which denotes God in his bending towards humanity, can be equalled to nothing but love, as love is a movement towards someone else that is ever new and elusive

---

11. Unger, "Marriage," 817.
12. Elwell and Comfort, "Marriage, Marriage Customs," 861–64.
13. Youngblood et al., *Nelson's New Illustrated Bible Dictionary*.
14. Richards, "Love," 418.
15. Elwell and Comfort, "Love," 827–29.
16. VanGemeren, "חסד," 212.

God's Love Languages 51

and that is characterized by complete self-abandonment. This is the way God loves man. . . . God's relation to man is this comparable to that of a lover and his or her beloved."[17]

God's relation to man is also comparable to the Old Testament concept of *covenant*. The biblical concept of covenant is the "central force behind the different forms of marriage imagery."[18] This is because "there are only two relationships that are appropriately exclusive: marriage and covenant. Rivals could not be tolerated in either relationship."[19] This is why God is described as a *jealous* lover. God's faithful *checed* requires the same from his intimate partner.

Now that we are equipped with the terms of God's love, let's track God's intimate relationship with humankind from Genesis to Revelation.

God as Lover in the Pentateuch

Before God even created mankind, as described in *Genesis*, he performed several actions that demonstrated his heart for his most beloved creation. First, he prepared a garden paradise, a home for a happy couple and their family. He created אדם (*adam*—humankind), stamped with his own image, and then provided for Adam's loneliness by forming a woman, Eve, as his companion. For the two of them, God designed a sacred act of intimacy that mirrored God's love for them. Through it all, God made himself known to the couple, communicating with them, and even hanging out with them in the home that he had prepared. This scene, which beautifully demonstrates God's heart for his human creation, sets the stage for the biblical imagery of God as Lover. Clearly, God was passionate about this couple from the beginning, and he wanted them to *know* it. He wanted them to know *him*.

This deep desire is why the rebellion of Adam and Eve carried such dire consequences. To know and love God is to keep his commandments (Exod 20:6; John 14:21). When Adam and Eve disregarded God's instruction, they were unfaithful to him. They committed spiritual adultery and were removed from the Garden sanctuary. Their independence created a distance in the relationship that only God could breach. Until God

---

17. Abma, *Bonds of Love*, 254–55.
18. Ibid., 24.
19. Dillard and Longman, "Hosea," 361.

found a way to dwell with them again, humankind remained outside of his presence, separated from him.

The rest of Genesis traces God's relationship with certain individuals (the patriarchs and Noah) by means of various covenants, some of which we've already talked about.

While God made himself known to individuals in Genesis, he revealed himself to a nation in *Exodus*. In this book, God reveals his personal name (*YHWH*) to a nation that he *chooses*: Israel. God sees a damsel in distress and comes to her aid. He delivers her from the bully and draws her to the place he has prepared for her. (Hosea 2:14–15 even uses the language of seduction to refer to the Egypt-to-wilderness event; God is pictured as a seducer and Israel a youthful maiden.) In Exodus 19–24, the author shows how God draws up and delivers his exclusive covenant offer to his new bride.

Cate, author of *Old Testament Roots,* describes the concept of covenant well, first explaining that covenant and choice are inseparably linked. Without God's choosing (*bachar*) Israel, there would have been no covenant.[20] Remember from chapter 1 that the covenant God established with Israel closely resembles an ancient suzerainty treaty, an agreement between a great king and his vassal, bound by an oath between the two parties.

When the covenant was offered to Israel on God's terms, she could accept or reject it. If she chose to accept it, she was obliged to be obedient to God's act of divine *bachar* and *checed*. Once committed, she had no right to withdraw. Such an action would be described as treachery and *infidelity*. We'll notice later that the prophets often drew upon the image of *adultery* to describe Israel's violation of the covenant.[21]

So, with the full understanding of this agreement, the bride, Israel, says "I do," in Exodus 19. Almost immediately, Israel is unfaithful to her new husband, breaking her promise to "have no other gods before *YHWH*." She didn't last a week. But because of his *checed*, God renews the covenant, and again Israel promises to obey (Exodus 23).

God then delivers his plan to dwell with his people, in a royal residence called the tabernacle. As he had in Eden, God again lives with his people. Although still somewhat removed, *YHWH* demonstrates his longing to be in the presence of the bride he has chosen.

20. Cate, *Old Testament Roots*, 116.
21. Ibid., 124.

Leviticus concerns itself with the chastity of the bride. Because of his own holiness, God expects holiness from his bride. Leviticus describes a system by which the people could re-establish purity regularly, so as to continually restore harmonious relationship with God.

The setting for *Numbers* isn't the Promised Land, the home God had prepared for his bride; it's the wilderness—hardly a place for a new bride to enjoy her new position. Because the people disobeyed, they ended up wandering around in the desert when they could've been enjoying their new home. Even so, the wilderness is elsewhere described in a positive way, highlighting the lack of distraction there (Hos 2:14–15). This could've been a time of intimate fellowship with God, the Divine Lover.

Instead, Israel is unfaithful. She commits adultery through unbelief, ingratitude, disobedience, idolatry, and sexual immorality again and again. Even so, the book ends on a note of hope. Perhaps the second generation of Israel would hold fast to the promises she had made with her Divine Husband.

Deuteronomy calls for a renewal of the covenant as the Israelites prepare to enter the Promised Land. Included in this renewal are blessings for keeping the covenant and curses for failing to do so.

While the Penteteuch introduces the imagery of God as Lover of the bride to whom he makes himself known (*yada*), and whom he chooses (*bachar*), loves (*checed*), and takes (*laqach*) as his own, the rest of the scriptures narrate various interactions in this relationship. Let's explore this motif through the Prophets, the Writings, and the New Testament.

God as Lover in the Prophets

While all of the prophets condemn Israel for her adulteries, Hosea, Jeremiah, Isaiah, Ezekiel, and Malachi develop the imagery of the unfaithful partner of the Divine Lover most explicity. *Hosea*, probably the first prophet to explicitly relate Israel's relationship with God to a marriage,[22] refers to Israel's disobedience as *harlotry* because the roots of the relationship are in the exclusive bonds of the Sinai covenant. "Only in light of this covenant relationship can Israel's inclinations towards other gods than *YHWH* be labeled as 'harlotry.'"[23]

---

22. Ryken, "Marriage," 539.
23. Abma, *Bonds of Love*, 139.

Hosea portrays the baals and *YHWH* as rival partners of Israel. In *YHWH*'s passionate *checed*, he cajoles, seduces, pleads with, rebukes, threatens, attacks, and persuades the people in order to restore covenant relationship. That Israel would even glance at another partner, especially considering her plight when *YHWH* first chose her and considering his *checed* toward her, is a shattering blow. Abma explains: "When Israel starts to consider the possibility of combining adherence to *YHWH* with the worship of other gods, the awareness of the uniqueness and distinctiveness of *YHWH* and his Torah have in fact vanished. The covenant relationship in its special sense is no longer effective. The 'harlotry' after other gods is taken so seriously because of a mistaken view of the relationship between Israel and *YHWH* that it implies."[24]

But despite Israel's prostitution, Hosea holds out tenacious hope for her marriage with *YHWH*. By lavishing the bride with gifts, luring her to the wilderness where there are no distractions, and placing her in view of the land of promise, *YHWH* hopes to seduce Israel back into an intimate relationship of the heart. His is a loving proposal that demands a response. She will no longer call *YHWH* her "master," but her "husband" (2:18). This relationship will not just be a reunion; it will be the dawn of a completely new bridal time, with new gifts (righteousness, justice, loving-kindness, compassion, and faithfulness) that cannot fade with time.[25] *YHWH* longs for Israel to acknowledge him as a "unique partner, the covenant God with whom Israel has a special alliance."[26]

Like Hosea, *Jeremiah* opens with the analogy of *YHWH*'s marriage to Israel. "I remember your youthful loyalty, / our love as newlyweds," he says. "You stayed with me through the wilderness years, / stuck with me through all the hard places. / Israel was God's holy choice, / the pick of the crop. / Anyone who laid a hand on her / would soon wish he hadn't!" (2:2–3). But this was a time long past, a short time of faithfulness and devotion contrasted with the faithlessness and disloyalty that Jeremiah condemns. *YHWH* even refers to sending Israel her certificate of divorce because of her adulteries (2:8), but he hardly gets the words out of his mouth before he pleads for Israel to return to him (2:12 ff.). Repentance, the crucial theme in Jeremiah 3, is put in the perspective of a restored

---

24. Ibid., 140.
25. Ibid., 191.
26. Ibid., 190.

marriage relationship, demonstrating the intimacy and deep mutual commitment *YHWH* desires.[27]

Jeremiah promises an even deeper restoration than had Hosea: "The time is coming," declares the Lord, "when I will make a brand-new covenant with Israel and Judah. It won't be a repeat of the covenant I made with their ancestors when I took their hand to lead them out of the land of Egypt. They broke that covenant even though I did my part as their Master. . . . This is the brand-new covenant that I will make with Israel when the time comes. I will put my law within them—write it on their hearts!—and be their God. And they will be my people. . . . I'll wipe the slate clean for each of them. I'll forget they ever sinned!" (31:31–34).

Like Jeremiah, *Isaiah* refers to a letter of divorce for Israel (50:1–3), although some argue that because Israel cannot produce it, it doesn't exist. This is a hopeful notion because it implies no finality for the divorce and creates an opening for restored relationship.[28] In chapter 54, the message of hope continues: "For your Maker is your bridegroom, / his name, God-of-the-Angel-Armies! Your Redeemer is the Holy of Israel, / known as God of the whole earth. / You were like an abandoned wife, devastated with grief, / and God welcomed you back, / Like a woman married young / and then left . . . I left you, but only for a moment. / Now with enormous compassion, I'm bringing you back" (5–7).

This language, along with expresssions such as "my people" (10:24), "precious and honored" (43:4), and "chosen" (43:10), reveals *YHWH*'s tender affection for Zion and emphasizes the element of intimacy that is central in the marriage metaphor.[29]

In *Ezekiel*, Israel is condemned for using the gifts and jewels with which *YHWH* had adorned her to attract other lovers. She is condemned for prostitution, but God promises to purify a remnant who will know (*yada*) him. The book also foreshadows God dwelling forever with his people (48:35).

The other prophets often present the imagery of God as Lover more subtly. *Joshua*, for example, predicts unfaithfulness (24:19–20), but focuses on covenant renewal (ch. 8). The book also focuses on the home God has prepared for and promised to his bride. *Judges* narrates Israel's disloyalty

27. Ibid., 252.
28. Ibid., 72.
29. Ibid., 109.

in terms of alliances with foreigners, and refers to this intermarriage as unfaithfulness and idolatry (2:10–3:5). The people are reminded that the blessings of the covenant are contingent upon their faithfulness to it. In *Samuel*, sexual purity is a significant motif, and the prophet reminds Israel that she must remain chaste in her relationship with God. Samuel also focuses on the temple, which indicates that God desires to be in intimate contact with his bride. *Kings* describes the unfaithfulness of Israel's leaders and records the seduction of Solomon's successors.

Joel, Amos, Micah, Zephaniah, Haggai, and *Zechariah* all address the problem of Israel's idolatry in terms of unfaithfulness to YHWH. All also look forward to the repentance of Israel (or of a remmant of Israel), redemption, and eventual restoration to covenant relationship. In this way, they foreshadow the new covenant, the covenant of the heart with spiritual Israel. *Obadiah* and *Nahum* show a different side of God, the protective lover. In these books, God promises to fight for his bride. He won't allow Israel to be destroyed by her enemies.

Jonah is unique among the prophetic books because it focuses on God's desire to see a non-Israelite nation come to him. (However, it's significant that God relentlessly pursues Jonah's hardened heart when he could just as easily have chosen another messenger.) Jonah's anger over God's withering a little plant while saving a great city (Jonah 4) demonstrates his ingratitude for God's choice of Israel, the smallest and most insignificant of all nations, to be his bride and his light for all peoples. The book of Jonah ultimately shows that God wants to show his *checed* to the world.

God as Lover in the Writings

While the prophets clearly refer to the marriage motif, the writings feature the imagery of God as Lover more subtly. The ancient Hebrew hymnal called the *Psalms*, for example, provides the soundtrack for the divine-human encounter, and presents this relationship using a variety of images. The Psalms express the intimacy of a relationship with God, and they do so using the foundation metaphor of the covenant.[30] For example, God is presented as a jealous husband, and his people are rebuked for their unfaithfulness in Psalm 78. Zion is the "focal point of

---

30. Dillard and Longman, "Psalms," 228.

God's election;"[31] she is extolled as the chosen place of God's dwelling (Ps 132:13) because he loved her (Ps 78:68). The Psalms also foretell God's most intimate love gift, the Messiah (Luke 24:44).

The *Song of Songs*, as it describes the mysterious passion God created between man and woman, presents the physical symbol of a spiritual relationship with God. While the divine-human love relationship isn't sexual, it's a passionate, vibrant affair that mimics the relationship between Christ and the church (Eph 5:22–23).

Job and *Habbakuk* present figures who remain loyal to *YHWH* despite the appearance that *YHWH* is unfaithful. In the end, of course, *YHWH* is proved to be both faithful and sovereign.

While Job and Habbakuk deal with individual suffering, *Lamentations* documents the anguish of a nation. Because Israel has broken covenant, she's experiencing the covenant curses, and she's desperate to know God's favor again. Significantly, the writer of the book recognizes that, were it not for God's *checed*, she'd not only be suffering, but would be completely consumed (3:22). It's important to remember that even God's discipline is because he jealously longs for requited love from his lover. The message of *Ecclesiastes*, too, is that faithfulness to God is the only fulfilling relationship; all others will fail.

In a curious twist on the image of God as husband, *Proverbs* presents God as Woman Wisdom in competition with Woman Folly for the attention of the young men of Israel. Both attempt to seduce the young men—Woman Wisdom to purity and faithfulness to *YHWH*, and Woman Folly to promiscuity and idolatry with false gods. Those who choose Woman Wisdom are praised for their wise choice of partner, *YHWH*.

The example of Boaz in the book of *Ruth* can be seen as a type of God (the wealthy redeemer) who chooses to rescue the distressed damsel, raising her from a position of poverty to one of honor and dignity. In *Esther*, God intervenes to save his bride, proving his love to the Jews even after their unfaithfulness resulted in being exiled. The message of *Daniel* is that *YHWH* will rescue the distressed damsel once and for all, a promise that John addresses again in the Revelation.

Ezra-Nehemiah addresses the problem of (literal) intermarriages and subsequent divorces, but the people reaffirm their marriage vows to *YHWH*, promising to remain faithful to their covenant with him (Neh 8–10). Like Ezra-Nehemiah, *Malachi* addresses the problem of inter-

---

31. VanGemeren, "רחב," 640.

marriage between Israelites and foreigners, and the resulting problem of divorce. However, the book begins with the assurance of God's love (1:2) as shown by his willingness to fight for Israel against Edom. While God loves Israel, he hates divorce (2:16), in that he hates when a relationship between a man and a woman, which is designed to mirror the relationship between *YHWH* and his people, doesn't reflect God's *checed*. He hates any kind of violence to relationship because it hurts people who are made in his image—people who are designed to mirror him.

In *Chronicles*, although words like *abandon*, *forsake*, *unfaithful*, and *rebellious* characterize the book, the geneaologies speak of "Israel's continuity and her election as God's people."[32] She is still his chosen bride.

After four hundred years of silence during the intertestamental period, it certainly must have seemed that God had abandoned and forsaken his unfaithful, rebellious bride. But when the fullness of time had come, God again visited Israel, this time in a body of flesh and blood. If there was ever a question about God's passionate love, Immanuel—God With Us (Isa 7:14; Matt 1:23)—dispelled all doubts about his unquenchable desire to dwell with the bride that he had chosen and taken for his own. The New Testament presents Jesus Christ as the bridegroom, the fulfillment of the old covenant and the bearer of the new (Jer 31:31; Luke 22:20).

God as Lover in the Gospels

In the *Gospels*, the Messiah unequivocally demonstrates God as Lover, for this new covenant requires the life of God himself, which he willingly sacrifices to buy back his bride (Luke 1:68). "Love one another the way I have loved you. This is the very best way to love. Put your life on the line for your friends" (John 15:13). As in the old covenant with God, true love in the new covenant is reciprocal; it requires that the beloved obey the lover's commands (John 14:15, 21, 23). Furthermore, Jesus makes it clear that he is the one who *chooses* his followers (Luke 6:13; John 15:16); they don't *choose* him. He still pursues the house of Israel, for salvation is of the Jews (John 4:22). But the Jews fail to understand his mission, and Jesus condemns them for their wicked and adulterous desires (Matt 12:39, 16:4; Mark 8:38). Fortunately for Israel, however, the Messiah has the authority to forgive the adulteress (Luke 7:48; John 8:11).

---

32. Dillard and Longman, "Chronicles," 173.

Knowledge of God is a significant theme Jesus champions during his ministry. In John 10, Jesus describes the intimacy he shares with those who love him. He *knows* his sheep by name, and they *know* him. And if they know him, they also know the father (John 14:7). In addition, Jesus prepares his followers for his departure, explaining that he will send the Holy Spirit to live within them until he can be reunited with them. The new covenant provides that God is not only *with* us, but *within* us; he penetrates us, and this is how we *know* him.

In the same chapter, Jesus promises to prepare a place for his bride, a room in his father's house, so that he can live for eternity with her. "There is plenty of room for you in my Father's home. If that weren't so, would I have told you that I'm on my way to get a room ready for you? And if I'm on my way to get your room ready, I'll come back and get you so you can live where I live" (John 14:2–3). Those to whom Jesus was speaking would have recognized the marriage imagery here, as it was customary in Hebrew culture for a betrothed man to prepare a place for his bride-to-be in his father's house, where they would consummate the marriage.[33] This is precisely what Jesus promises to do here.

Jesus presents himself as the bridegroom in other passages in the Gospels, as well. This imagery was familiar to the Jews, not only because of its use for Lover God in the Old Testament, but also because the Jews sometimes used bridegroom imagery in connection with Messiah's coming or with the messianic banquet.[34] When Jesus presents himself as the bridegroom, he's putting himself in a position occupied exclusively by God in the Old Testament. The message is clear: Jesus = Bridegroom = Messiah.[35]

God as Lover in the Letters

In *Acts*, Luke continues the story of the pursuit of the bride after Jesus' ascension. In this book, the promise of Jesus Christ to be within us (John 14) is fulfilled by the coming of the Holy Spirit. The book also recounts how the Gospel is taken first to chosen Israel, and then to the chosen Gentiles. In *Romans*, Paul continues spreading the good news of the new covenant, "starting with Jews and then right on to everyone else" (1:16).

---

33. Youngblood et al., *Nelson's New Illustrated Bible Dictionary*.
34. Barker and Kohlenberger, *NIV Bible Commentary*, 2:45.
35. Ibid., 113.

His purpose is to describe how to harmonize the covenant promises given to Isreal with God's present plan to bless the Gentiles.[36]

Ephesians also refers to marriage in the loftiest of terms. There, Paul interprets human marriage as representing the relationship between Christ and the church (5:21–33). In this epistle, Paul explains that husbands are to care for their wives as Christ cares for the church (28–30). This love sometimes shows itself in the ultimate sacrifice, as demonstrated by Christ's sacrificial death (25). Paul explains that in dying for his bride, Christ cleansed her and made her holy (26), so that she would be "dressed in dazzling white silk, radiant with holiness" (27). This, Paul says, is how husbands should love their wives because husbands represent God, the ultimate lover. In a final note, Paul addresses the fidelity that should be present within marriage, as it represents the union of Christ and the church: "No longer two, they become 'one flesh'" (31).

In his first letter to the *Corinthians*, Paul takes up this subject again. Apparently, the Corinthian church was riddled with sexual immorality, and in 1 Corinthians 6–7, Paul addresses the problem.

> Remember that your bodies are created with the same dignity as the Master's body. You wouldn't take the Master's body off to a whorehouse, would you? I should hope not. There is more to sex than mere skin on skin. Sex is as much spiritual mystery as physical fact. As written in Scripture, 'The two become one.' Since we want to become spiritually one with the Master, we must not pursue the kind of sex that avoids commitment and intimacy, leaving us more lonely than ever—the kind of sex that can never "become one." (6:15–17)

This is perhaps the most explicit reference comparing the physical/sexual union between human partners with the spiritual union between Christ and believers.

In his second letter to the *Corinthians* (chapter 11), Paul takes up the marriage imagery again, this time likening himself to the father of the bride, whose responsibility it is to present his daughter as a pure virgin to the bridegroom. Paul explains that he's afraid that the loyalty of the bride at Corinth may be in jeopardy, and he fears their hearts are adulterous. He desires to present the church as purely devoted to her husband, Christ, and he is afraid that they may be lured away just as Eve

---

36. Gromacki, *New Testament Survey*, 182.

was seduced by the serpent. He promises to visit soon to ascertain their degree of loyalty to their first love.

The unique letter to the *Hebrews* describes much of the new covenant, prophesied in Jeremiah 31:31. This covenant will be written within, and those who receive it will know the Lord in their hearts. In the intimate terms of *YHWH* the Lover, God claims his people as his own and promises to forgive them. Hebrews presents the faithfulness of Christ over and against the unfaithfulness of Israel. It's because of Christ's spotless holiness that he can enter the dwelling of God to offer himself, so that we may be "confident that we're presentable both inside and out" (10:22).

All of the letters to the early church employ terminology from the semantic field of marriage. Believers are encouraged to be *sexually pure, holy, faithful, loyal,* and *steadfast* to the God who loves, choses, lives within, and is preparing a place for them. And because of this covenant relationship, believers are expected to live a life of love toward others as well (1 John 3:16, for example).

God as Lover in The Revelation

Finally, the marriage motif is found in *Revelation*, which describes how "his Wife has made herself ready" (19:7) for the marriage supper of the Lamb. Here the bride stands in direct contrast to the prostitute and her immoral lovers of the preceding chapters. She is a chaste bride, dressed in bright, clean, fine linen (8). The image is expanded in Revelation 21, where the bride is defined as the New Jerusalem, the holy city. This city is the ultimate Promised Land, a remake of Eden's Paradise. In this city, God is once again reunited with his bride, and will remain so forever: "God has moved into the neighborhood, making his home with men and women! They're his people, he's their God" (3).

A PERSONAL REFLECTION

I first learned about covenant relationship as I prepared to write about it in Dr. Wilbur's "Old Testament Genre" class in seminary. Some traditions, such as the Reformed tradition, base their entire doctrinal system and practice on various interpretations of covenants, but I had never before studied the concept of covenant, though I had grown up in a faith community that based its belief and practice on the Bible.

As I began to consider the foundations of my own marriage, it became critical for me to plumb what the scriptures had to say about covenant. I was both pleasantly surprised and deeply disturbed by what I found. The pleasant surprise came about as I discovered a picture of God whose *checed* moved my heart. The dread occurred because my own marriage came nowhere close to fulfilling the most rudimentary characteristics of covenant.

As I continued to consider what intimacy really is (the mutual vulnerability of knowing and being known), I began to long for it with my husband, but I wasn't sure how to go about either offering or inviting it. My answer came in one of my counseling classes, "Issues of Abuse," in which Dr. Templeton worked with a student volunteer in four counseling sessions, which were simulcast live into our classroom.

I'll never forget Freda's courage as she poured out her story to Dr. Templeton. With absolutely no visible resistance, Freda told heart-wrenching stories of sexual abuse. She described the molestation by her father when she was four years old and by an uncle when she was a young teen. As she re-lived the horror of these experiences right before our eyes, Dr. Templeton's kind presence changed Freda's experience of the scenes. No one had ever entered her story with compassion, care and pursuit like Dr. Templeton had, and the transformation on her face was amazing. The shame dropped from her features and was replaced with softness. She had come into the class a naturally pretty woman . . . she left radiantly beautiful.

In the last session, Dr. Templeton commented on Freda's intimate sharing with him and challenged her to share with her husband in the same vulnerable way that she had shared with Dr. Templeton. It was a suggestion that I decided to take into my relationship with Chip. The class had stirred up old sexual abuse memories of my own, and in an effort to be more intimate with my husband, I determined to share with him what was on my heart.

I thought primarily of Ryan, a family friend whom I had seen a couple of years before at my sister Suzie's funeral. As I reflected on that grief, I shared with Chip about how regretful I was that I had, at the luncheon after Suzie's funeral, tried to present to Ryan the image that I was fine. My whole demeanor at the funeral was an unconscious attempt to seem like I hadn't been hurt by Ryan's abuse. I'd even commented from the platform during the funeral service that my sister had helped me walk the path to forgiveness of several in the audience who had been harmful. But the soul-searching I was doing in graduate school was making me aware of the unconscious motivations for my tough demeanor, and I could no longer pretend that I hadn't been hurt.

When I came home from the last "Issues of Abuse" class, I told Chip that I was sorrowful that I had sat across from Ryan at the luncheon after Suzie's funeral reminiscing about old times as if nothing bad had ever happened. I'd ignored the elephant in the room, and I was ashamed of myself. Chip, who'd been sitting beside me, acknowledged that my casual attitude with Ryan had confused him, because it was inconsistent with what I'd shared with him concerning how much Ryan had hurt me. And even worse, Chip said that he'd felt shut out of the conversation.

As Dr. Templeton had suggested to Freda, I shared vulnerably with Chip my regret about my behavior at the luncheon, and how I was angry with myself for not picking up on Ryan's subtle guilt messages about my father's emasculating comparison of my accomplishments to his and to Davie's (my brother) failures. As I was talking, Chip stopped me. "That reminds me of the time just before we were married," he said, "when you, your mom, Ryan, Davie, and I were sitting in your mom's living room, and all of you were reminiscing about old times, and you went over and sat on Ryan's lap and stayed there for a while. I felt confused and left out and rejected."

Immediately, my heart was broken for how I had treated Chip. I burst into tears. Because of my refusal to simply recognize that I was "hurtable," that I wasn't as tough as I wanted others to think I was, I'd deeply wounded him. For the first time, I allowed myself to feel the full weight of the pain of Ryan's abuse. He'd intended to hurt me, however unconsciously, and he had, and as a result of that, I'd wounded others, like Chip, making them powerless, as I had been. I was humbled, broken, soft, sorrowful. In a word, I was repentant.

That conversation was the first in which I invited Chip into the deep core of my soul. We'd shared some sorrowful moments together, but I'd never allowed Chip to see how vulnerable I was with regard to the sexual offenders in my history. I determined to be vulnerable with Chip no matter how well or how poorly he received my heart. As it turned out, Chip didn't receive my vulnerability well, at all. Considering that he'd been drawn to my toughness before we were married, perhaps it was disconcerting for him to find out that I really was a sensitive and hurtable person.

In the interest of increasing the intimacy between us, I also began to bid for Chip to share his heart with me, but to no avail. Again, this hadn't been a pattern in our relationship, and Chip didn't indicate interest in changing our emotionally distant dynamic. As I share in chapter 9, the end of our relationship featured a few precious moments between us, but Chip was as afraid to know who I really was as I had been to accept my vulnerability.

I still long to know and be known. Perhaps you do, as well, but can't quite envision what this might look like. Or perhaps it just seems terrifying to consider letting your partner into the deepest parts of your soul. Let me encourage you to begin sharing your secrets and your feelings with your partner at whatever level challenges you to risk without creating crisis for yourself.

A THERAPEUTIC REFLECTION

Iris and Sean

Knowing. I've never been more impressed with the willingness of a couple to know and be known than I've been with Iris and Sean's commitment to it.

I began working with Iris when she and Sean were living together, as parents of a little girl, Elisa. Iris entered therapy with an open heart and very little resistance, and she made quick progress in therapy around issues of childhood sexual abuse. However, the focus of our therapy shifted for a time when problems cropped up between she and Sean after they became engaged and started to plan a wedding. Iris became unsure about whether Sean was "the one for her," so we explored that question together.

Before long, we invited Sean to come to counseling with Iris, which he did. As Iris and Sean interacted, it was clear to me that they were hiding their hearts from one another. They fought over the same petty issues over and over again, without ever really getting to the real motivations driving their arguments.

We discussed various ways that they were distancing themselves from each other, and then I told them a story: When I was twelve years old, we acquired a really cool orange soap box car with black trim. We lived on a dead-end street, and our driveway had two hills and a strait-away that led out into the road. One day, when my brother, sister, and I discovered that the soap box car had developed steering and brake problems, Davie decided to fix the steering and brake cables with duct tape. Once the repairs were made, the three of us took the newly repaired car for a test drive.

Down the driveway we went, enjoying the wind in our hair ... until Suzie tried to brake and turn. The duct-taped cables snapped, and we had no way to steer or to stop. Instead of guiding us skillfully to the side of the road as she usually did, Suzie just screamed. Before we knew it, we had crashed into the guardrail at the end of our driveway. Davie flew over the guardrail and landed fifteen feet on the other side, unharmed. Suzie jolted forward in the driver's seat, and was also unharmed. I pitched forward into Suzie's back, and got off the soap box car mildly stunned.

Then Davie pointed at my right knee. I looked down and saw blood streaming from a gash in my leg. When I had careened forward, an unsecured piece of metal trim had pierced my skin all the way down to the bone. At the sight of it, I let out a pitiful wail and went limping back to the house.

My mother cleaned the wound and took me to the hospital where they stiched up the gash. The trim had severed a nerve, which explained why I had not felt the pain of the injury. However, when the injury healed, the nerves remained close to the skin, and to this day, when something makes contact with the old wound, the exposed nerve stings to high heaven. For the rest of my life, I must be extra protective of the scarred patch just below my right knee.

I asked Iris and Sean how they would feel if they accidentally bumped me in my old wound and I hopped around in pain, holding my stinging wound. Both of them cringed to think of it, and said that they'd feel horrible and that they'd be extremely apologetic. I asked them if they'd feel any differently if they bumped me in my other knee. Although they said they'd be sorry, they wouldn't feel nearly as bad as they would if they re-injured an old wound.

I explained to them that in order for them to work through their conflicts together, they'd have to be willing to understand how they were injuring each other in their old wounds, however inadvertently they were doing so. I knew something of both Iris's and Sean's stories, and

I could see how they were unintentionally hurting one another in raw places. If there were to be any hope of moving from gridlock to dialogue in their conflicts, they would have to be willing to vulnerably share their old wounds with each other.

This metaphor helped us work through some deeply sensitive areas for both of them. I've never seen a couple navigate such precarious waters with so much courage and tenderness, and it wasn't uncommon for all three of us to cry over the wounds they described and how their conflicts tapped into these raw places. That's what knowing and being known is all about.

SNEAK PREVIEW OF THE NEXT CHAPTER

Now that we've painted a picture, in broad strokes, of what covenant looks like when it's whole (chapter 1) and broken (chapter 2), and then taken a peak into God's intimate relationship with people (chapter 3), let's zoom in for a closer look at some of the finer details of cultivating healthy relationships.

PART 2

Honest Evaluations—The Spirit of Reality Present

4

E.Q.: Don't Be Home Without It

ONE OF MY CLIENTS, Kady, was feeling her desperation keenly. A year before, Kady had discovered that her husband, Pete, had been sexually involved with their live-in babysitter, but Kady had been too paralyzed to separate from him then, so she felt that she had no grounds to do so now. She also questioned whether she could survive financially on her own, and was beside herself to think about how separating from Pete would impact their little girl, Rosie, whom they had adopted at her birth three years before. And recently, Pete had added physical abuse to the list of ways he had broken their marriage covenant.

On this particular day, Kady's work as a sign language translator took her into an unfamiliar part of her city, where she stopped to get some lunch. As she left the restaurant, her attention was drawn to a homeless woman who was talking stridently into the air, livid that a local hotel had refused to give her a room so that she could take a shower. Kady sensed the woman's desperation and was compelled to her, and despite Kady's personal struggles, as well as her uncertainty about the woman's state of mind, she approached her and asked about her story.

Tears streamed down the woman's face, and, as she told Kady about her predicament, she tightly hugged her. As Kady held the woman, she felt their kindred spirit of desperation. Lending the woman her ear and offering her compassion diffused the woman's bad temper.

Kady offered to buy the lady a meal, led her into the restaurant where Kady had just eaten, and for the next half hour, Kady donated her time and her presence to the woman. To curtail the woman's escalating rant, Kady asked the woman about her childhood—what she wanted to be when she was a little girl, her hopes, her dreams. The woman told Kady that she had wanted to be a writer, and as the woman talked about herself, she returned to her senses.

When the two women parted ways, a restaurant patron approached Kady. "I couldn't help but notice how you calmed that woman," he said. "At first, I was bothered that you had brought her in here and disrupted my lunch, but as I watched how you worked with her, I could only be amazed. Are you a counselor?"

As Kady shared this story with me, tears filled my eyes; I was in the presence of beautiful character. In response, I read Kady a story from Daniel Goleman's book *Emotional Intelligence*,[1] in which the author tells the story of how one man's exceptional relational skills quieted a large, volatile drunk man on a train, saving the passengers from imminent danger. Goleman attributed the man with emotional brilliance. I felt the same way about Kady.

A THERAPEUTIC REFLECTION

Daniel Goleman refers to the skill of interpersonal relating as "emotional intelligence." Citing research by Peter Salovey and John D. Mayer, Goleman describes five domains of emotional intelligence: 1) knowing your emotions, 2) managing your emotions, 3) motivating yourself, 4) recognizing emotions in others, and 5) handling relationships.[2] Let's take a quick look at each of these domains and then apply this information to the specific relationship of marriage.

Knowing your emotions—being able to recognize a feeling as it happens—is the keystone of emotional intelligence, and it is crucial to intrapersonal insight and self-understanding. If we don't know our emotions in the moment, we're at their mercy, and we have less control over our lives and our choices. People who are emotionally flat—alexithymics—are boring, colorless, bland. This doesn't necessarily mean that they have no emotion, but simply that they may not have words for what they're feeling because their emotional vocabulary is severely limited. Often, alexithymics can describe the bodily symptoms that accompany a feeling, such as sweating, accelerated heart rate, dizziness, and fluttery stomach, but they wouldn't know they were anxious. Having no words for your feelings tends to leave you acting like you have none. This can be particularly distressing, and even dangerous, when you have to make

---

1. Goleman, *Emotional Intelligence*, 124–26.
2. Ibid., 33–126.

a decision that requires emotion but are unable to tune into intuition and into the emotional wisdom gained through past experiences.[3]

Managing your emotions, the second skill of emotional intelligence, requires first that you know them. The goal of emotion management is balance, what used to be called temperance—neither emotional excess nor emotional poverty, but able to feel and utilize whatever emotion is appropriate for the circumstances. Anger, anxiety, and depression are particularly difficult emotions to manage, especially if you cannot recognize their presence.[4]

Motivating oneself refers to the twin emotional competencies of self-control and ambition. Self-control—the ability to stifle impulsiveness and to delay gratification in pursuit of a goal—has been shown to be a better predictor of SAT scores than has IQ. Hope and optimism are excellent antidotes to helplessness and despair, and they need to be accessible when anger, worry, and melancholy threaten to give way to the desire for instant gratification.[5] Like helplessness and despair, hope and optimism can be learned. Of course, if in your optimism you are too naïve, or you use optimism to cover up legitimate pain, you can find yourself exposed to real danger.

Knowing your emotions is a prerequisite for *recognizing emotions in others*. Alexithymics are unable to know what others are feeling because they don't know what they themselves are feeling. They fail to tune into emotional messages of tone and body language, creating distance in relationships. Empathy, the ability to know how another feels, is *the* fundamental people skill. Because people's emotions mostly are expressed nonverbally—through tone of voice, gesture, body language, etc.—those who miss these cues can miss up to 90 percent of a message.[6]

The roots of empathy begin in infancy with the emotional attunement, or lack thereof, between a child and his or her mother. When a child's emotions are met with empathy, acceptance, and reciprocation, he or she is able to internalize these skills and take them into his or her relationships through the rest of life. A lack of attunement also leaves its imprint on a child, exacting a tremendous emotional toll. When a child's emotions are not met with empathy, he or she will learn to avoid ex-

3. Ibid., 46–55.
4. Ibid., 56–77.
5. Ibid., 78–95.
6. Ibid., 96–7.

pressing feelings and may even stop feeling them altogether. Emotional neglect and emotional abuse (cruel words, threats, and humiliations) can have impact on an individual and on the people who are in relationship with that individual for a lifetime.[7]

Empathy, like optimism, has its downside, however. Children who endure covert and/or overt abuse can become hyper-empathic, a condition in the therapeutic world called hypervigilance, referring to over-alertness to the people around them. Such anxiety comes from having to constantly monitor for cues that signal danger, leaving the individual too preoccupied with others' emotions to be aware of and to take care of his or her own emotional state.

Handling relationships is the art of managing emotions in others, and those who do this well are effective interpersonally. This skill requires the ability to recognize emotions of others, so as to tune into them, as an attentive mother does with her child. How deftly one does this largely determines the quality of a person's relationships. People who are poor at receiving and sending emotions are prone to have relationship problems, whether in friendship, business, or marriage.[8]

A partnership that is characterized by these emotionally intelligent qualities shares an intimacy of the deepest kind, as it mimics in adult life the intimate attunement between infant and mother. The intimacy of making love requires that lovers respond to one another with shared desire, aligned intentions, and a synchrony of simultaneously shifting arousal. Goleman says, "Lovemaking is, at its best, an act of mutual empathy; at its worst it lacks any such emotional mutuality."[9]

Lovemaking often gets jettisoned long before couples hit the bedroom, however. In fact, a partnership with a lack of emotional intelligence on the part of one or both individuals is likely to end in divorce. The maintenance of such a relationship may be possible, but it would have no heart and be covertly oppressive, or it would be overtly abusive or neglectful, characterized by violence of some kind or another (emotional, verbal, physical, spiritual, sexual).

The current trends in marriage and divorce make emotional intelligence fundamental to the sacredness of a covenantal relationship. The stigma of divorce and the economic dependence of wives on their hus-

---

7. Ibid., 98–106.
8. Ibid., 111–26.
9. Ibid., 101.

bands are no longer strong enough to keep couples together in miserable matches, so we need to face and deal directly with the problems that prevent emotional intelligence.[10] Otherwise, intimate partnership may be threatened to extinction.

Emotional Intelligence Prevention

So what prevents emotional intelligence? As you might have suspected, the problems start in infancy. Little girls and little boys often are taught different lessons about handling emotions.[11] Parents tend to discuss emotions more with their daughters than they do with their sons. In this way, some boys become largely unconscious of their emotions and how to articulate them. Also, girls more naturally seek emotional connection with their friends while boys favor independence. This is simply a neurobiological difference—females tend to feel their emotions more strongly than males.

Given this state of affairs, Goleman says, women usually enter marriage with more refined emotional managing skills while men enter marriage with a diminished appreciation for the importance of the task of helping a relationship survive. While men talk more often with their wives before marriage, they tend to measure closeness after they're married by doing things together, not by talking things over.[12]

Women tend to have a natural proclivity for tuning into the trouble spots, while men tend to have a proclivity for tuning them out. Women also tend to initiate conversation about these trouble spots much more often than men, which leaves both partners feeling less than satisfied.[13]

This is not to say that women don't contribute their fair share of emotional unintelligence. They do. Especially if they've learned to protect themselves from getting hurt in relationship. In such cases, women often shut down their natural connective tendencies and adopt a style of relating that keeps them from having to get too close. I've treated plenty of women who've had to work for years to be restored to their natural ability to connect with people.

10. Ibid., 129.
11. Ibid., 131.
12. Ibid., 132.
13. Ibid., 132–33.

When trouble spots do occur in a relationship, *how* a couple discusses them is most important;[14] this topic will be addressed in the next chapter and in chapter 7. Suffice it to say for now that it's possible to learn to fight well, as long as both parties are equally motivated and committed to cultivating their shared emotional intelligence. Depending on the history that each individual brings to the relationship, this task will be more or less difficult. For many, it requires, first and foremost, a commitment to resolving the traumas from childhood that have left footprints on their style of relating.

In intimate partnerships, healing these old wounds is critical because much is at stake. Managing impulses in relationships that tap into our deepest longings is difficult, even in the healthiest of covenants, so relationships that hold the trauma of one or both partners have a doubly difficult animal to tame. However, when individuals can resolve these conflicts and emerge with whole hearts, they can enter, or re-enter, into relationships with an emotional savvy to which they had no access prior to their individual healing journeys.

As we'll notice in chapter 6, individuals who've experienced childhood trauma tend to find partners who have also experienced childhood trauma. We tend to marry into a situation that feels familiar, so it stands to reason that if your spouse has issues to resolve, you likely have issues to resolve, as well. What often happens in marriages with traumatized individuals is that one partner will assume all the responsibility for the pain in the relationship, and is usually the first (and only) partner to seek help. This dynamic itself suggests that there are hidden issues that need to be addressed by the spouse who takes no responsibility for the relational breakdown. The old saying, "It takes two to tango" is a good rule of thumb when it comes to working with couples in crisis.

Gabby and Neil

The five domains of emotional intelligence were partially present in Gabby's relationship with Neil, creating the illusion of healthy relationship for years. Eventually, however, the deficits of their emotional intelligence package resulted in a divorce that was disillusioning for both partners and their children.

---

14. Ibid., 133.

Everyone approved when Gabby and Neil were married. Neil was a stable, rational, responsible engineer type, and Gabby was a bubbly, emotional social butterfly. Not that she would've fit the dumb blonde jokes that are so popular these days, but she loved to play, party, and have a good time. She was full of heart and deep emotion. However, when she met Neil, she started attending a church that measured a person's spiritual life by certain behaviors: no dancing, no alcohol, no this, no that, and plenty of rigid, spiritual disciplines (church attendance at every service and function, fasting, praying, reading scripture).

In the course of time, Gabby and Neil had two boys, and while they didn't always see eye to eye on how to rear them, Gabby and Neil tried to honor one another as individuals, and they were able to come to consensus about most of their disagreements. Gabby and Neil seemed to be models of respectful treatment within marriage, and because of their exemplary, non-conflicting relationship, they often led couples groups at their church, passing along helpful communication tips that they'd learned at the marriage workshops they'd attended over the years.

Each of them fulfilled a traditional role, Neil working to support the family, and Gabby staying at home to rear their two boys. They had sex once a week, although Gabby could never climax. Neil knew that he was supposed to please her, but Gabby never felt drawn to give herself completely to him. According to Neil, they didn't have sex frequently enough, and according to Gabby, they had sex more often than she could stand. They went on vacations together, attended church together, and engaged in denial together.

No wonder it confused so many people, including their children, when Gabby and Neil announced that they would be separating on a trial basis. While Neil opposed this idea—he thought that they should stay together while they tried to sort through things—Gabby said that if she stayed in that environment, she was afraid she'd either commit suicide or succumb to an affair so as to feel alive.

A colleague and I worked with Gabby and Neil to help them determine what had gone wrong and what would need to happen differently if they were going to get back together. We had each spouse complete a "Trial Separation Agreement" form (See Appendix B), which is designed to help couples get to the heart of the issues between them and to come to consensus on what to do about their relationship. The hope is always that couples will be able to identify the problems and to commit to working through them.

As Gabby poured out her soul concerning the lack of intimacy in their marriage, Neil listened politely and impassively. Gabby shared with painful vulnerability the poverty of heart connection that she and Neil shared. Neil seemed confused and often stared out the window as Gabby spoke.

Neil brought his own concerns to the table. He couldn't in good conscience separate because it would, in his view, be contrary to the teaching of the scriptures. And divorce was absolutely out of the question because neither of them had repeatedly committed adultery (which would indicate a pattern of hardheartedness), neither had deserted the other (which only applied to marriages where one partner was a believer and the other was not), and neither had engaged in a pattern of abuse or neglect (although Neil couldn't really define what either really was).

Although Gabby and Neil's relationship appeared to have all the characteristics of a solid friendship, it suffered from a severe lack of certain emotionally intelligent qualities. There was no heart in the relationship. For twenty years, they had related to each other in an almost exclusively masculine way, like two computers communicating remotely. Gabby had squashed her feelings, along with almost everything else about her that was feminine, because she had been taught that feelings were irrational and suspect, and that they were supposed to serve the intellect.

Without Gabby's feminine contribution, including her unique ability with regard to emotional intelligence, the relationship was as lifeless as Pinocchio before he took his first breath. Over time, Gabby's spirit started to die, too. In desperation, she pled with Neil to consider her feelings, her feminine needs, but he seemed baffled by her request. Gabby wasn't behaving like the woman he'd married, and he had no idea what to do with her emotions. The only time Neil showed emotion in sessions was when he considered what it would be like for their boys to be the innocent victims of a divorce. I was encouraged by Neil's empathy for his sons, but his compassion seemed to harden whenever Gabby expressed her own feelings.

Gabby and Neil sought counsel with their pastors and with three professional, Christian counselors, but they were unable to find a way to bridge the gap between the masculine and the feminine . . . and between the unresolved childhood wounding that each had brought to the relationship. They couldn't find a way for Gabby's feelings to matter, and in the end, this failure cost them their relationship, leaving two adults and their two children severely shell-shocked and deeply wounded.

A PERSONAL REFLECTION

Emotional Intelligence Untapped

I'm not proud to admit that my history with Chip doesn't include much emotional intelligence on either side. Before Chip and I were married, it seemed to me that it was only fair that he knew about the sexual events that had happened in my childhood. I thought he should have the chance to decide whether or not to be in relationship with me, a tainted, sullied, defective individual—for that's how I saw myself at the time. Back then, I hadn't identified the sexual events in my childhood as abuse, as is typical of most abuse survivors, so when I shared with Chip those events, I simply told him that I'd been sexually involved with my older brother's friends from the time I was about nine years old until the time I was about thirteen.

I remember that my first disclosure about these events took place in Chip's car in the parking lot of my college dorm. I was afraid to tell him, but I eventually mustered the courage to say that there was something about me that he should know. I shared the information like a reporter with a news story. Hiding my dread of how Chip would respond, I spoke with little emotion—I hadn't been connected to my emotions of those events since I had cut them off at age thirteen, when I finally realized that I'd been used for someone else's pleasure. I wanted Chip to see me as tough and resilient, so I didn't show him the pain of those events, only that I had overcome it. (Or so I thought.)

Chip listened and then responded with shock, disappointment, and blame. "How could you have done those things?" he asked.

I had no answer, so I remained silent, but the shame inside of me threatened to shrink me to nothing until something else took over and hardened me up. Chip's response was exactly why I'd never told anyone about those events—I'd expected them to blame me, and I'd expected to be punished. I don't remember the rest of that conversation, but I do remember going to my dorm room in a daze. I hadn't known exactly what Chip would do with the information, but he'd confirmed my worse fears: I was damaged goods.

As I recall, our relationship became strained at that point, and although we rarely discussed these events, they hung in the air between us. We no longer simply enjoyed our budding romance; we no longer played with innocence and enthusiasm. Something had come between us, and things were no longer the same. We began bickering about meaningless things, and we continued to do so for the next couple decades.

If either one of us would have been emotionally intelligent, we would've realized that our relationship held too much pain for us to manage and contain. Both of us, however, were in a pattern of denying our emotions and of fearing the abandonment of the other. Neither of us felt safe in the relationship, but we had no words for that reality.

Our dating relationship was rocky, and I took much of my pain to my journal, which had been my closest friend since tenth grade. Several times, I considered breaking off the relationship, but I couldn't bring myself to do it. I didn't want to hurt Chip, I didn't want to deal with the pain of breaking up, and staying in the relationship seemed to be less painful than letting it go. I never gave much weight to the reality that Chip was hurtful to *me*; I was more concerned with making sure *he* wasn't hurting so that he wouldn't leave me.

So we married—two emotionally unintelligent people who continued to bicker, never really getting to the real issues between us. When my pain was more than I could bear, I sought solace in my journal, and when I read my journals seventeen years later, I noticed some disturbing themes.

First of all, I noticed that my words described my emotions pretty well, so it seemed like I had a good grip on *knowing my emotions*. The problem was that I didn't trust them. I constantly second-guessed myself, always deciding that Chip's perspective on our arguments must be more accurate than mine.

In this context, *managing my emotions* meant denying them or stuffing them in favor of Chip's. This may seem noble, but I must admit that it was really nothing more than an unconscious strategy for me to avoid the pain of acknowledging that my perspective and my feelings didn't matter to Chip. Instead of facing that reality, I simply tapped into my naturally empathic nature and used it to avoid having to admit the truth about our destructive relationship.

Motivating myself had always come easily, but again, I used this legitimate personality trait in an illegitimate way: I over-functioned in order to survive. I threw myself into undergraduate and graduate school and into work, spending very little time at home with Chip. Unconsciously,

I desperately wanted him to acknowledge my intelligence, my creativity, my talents. I wanted him to think well of me and to be proud of me, to stamp out the chronic ache in my soul from the disregard of my brother, whom I had idolized. I didn't realize that I was searching for external affirmation when there was none internally, so I continued to mercilessly drive myself for approval. In turn, Chip unwittingly became the innocent casualty of my desperate striving for affirmation. I realize now that even if affirmation had been offered, it would've had nowhere to land, nothing to attach to, and I wouldn't have believed it. Of course, I wasn't consciously aware of any of this at the time, so I had no way of communicating it to Chip.

As a result of my childhood trauma, I had also become hypervigilant—acutely sensitive to the subtle emotional messages that people provide through body language, tone, and other non-verbal means. This survival skill isn't what Goleman means when he refers to *recognizing emotions in others* or *handling relationships*. Certainly, hypervigilance notices emotions in others, but not for the purpose of loving them well. People in survival mode notice things to help them come up with strategies to generate a sense of safety in a world of potential harm.

Perhaps the pattern is becoming clear. While I possessed the qualities of an emotionally intelligent person, I over-used some and under-used others, making it impossible for me to handle relationships well. I carried the emotional burden of my marriage for as long as Chip and I were together without helping either of us in our relationship.

Emotional Intelligence Tapped

Over a season of deep soul-searching and wise counsel, I was able to realize these destructive patterns of relating. I also found that I was able to change my way of being regarding all five of the qualities of emotional intelligence once I became strong enough to feel whole and worthwhile, even without Chip's approval.

When I became more secure in who I'd been designed to be, I was able to release Chip from the demand that he save me from my wounded past. As my broken heart mended, I developed the ability to know and manage my own emotions. I remain internally motivated, but I'm no longer compelled to accomplish things in order to get the approval of others. Instead, I do what I do simply because I'm living out what is inside me to do.

I'm also able to *recognize the emotions in others* for other purposes than protecting myself—my work as a counselor requires that I empathize with people and that I have compassion—and I allow my own feelings to matter, as well. Outside of my therapy office, I no longer have one-sided relationships, and I share comfortable give-and-receive friendships. My feelings matter to my friends and theirs matter to me. Given my history, I shouldn't have such healthy friendships, so I'm deeply grateful for the beautiful relationships that I share.

I've had the opportunity to practice handling interpersonal relationships in a new way, and I've found that being secure within myself makes all the difference. When I'm not operating out of a feeling of deficit and survival, I'm able to share my heart with others without feeling destroyed if they don't receive me well.

For the last two years of our marriage, while Chip and I were separated in our house, I aspired to change my way of being in our relationship, no matter how Chip responded. I discovered that I could refrain from engaging in arguments, that I could control my responses, even when Chip said deeply hurtful things. I found that I could hurt for him and I could empathize with his pain without having to lose sight of my own. I realized that it's possible to name what is true without being contemptuous, condescending, or resentful. I learned that Chip couldn't *make* me react, even if he was completely insensitive. I had control over my own responses, no matter how Chip treated me. I could always choose to be emotionally intelligent.

During this time, our arguments diminished to almost nothing. I cried alone in my room a lot, but once I got my emotions all cried out, I could be kind to Chip, knowing that God would hold my pain with me, even if Chip wouldn't. I began to see Chip in a whole new light during those two years, and my compassion for him grew.

A THEOLOGICAL REFLECTION

What the Bible Has to Say about Emotional Intelligence

Let's take a theological perspective for a minute. I suspect that it's fairly clear that "emotional intelligence" is simply a new name for competencies that the Bible addresses. If God is our example, the Bible often describes God's emotions: we read that he grieves, gets angry, feels compassion. We also read that he manages his emotions in that he has patience, he restrains himself, he understands when people rebel against him, and he has an almost endless ability to withhold judgment. In addition, he is internally motivated to create, to convict, and to remain active in our lives. He's a master of recognizing emotions in others, knowing the thoughts and intents of our hearts. And with regard to handling relationships, God doesn't feel out of control when we respond to him poorly. Instead, his temperate control of his reactions provides the standard by which we're to measure our own skill at handing relationships (by responding rather than reacting).

Chapter 1 highlighted several verses that describe different aspects of emotional intelligence, and we could highlight many others. The passage in Galatians 5:22–23, however, provides an excellent summary of emotional intelligence:

> But what happens when we live God's way? He brings gifts into our lives, much the same way that fruit appears in an orchard— things like affection for others, exuberance about life, serenity. We develop a willingness to stick with things, a sense of compassion in the heart, and a conviction that a basic holiness permeates things and people. We find ourselves in loyal commitments, not needing to force our way in life, able to marshal and direct our energies wisely.

As we noticed in chapter 1, if all the scripture we had were the book of Genesis, we would have enough instruction on how to live in harmony with one another for our entire lives. Unfortunately, we would also see example after example of how far short our ancestors fell with regard to following that instruction, and how we've been failing in relationship in the same ways ever since.

The first chapter of the Bible gives us the most fundamental guiding principle of relationship in all of scripture. Genesis 1:26–28 reads:

> God spoke: "Let us make human beings in our image, make them
>   reflecting our nature . . ."
> God created human beings; he created them godlike,
>   Reflecting God's nature.
> He created them male and female.

From this passage we learn that human beings are stamped with the insignia of God, that we reflect the very nature of the Creator. You are imprinted with this mark, as is your spouse, your children, your parents, your siblings, your friends, your enemies. Everyone, with no exceptions, is born into this world with the mark of God built into his or her design.

Whether we understand what that means or not, it should leave us in awe of every person who has ever graced the face of this planet as it whirls through the vast eons of space and time. Somehow, our souls reflect the nature of the Divine. If we could grasp that principle and live it out—if we would behave in an emotionally intelligent manner—we would live reverently, respectfully, and full of wonder toward everyone with whom we come in contact. Ultimately, this would bring perfect peace and harmony all over the world.

Unfortunately, it wasn't long before we began to relinquish emotional intelligence, and this Genesis 1 sense of wonder was forgotten. In fact, people began to treat one another with such disregard and contempt that the first recorded blatant crime in relationship is murder. After Cain killed his brother Abel, it wasn't long before evil ran rampant all over the earth: "God saw that human evil was out of control. People thought evil, imagined evil—evil, evil, evil from morning to night. God was sorry that he had made the human race in the first place; it broke his heart" (Gen 6:5–6).

God decided to wipe out the evil and start over, but chose to spare Noah because he was moved by the integrity he saw in this man. Scripture says that, "Noah was a good man, a man of integrity in his community. Noah walked with God" (Gen 6:9–10).

So God destroyed the land with a flood and re-established relationship with his image-bearing creatures through a new representative. The first crime God addressed when he covenanted with Noah was murder:

> Whoever sheds human blood,
>   by humans let his blood be shed,
> Because God made humans in his image
>   reflecting God's very nature.
> You're here to bear fruit, reproduce,
>   lavish life on the Earth, live bountifully.
>   (Gen 9:6–7)

There's that phrase again: "Because God made humans *in his image* reflecting God's very nature." We don't need commentaries and a thorough study of social and literary context to know that this phrase, and each person to whom it refers, deserves respect. And it refers to *every* person.

How are we to treat our fellow human beings? With emotional intelligence and the respect that we would give an emissary of the Master of the Universe. This means that our spouses, our children, our parents, our siblings, our friends, and everyone with whom we have relationship is deserving of our awe and reverence. In chapter 1, we looked at the reverent view of people that C.S. Lewis presents in *The Weight of Glory*. Although he affirms that there are no ordinary people, we act like ordinary people as often as not. We were created to reflect the nature of our Creator, but instead we act more like scavengers, murdering with mean looks, cruel words, murderous tones, and otherwise showing utter contempt for the image of God in the people we claim to love.

This, of course, begs the question about what to do when we don't act like image-bearers. What do we do about the mean store clerk, the belittling spouse, and the serial killer? How can we have respect for such individuals? If all we have is awe for them, will we not give them free license to do whatever they want? Is it loving to withhold consequences from people who behave badly toward their fellow image-bearers?

Fortunately, the first book of the Bible addresses these questions, too. It's precisely *because* human beings are made in God's image that there are consequences for acting as if we are not. Adam and Eve, for example, didn't honor the instructions of the one who breathed into them the breath of life and who designed them with his very nature, so they were banished from the Garden of Eden and were subjected to the curse, about which they had been warned. We cannot act like animals if we want to be treated like image-bearers.

This principle applied to Cain, as well. When he murdered his brother, he suffered consequences at the hands of the one who'd given him life. Cain had no right to take Abel's life away, and his act of rage led him to behave in a way that didn't honor the image of God in him or in his brother. That attitude had to be avenged, and God did just that.

By Noah's time, people were acting so shamefully that it was all but impossible to tell that they were made in God's image, and God was grieved. He put into motion the consequences of such disrespectful treatment.

From these examples we learn that, out of respect for the divine image in humanity, we must take action against attitudes and behaviors that harm others. If we don't, we invite the fallen part of us to run rampant on the earth. The punishment must fit the crime, of course, so our action toward a serial killer needs to be different than our action toward a store clerk who is snippy with us because he or she is having a bad day. The serial killer needs to be taken off the streets so that he or she can't harm others. The offense of the store clerk who snaps at you for accidentally presenting the wrong currency may need to be overlooked.

Genesis details story after story in which our forefathers both harmed and helped one another, and there are always consequences for attitudes and behaviors that show disrespect for God and people.

In Exodus, God gives Moses the Decalogue, a list of ten commandments that are in keeping with treating God and human beings with the circumspection that is due the Creator and his creatures. Later, Jesus summed up these commandments: "'Love the Lord your God with all your passion and prayer and intelligence.' This is the most important, the first on any list. But there is a second set alongside it. 'Love others as well as you love yourself.' These two commands are pegs; everything in God's Law and the Prophets hangs from them" (Matt 22:37–40).

If we committed to follow these two commands and pulled it off for the rest of our lives, we would live a life that is exemplary, a life in which we harm no one, and a life that is characterized by emotional intelligence.

Jesus mentions the Law and the Prophets. In our current cannon, we also have the Writings of the Old Testament and the whole of the New Testament. Nothing in these scriptures detracts from the requirement to live in reverence of what God has created. Passage after passage after passage tells us to be simultaneously strong and tender, compassionate and firm, merciful and just, protecting of those who are weaker and allowing consequences to come to bear on those who abuse power. (For some specific examples, see chapter 1).

A plain reading of scripture with regard to how we're to treat fellow image-bearers is consistent. How we go about it is controversial, but respect and reverence are easy to spot. So are their opposites: disrespect and disregard. Be sure you're treating others respectfully or expect to suffer distance and discord in your relationships. It's just how relationships between image-bearing creatures work.

SNEAK PREVIEW OF THE NEXT CHAPTER

At last, marriage takes center stage in the next three chapters. Vows. What do we mean when we gaze into the eyes of our partner and promise to love, honor, and cherish the other in sickness and in health, for better or for worse, for richer or for poorer as long as we live? And more importantly, what *don't* we mean?

5

'Til Homicide Do Us Part

When pop star Britney Spears, on a whim, married her childhood friend, Jason Allen Alexander, January 3, 2004, the country shook its head in disbelief, disgust, and disappointment. Just fifty-five hours later, the country breathed a collective sigh of relief when the marriage was annulled on the grounds that Britney "lacked understanding of her actions to the extent that she was incapable of agreeing to marriage because, before entering into the marriage, the Plaintiff and Defendant did not know each others' likes and dislikes, each others' desires to have or not have children, and each other's desires as to State of residency."[1]

These are just a few things that these childhood friends didn't know about each other. They didn't know what, unfortunately, most couples don't know when they marry one another: who they are as individuals and what kind of person would make a good fit with them. They had never tried to envision what kind of puzzle piece would match theirs.

People who enter marriage before defining and knowing themselves inevitably set themselves up for tremendous tension in their relationship. As we found in chapter 2, we seek out what's familiar, even if what's familiar is destructive. Chip and I were no exception.

A PERSONAL REFLECTION

The Marriage Vows

On October 22, 1988, Chip and I were married in a small, nondescript church building. Although neither one of us was a member of the church, it was the denomination of my childhood, and it was all I knew,

---

1. Associated Press, "Judge Dissolves Britney's 'Joke' Wedding."

and Chip had become familiar enough with it through a high school friend to get married there.

Ours was a traditional wedding for this denomination, which meant that if we wanted music, we had to rent a piano; no musical instruments were in the building because the New Testament doesn't mention any musical instruments other than the voice. Based on their hermeneutical argument from silence, whatever wasn't mentioned in the New Testament wasn't permitted because it didn't fit what they believed was the prescriptive "pattern" of the first century church.

Our ceremony was simple and our reception was both alcohol- and dance-free, except for a disjointed dance to our theme song, "Lean on Me," with which my sister surprised us. The church guests glared at us as we danced, to Chip's mortification, and he never did forgive my sister for her attempt to give us a normal moment in an otherwise legalistic day.

In the weeks preceding the wedding, Chip and I met with the preacher whom we had chosen to perform the ceremony to determine what we wanted to vow to one another. We chose to say traditional vows, without really understanding to what we were agreeing. Let's look at the text of the ceremony and try to understand what the words really mean.

The Wedding Ceremony

The following is a transcript of the wedding ceremony:

Preacher: *We are gathered together here in the sight of God and in the presence of these witnesses, to join together this man and this woman in the holy state of matrimony.*

Marriage was instituted by God in the beginning, as it is written, "The Lord God said, '[It is] not good that man should be alone; I will make him an help meet for him....' Therefore shall a man leave his father and his mother, and shall cleave unto his wife: and they shall be one flesh." [Gen 2:18, 24, KJV]

Marriage depicts the union of all believers, collectively spoken of as the Bride of Christ, with the Lord Jesus, the Heavenly Bridegroom. In this ideal union mentioned in the Epistle to the Ephesians, the Lord Jesus is called "the saviour of the body" showing that the union should be characterized by protection and care.

In this happy relationship, there should be mutual sharing of the responsibilities of life, with the husband taking the lead in spiritual and material matters making sure every need of the home is being met. The wife has her God-appointed place in submission to loving leadership, helping to produce a home where the fragrance of Christ will permeate the atmosphere.

Chip and Jade, our prayer for you would be that your home will increasingly become, as the years go by, a fulfillment of every thought and ideal that arises in the heart when we hear the mention of that simple word, "home."

Ephesians 5:22–33 [KJV] *explains the way to bring this to pass where it says, "Wives, submit yourselves unto your own husbands, as unto the Lord. For the husband is the head of the wife, even as Christ is the head of the church: and he is the saviour of the body. Therefore as the church is subject unto Christ, so [let] the wives [be] to their own husbands in everything. Husbands, love your wives, even as Christ loved the church, and gave himself for it; That He might sanctify and cleanse it with the washing of water by the word, That he might present it to himself a glorious church, not having spot, or wrinkle, or any such thing; but that it should be holy and without blemish. So ought men to love their wives as their own bodies. He that loveth his wife loveth himself. For no man ever yet hated his own flesh; but nourisheth and cherisheth it, even as the Lord the church: For we are members of his body, of his flesh, and of his bones. For this cause shall a man leave his father and mother, and shall be joined unto his wife, and they two shall be one flesh. This is a great mystery: but I speak concerning Christ and the church. Nevertheless let everyone of you in particular so love his wife even as himself; and the wife [see] that she reverence [her] husband."*

This institution was sanctioned and honored by the Lord Jesus by His presence and that of His apostles at the wedding in Cana of Galilee and in the epistles is declared to be "honourable in all" [Heb 13:14, KJV]. This union is to be a lifetime union; therefore, it should not be entered into lightly, but discreetly, advisedly, and in the fear of God.

I require and charge you both that if either of you know any lawful impediment why you may not be united in marriage, you do now declare it, for be well assured that if persons are joined together otherwise than God's Word allows, their union is not blessed by Him.

To the bridegroom: Do you, Chip Strong, take this woman to be your lawful wedded wife, to dwell with her, to love her, to honor her, to cherish her, in sickness and in health, for richer or poorer, for better or for worse, and forsaking all others, to cleave to her and to her only as long as you both shall live? His response: *I do.*

To the bride: *Do you, Jade Stone, take this man to be your lawful wedded husband, to dwell with him, to love him, to honor him, to obey him as is fit in the Lord, to cherish him, in sickness and in health, for richer or poorer, for better or for worse, and forsaking all others, to cleave to him and to him only as long as you both shall live?* Her response: *I do.*

To the bridegroom: *Repeat after me. In the presence of God and these witnesses, I, Chip Strong, take you, Jade Stone, to be my lawful wedded wife, from this day forward, to love, honor, and cherish, until death do us part, or until the Lord come.*

To the bride: *Repeat after me. In the presence of God, and these witnesses, I, Jade Stone, take you, Chip Strong, to be my lawful wedded husband, from this day forward, to love, honor, and cherish, until death do us part, or until the Lord come.*

In pledge of these vows give and receive a ring.

For as much as you have consented to dwell together in the state of matrimony and have made these vows before God and these witnesses, and according to the laws of the state of Pennsylvania, I now pronounce you husband and wife.

What God hath joined together, let no man put asunder.

You may now kiss your bride.

The Lord bless thee and keep thee. The Lord make his face to shine upon thee and be gracious unto thee. The Lord lift up his countenance upon thee and give thee peace.

What Did These Words Mean?

When Chip and I made these promises to one another, we did so without truly understanding what they meant. We had entered into marriage in just the way we'd been warned not to: lightly, indiscreetly, and ill advisedly. I wish that we'd stopped to consider what we were really saying when we spoke these words to one another. Both sets of our parents had made similar vows, and both sets of parents had miserably kept their promises to one another, but they had remained married—at least on paper—and the message we received was that marriage, even with broken vows, was to be endured at all costs.

Now that I have taken stock of those promises and how poorly Chip and I kept them, my mind is free to consider that these vows are actually *impossible* to keep. What presumption to vow before God something that is impossible to do!

Appropriate Marriage Vows

If we'd been encouraged to say what people are really promising when they make an unconditional commitment to a partner, the vows may have looked something like this:

"Do you, Chip, take this woman to be your lawful wedded wife; to live with her; to cope in silence with the impact of sexual abuse on her life and with all the other issues that will surely keep her from loving you with both tenderness and strength; to remain with her even if she proves to be or become physically or emotionally unable or unwilling to be in intimate relationship with you; to accept the television as your closest friend when Jade proves to be more loyal to her education and to her professional work than to being present with you; to accept whether she puts you in debt up to your ears or whether she makes you rich beyond comprehension; to allow her to treat you like you are worthless; to ignore the issues that she brings into the relationship from her family of origin; to stick to her like glue even if she decides she doesn't want to be with you, pridefully refuses to admit when she is wrong, and never tries to genuinely repair the harms she does to you; and do you promise to do this until one or the other of you dies?"

Would Chip have been fool enough to respond, "I do"?

And what if the preacher had said to me: "Do you, Jade, take this man to be your lawful wedded husband; to dwell with him; to cook, clean, and to finish school so that you can get a lucrative job while Chip works part time and shares minimally in domestic responsibilities; to acquiesce to any belittling you may experience as a result of Chip's dissatisfaction from his sexual compulsions; to ignore all the other issues that will prevent him from being faithful to you in his mind and body; to not hold him accountable for dealing with his divided heart and his bound soul; to ignore the issues that he brings into the relationship from his family of origin; to comply with his attempts to control and to dominate you; to keep your heart open to him no matter whether he chooses to treat you with dignity or not; to submit to his negativity and to his passivity; to enable him to hurt you but to not let anyone know it; to give your heart and body to him regardless of whether he is strong enough to bear your burdens with you; to stay with him even if he refuses to get help to genuinely repair your relationship when you hurt one another; and do you promise to do this until one or the other of you dies?"

If I knew I was signing up for this, I hope I wouldn't have been so quick to speak my vows and agree to such foolishness. On the other hand, it would have been much more honest to agree to vows that included *conditions* for both of us. Healthier and more realistic vows might sound something like this:

"Do you, Jade, take Chip to be your covenant companion, equal partners with differing strengths; to treat him with dignity as one created in the image of God, and to kindly but firmly require that you also be treated as a fellow image-bearer; to seduce him with your feminine design into intimate relationship; to allow yourself, both soul and body (in that order) to be intimately known by him, under the condition that he treasure your soul and body like rare and priceless gems; to require that he allow himself to be known by you in the same vulnerable ways, both emotionally and physically; to encourage and support his growth into more and more of who God designed him to be; to be held accountable by him? And do you agree to break from all emotional attachments to people, activities, ideas, or a way of being that divide your loyalty to him? To enjoy your similarities; to honor and to come to appreciate your differences, humbly and frequently seeking wise counsel to help you appreciate those differences; to genuinely work to repair every breach in your relationship, accepting the emotional and physical consequences of breaking these promises, which may include separation and/or divorce due to a perpetually stubborn and unrepentant heart, so as to demonstrate your reverence for your union as a physical representation of your spiritual covenant with God?"

Comparably, Chip's vows would have been more in keeping with the spirit of a true covenant if they had sounded something like this:

"Do you, Chip, take Jade to be your covenant companion, equal partners with differing strengths; to treat her with dignity as one created in the image of God, and to require, with tenderness and strength, that you also be treated as a fellow image-bearer; to protect her heart from harm with your masculine strength; to allow yourself, both soul and body (in that order) to be intimately known by her, under the condition that she honor your soul and body like rare and priceless treasures; to require that she allow herself to be known by you in the same vulnerable ways, both emotionally and physically; to encourage and support her growth into more and more of who God designed her to be? And do you agree to be held accountable by her; to break from all emotional attachments to people, activities, ideas, or a way of being that divide your loyalty to her? To enjoy your similarities; to honor and to come to appreciate your differences, humbly and frequently seeking wise counsel to help you appreciate those differences; to genuinely work to repair every breach in your relationship, accepting the emotional and physical consequences of breaking these promises, which may include separation and/or divorce due to a perpetually stubborn and unrepentant heart, so as to demonstrate your reverence for your union as a physical representation of your spiritual covenant with God?"

This is what covenant commitments are supposed to include: sincere and firm commitments, as well as real consequences for unfaithfulness. But our practice falls far short, particularly when we insist that people remain in harmful relationships that don't honor God or one another. If Chip and I had agreed that we'd suffer consequences for our poor treatment of the other, I suspect that we would've been a little more careful about getting married without much consideration for the realities of covenant, and I expect that we would've had more incentive to treat each other with dignity.

I do realize that some could read those words of commitment and claim that they aren't commitment at all. How can you say you're committed when your commitment is conditional? Isn't it a recipe for people to get married without much stock in their vows if they think they can just get divorced when the going gets tough?

These are legitimate questions. We must distinguish between "tough going"—which includes life's hardships, like a friend's betrayal, being laid off from gainful employment, and the death of loved ones—and covenant-breakage. *"Tough going" doesn't refer to abuse and neglect*, but to those times in life that are hard to weather alone, those times when we need a strong companion and friend to help us. Chronic neglect of marriage vows and abuse, on the other hand, isn't a hardship; it's a violation of the sacred ground of relationship, and it needs to be addressed as such.

Abuse and neglect aren't merely relational storms or tough times—they're violations of relational promises, and God doesn't require that we weather them without addressing them with intentional and meaningful intervention. No one ever vows, "If you harm me or others, such as any children we might have together, I promise to allow your abuse or neglect to continue with impunity." God doesn't expect this, either, unless your name is Hosea and you have been specifically called by God to be a living object lesson for God's relationship with Israel during a specific period of time in history. I doubt that you fall into this category!

Just as we must interpret scripture in its context, it's important not to divide the statements concerning the *conditions* of covenant from the statements regarding the promises to *bless* one another in such a covenant. If the promises are kept, there's no need for the conditions to come into play at all. Following through on your commitment to bless your spouse provides appropriate grounds for marriage. If we can't commit to bless, then we shouldn't be promising to do so. Just as a violation of one commandment constitutes a violation of the whole Law, so it is with the marriage covenant. You can't keep only one stipulation of the covenant and claim that you've kept your promises. You haven't. If you haven't loved *and* honored *and* cherished your spouse, as you promised to, it means nothing that you remain together. If you can't honestly commit to loving, honoring, and cherishing your spouse for a lifetime, don't promise to. And you shouldn't commit to such a union if you can't commit to requiring your spouse to do the same for you, either. To fail to hold yourself or another accountable for continuous failure of promises isn't honoring to either party. It would be as foolish to make such a business deal as it is to commit to such a marriage.

This is a high view of marriage, but that's the nature of a God-honoring covenant. Only make covenants that you can uphold. Otherwise, you're asking to be forsaken as a result of your forsaking the covenant you made.

A THERAPEUTIC REFLECTION

Although we promise to love, honor, and cherish our spouse and to give him or her our first priority in attitude and action, none of us keeps our promises perfectly. We're quick to point out this failure in our spouse and much less eager to take responsibility for our own failures of our covenant companion.

However, if we all took individual responsibility for fulfilling our vows and for making genuine effort to repair as soon as we failed to do so, we'd have no need of divorce. So, let's take a look at what characterizes a healthy marriage (loving, honoring, cherishing, and being faithful) before we address the last vow we make: to do these things "as long as we both shall live."

To love, honor, cherish and be faithful to our spouse is what intimacy is all about. The scriptures capture this concept with the word "know," as we saw in chapter 3. To know and be known more and more deeply is the exclusive privilege of covenant companionship. Our culture has come to use the words intimacy and sex interchangeably, which is unfortunate, because many people have sex without true intimacy, and it's possible to share intimacy without engaging sexually. Intimacy is a matter of the heart, which, when expressed with vulnerability in a context of safety in a covenant, inevitably leads to sexual intimacy. As noted in chapter 1, emotional and sexual intimacy mirror on a physical level the kind of relationship that we can have with God on a spiritual level. Adam and Eve *knew* one another, and the result of their union was the conception of a child. (We'll specifically address covenant sexuality in the next chapter.)

I'm sorry to say that I know very few couples who wholly fulfill their promise to love, honor, cherish, and remain faithful to one another. More often than not, we begin to take one another for granted over time, and we forget about the courtesy and the consideration that we're careful to offer everyone else. We neglect our spouse in ways we'd never neglect our cars or our homes. We stop treasuring the other as a unique and fascinating specimen who reflects God's image.

A plethora of resources is available to us today to help us get a picture of what intimacy looks like. In *Every Man's Marriage*, for example, Arterburn and Stoeker describe the oneness of intimacy in their exegesis of Ephesians 5:28–31:

> Who sets the terms for oneness in marriage? Your wife. More accurately, your wife's essence. And that means there will be some sacrifice on your part. . . . Oneness lies not in the *sentiment* of loving your wife as ourselves, but in the *act* of loving her as ourselves. . . . The whole plan of marriage was designed that you might be one with her. And because women were created for relationship, her highest priority is that you would honor her essence as you do your own, living in mutual submission with her. We must treat the convictions and gifts of her essence exactly as our own.[2]

---

2. Arterburn and Stoeker, *Every Man's Marriage*, 53–4, 58.

The phrases, "'til death do us part," and, "as long as you both shall live" refer to this oneness, but they have been grossly misunderstood and misinterpreted. At face value, they express the sentiment of eternal love that children inscribe into the condensation on a school bus window: "John and Jane *forever*." No one enters marriage hoping it will fail; we all want to live happily ever after. In our practice of these sentiments, however, some of us act as if we promised to agree to be emotionally, physically, sexually, or spiritually battered, abused, and neglected for as long as we live.

So, when we utter the phrase "'til death do us part," after we have promised to love, honor, cherish, and give our spouse first priority, we're saying that we are committing to do *this* until we die. We are *not* promising that if our spouse beats us to a pulp that we will endure the abuse without addressing it. We're *not* promising that if our spouse comes to treat us with contempt that we won't approach the issue. When we utter those words, we do *not* mean "'til we kill one another." Emotional homicide is not what we refer to when we promise to love, honor, cherish and remain faithful *until death*. When we utter those words, we're making a promise from a positive orientation, not a negative one. When I spoke my vows, I promised to love Chip until he died, not to ignore when he didn't love me; similarly, he promised to cherish me, not to disregard my failure to cherish him.

When we make these promises, we mean that we intend to love, honor, cherish and remain faithful to our spouse until we die, and we expect that our partner will do the same. We promise to fulfill our vows, not to remain in a situation where our spouse has promised these things and refuses to follow through. We aren't promising to merely *cohabitate* (live together) until death parts us . . . we're promising to *collaborate* (labor together) until death parts us. Cohabitation by itself doesn't provide grounds to make a covenant. When we sign a promise to pay our rent on time, we give our word that we intend to do so. If it becomes clear that we haven't intended to do so, there are consequences that we can expect to suffer, namely eviction. A marriage contract is no different. If I make a promise to love someone and I don't keep my promise, I should expect to suffer consequences, including eviction from the relationship if the infraction is severe or incessant.

We've already acknowledged that none of us perfectly keeps our vows to love our spouse. Does that mean that we all have grounds for divorce? By no means. Grounds for divorce only come into play when the grounds for marriage (vows) have been broken consistently or deeply and without genuine repair. A repair and restoration process supersedes broken promises, and it's a process that re-enacts the gospel of Jesus. There are penalties for disrespecting our promises before God, but if we come to him in genuine contrition, he's faithful and just to forgive us—to restore us fully to our covenant with him. If we don't, we can expect that our relationship with God will remain distant and broken. Human covenant is no different.

Included in grounds for marriage is the understanding, whether written or not, that we will hurt our spouse and that our spouse will hurt us. There's no way that two human beings can live together day after day without hurting one another at times. Fortunately, while failure will inevitably occur in all relationships, "trust is not built on the absence of failure as much as on the willingness of each party to own and rectify each harmful break in the relationship."[3] It's an amazing feature of healthy relationship that we can become even closer to our partner after a breach that is skillfully and genuinely repaired than if the breach had never occurred! So the question becomes, how can breaches in the relationship be repaired well?

Just as our attitudes and behaviors create divided loyalties in our hearts toward God, so they create divided loyalties toward our spouse. And just as we can be restored to relationship with God through confession, repentance and repair, so we can be restored to our spouses by the same process. That's the good news.

The bad news is that few couples seek to keep their relationships free of built up resentments and spend little time in regular, intentional relationship evaluation and repair. This kind of neglect is emotionally unintelligent. (For more on the concept of "emotional intelligence," I highly recommend Goleman's book by that title; a brief summary of the concept is presented in the previous chapter.) By the time couples finally acknowledge that they've hurt one another, they've typically been doing so for years, ignoring each breach as it arose in relationship.

Repairing relationship is hard work, of course, because many people come into marriage with issues that they didn't create, and that they're often unaware of. Marriage tends to be the crucible in which all the uglies of the histories of two people get fired up together. We can either

---

3. Allender, *Wounded Heart*, 127.

allow marriage to help reveal and heal those old hurts, which requires intimacy and vulnerability, or we can deny our hurts until they build to a degree that feels too burdensome to repair.

What Makes Marriage Work

The most compelling research I've found to help people uphold marriage vows is recorded in Gottman's book, *The Seven Principles for Making Marriage Work*. After extensive work with couples in a controlled environment for fourteen years, Gottman came to one, simple conclusion: "[H]appy marriages are based on a deep friendship. By this I mean a mutual respect for and enjoyment of each other's company."[4]

Gottman spent years analyzing real-life marital interactions in an apartment on the campus of the University of Washington in Seattle, affectionately dubbed the Love Lab. When couples arrived at the apartment, they were instructed to act as naturally as possible, despite the team of scientists observing almost every interaction, the cameras recording nearly every word and facial expression, and the sensors constantly tracking bodily signs of stress, such as heart rate and blood pressure.

As a result of his work and his analysis of the data collected from these couples' interactions, Gottman was able to learn how to predict with over 90 percent accuracy whether a couple would stay happily married or not, based on their "mutual respect for and enjoyment of each other's company."

If it's true that happy marriages are based on mutual respect and enjoyment of one another, it should be good news that all we have to do to cultivate a healthy marriage is uphold our vows to love, honor, cherish, and remain faithful until death. If we do that, our marriage will have an overwhelming chance of success.

Of course, every marriage will have its difficult times. You can't throw two people together who have differences in lifestyle, personality or values and expect that the relationship will be conflict-free. And as Gottman found out, "most marital arguments cannot be resolved"[5] because they simply stem from fundamental differences. "Instead," Gottman says, "you need to understand the bottom-line difference that is causing the conflict between you—and to learn how to live with it

---

4. Gottman, *Seven Principles*, 19.
5. Ibid., 23.

by honoring and respecting one another. Only then will you be able to build shared meaning and a sense of purpose into your marriage."[6]

This type of conflict negotiation is not a novel concept. It's simply how relationships, of all kinds, work, and the Bible has attested to it for thousands of years. Of course, there are those times when couples need help in getting to the "bottom-line differences" between them, and emotionally intelligent couples seek good help early and often. They know that preventative maintenance is much less costly, emotionally and financially, than crisis management. It's also better for the children . . . but we'll address them in chapter 10.

When we promise to love, honor, cherish and remain faithful to our covenant companion until death parts us, we seldom consider *how* we're going to do this. Let me briefly present here Gottman's seven principles for making marriage work, and encourage you to get a copy of his book for yourself and begin (or continue) to practice these principles.[7]

Gottman's first principle is to get to know your partner. He calls this *enhancing your love map*, a love map being "that part of your brain where you store all the relevant information about your partner's life."[8] Again, this isn't a new concept. Knowing and being known, mutual vulnerability, is foundational to intimate friendship. Such knowing is not merely factual knowledge. Intimate partners share their inner world with each other—their deepest longings, beliefs, dreams and fears—and they do this on a regular basis. In sum, they share their hearts with each other.

The second principle is to *nurture your fondness and admiration*. The belief that your spouse is worthy of honor and respect will prevent contempt from creeping into the relationship and eroding its foundation. Couples who remember their *history* with a positive spin are more likely to have a happy *future*, as well. Again, nurturing fondness and admiration is simply what people promise to do in their vows.

Turning toward each other instead of away is Gottman's third principle for making marriage work. This principle is about romance. Staying in touch with each other in little ways builds up an emotional savings that can cushion a relationship when conflict arises. See Gottman's book

---

6. Ibid., 24.

7. From THE SEVEN PRINCIPLES FOR MAKING MARRIAGE WORK by John M. Gottman, Ph.D. and Nan Silver, copyright © 1999 by John M. Gottman, Ph.D. and Nan Silver. Used by permission of Crown Publishers, a division of Random House, Inc.

8. Ibid., 48.

for excellent exercises to help you understand and practice the art of keeping the fire burning. People have unique ways in which they feel loved (see Gary Chapman's *The Five Love Languages*), so it's important to know how to touch your spouse's heart in his or her special way. Then do that. Often. You promised to do this, too, when you vowed to love him or to cherish her.

The fourth principle for making marriage work is to *let your partner influence you*. In his research, Gottman found that "most stable marriages in the long run were those where the husband treated his wife with respect and did not resist power sharing and decision making with her."[9] While it's just as important for wives to let their husbands influence them, Gottman found that women tend to do this more naturally than men, while men have to work harder at letting their wives influence them. The concept of yielding to win, however, is as old as the Bible, as well: "Out of respect for Christ, be courteously reverent to one another" (Eph 5:21). In some circles, this is referred to as, "servant leadership," or, "mutual submission."

Perhaps you're starting to see a pattern here. Following through on your promise to respect your partner until you die will likely guarantee that you'll share many good years beforehand. It's a matter of emotional intelligence.

The fifth principle for making marriage work is to *solve solvable problems*. This implies, of course, that there are some problems that aren't solvable—69 percent, according to Gottman's research. Unsolvable problems arise from various fundamental differences between two people, and when these can be identified and defined, they can be managed. Given that when you marry someone you also marry their problems, it's emotionally intelligent to find someone whose problems are ones you can cope with. These problems will never leave completely, but you can move from gridlock to dialogue in these conflicts.

In training couples how to solve solvable problems, Gottman teaches the art of: 1) softly approaching the conflict; 2) using repair attempts effectively; 3) monitoring yourself during tense discussions so as to avoid escalating beyond a productive level; 4) reaching mutual compromise; and 5) becoming more tolerant of each other's imperfections. Ultimately, Gottman says that the basis for coping effectively with both solvable and unsolvable problems is the same: "communicating ba-

---

9. Ibid., 101.

sic acceptance of your partner's personality."[10] Need I say it again? This is what you promised to do when you exchanged your wedding vows, it's emotionally intelligent, and God has been telling us this from the beginning.

The sixth principle for making marriage work is *overcoming gridlock*. When couples find themselves in an unsolvable conflict, the best they can do is move from gridlock to dialogue. Gridlock indicates that you and your partner have hopes, aspirations, wishes, and dreams that aren't being respected by the other. When these differences remain unidentified and unaddressed, couples find themselves fighting over mundane things like whether the toilet paper is supposed to go under or over, who takes out the trash, or which in-laws to visit for Thanksgiving. Whenever the tense energy is disproportionate to the issue at hand, a couple is likely dealing with deeper issues that are being played out in a surface conflict. Their core values and differences are often rooted in childhood, which means that it takes soul-searching and a safe marriage to identify them. Safe places are created by loving, honoring, cherishing and treating your spouse as first priority. Lucky for you, that's what you already promised to do for the rest of your life.

When you've created a safe place for dreams to be shared together, you can participate in them on three levels: 1) you can listen to the dreams of your spouse, even if you don't share them; 2) you can offer financial support of the dream; and 3) you can become part of the dream. We'll never get everything we want, but if we get the most important things, we can compromise and live without the rest. Doing this together is one of the sweet rewards of a loving, covenantal relationship. You signed up for that, too, when you promised to love, honor, cherish and give your spouse first priority "forever."

The last principle for making marriage work is *creating shared meaning*. Covenant partnership isn't meant to be about parallel living. The richest and most intimate of covenant partnerships cultivate a spiritual dimension, one in which there is an inner life together, complete with symbols, traditions, appreciation of what each offers the relationship, and goals for your life together. Your covenant companion is the person you've chosen carefully to love, respect, cherish, and be faithful to for all of your days. Choose well, so that you can honor your promises to your spouse "for as long as you both shall live."

10. Ibid., 149.

(For another excellent description of what makes intimate partnerships work, see the chapter titled "Intimate Enemies" in Goleman's *Emotional Intelligence*.[11])

Emma and Terry

Remember Emma and Terry from chapter 2? When Emma came to me, she was torn about her choice of spouse because her parents had insisted that she marry Terry when it was discovered that they had been sleeping together. She felt that her choice about who to marry had been stripped from her. Having grown up in a household with a mother who was diagnosed with borderline personality disorder and other mental/emotional issues and a father who tried to avoid conflict at all costs, Emma had learned before she even went to kindergarten to set her own needs aside in favor of her mother's needs. So when her mother and father insisted that Emma marry Terry, she complied, so as not to raise the ire of either.

The day came when Emma promised to love, honor, cherish, and be faithful to Terry until she died. She never stopped to consider that she hadn't loved, honored, or cherished Terry *before* they got married, and she certainly wasn't more faithful and loyal to him than to her parents. She hadn't left home emotionally which made it impossible for her to give Terry first priority in her life. Her parents still came first.

In the course of time, Emma's attempt to get the attention she'd never received as a little girl manifested in several extra-marital relationships, and she emotionally and physically broke her promise to Terry to forsake her loyalty to all other lovers.

Terry, too, had significant unresolved childhood trauma that he'd lugged into the marriage, and it wasn't long before the two of them were in gridlocked conflict. Terry's own childhood had emasculated him, making it impossible for him to insist on Emma's faithfulness—he needed her to mother him, and that loyalty was more important to him than his loyalty to his marriage vows. Both Emma and Terry were more loyal to "a way of being that comes from a wounded past"[12] than they were to each other.

---

11. Goleman, *Emotional Intelligence*, 129–47.
12. Allender and Longman, *Intimate Mystery*, 52.

Although Emma claimed to want to be honest about the dynamics of her relationship with Terry, her fear of an angry God prevented her from facing the truth. Emma's view of God was much like her view of her parents: her job was to set aside her feelings in order to appease an emotionally unstable or distant and unprotective parent. Emma was afraid of God, and it was out of this terror that she asked me about Jephthah, the man described in Judges 11 who, in his lust to be ruler of the Gileadites, vowed to sacrifice to God the first thing that came out of his house if God would give the nation of Israel victory over the Ammonites. When the Israelites won the battle, Jephthah followed through on his promise, sacrificing his own daughter, the unfortunate and innocent victim of Jephthah's rash vow.

Human sacrifice was expressly forbidden in the Mosaic Law (Lev 18:21; Deut 12:31), so Jephthah should have known that God would be displeased if he followed through with his vow, particularly when it resembled the custom of the Ammonites who ritually sacrificed their children. He also would've known that God commands us to keep our promises (Num 30:2), so Jephthah trapped himself in his own double-bind, and his daughter paid for it with her life. As Barker says so simply, "Though Jephthah sincerely believed God required him to go through with his promise, he was badly mistaken."[13] Two wrongs didn't make a right back then any more than they do now. What would've made the situation right was for Jephthah to have softened his heart, humbly acknowledging and turning from the pride that led him to make his rash vow.

Emma's hermeneutic, her approach to interpreting scripture, allowed her to lift and isolate these scriptures from their historical-social-grammatical contexts and out of the context of the entire cannon, as she superimposed her own sub-culture and contexts over them. This is how people can find meanings in scripture that aren't there—they don't represent what the text originally meant.

Although Emma didn't want to be married to Terry, she was afraid, like Jephthah, to experience the wrath of God should she not remain with Terry until death, although she had already repeatedly broken the vows she had promised in God's presence at her wedding. I wondered how Emma would explain why a God who "hates divorce," *commanded* the men of Israel to divorce their foreign wives in Ezra's time (see chapter

---

13. Barker and Kohlenberger, *NIV Bible Commentary*, 1:352.

7 for more context on this event), which broke up families—the children were to be sent away with their mothers to their foreign lands. And what is the point of repentance (admitting and turning from wrong) if we can do penance and pay for our own wrongdoing (by remaining in harmful circumstances, for example)? Certainly, there are consequences to our poor choices, but staying in a marriage that is a false covenant doesn't correct the original mistake. Again, two wrongs don't make a right.

But Emma lived in fear that if she honestly appraised her relationship it might leave her divorced, and this possibility was much more distasteful and terrifying than facing the truth about her failure to keep her vows. While she knew cognitively that there was forgiveness from God for sincere repentance of her *sexual* unfaithfulness to Terry, she was blind to her failure of her other promise to be *emotionally* faithful to Terry. She seemed to think that she'd promised to simply remain under a shared roof until death took either her or Terry, not that she'd promised to love, honor, cherish, and remain faithful to him until death came knocking.

So why did Emma fear that she wouldn't be forgiven for breaking a vow that she hadn't even made (to merely cohabitate)? From what I could tell in my work with her, it was safer for her to fixate on this unmade vow than on the vows she did break, which would have required humility and brutal honesty. It was easier to fathom that God could forgive murderers like Moses and David than to throw herself on his mercy to forgive her for making rash vows that she'd broken over and over again. Plus, facing the truth about her marriage would have required her to face the truth about the pain in her family of origin, as well—a daunting prospect when you haven't emotionally left home.

As we noticed earlier in the chapter, when we speak the words, "in sickness and in health, for richer or for poorer, for better or for worse," we say them in the context of *loving* the other person through tough external pressures, not staying together when abuse, neglect, or unfaithfulness occurs within the relationship. If we keep the promise to *love* each other when times are tough, we'll find ourselves together on the other side of whatever hardships arise. Tough times don't include living by lies and hurting others with our entrenched, unquestioned ideas about the marriage covenant.

Because Emma's God was made in her parents' image, she couldn't see that God desires truth above all else—above all the lies that her upbringing had modeled for her—and that he doesn't despise a broken and contrite heart (Ps 34:18; Ps 51:17; Isa 57:15; Isa 66:2). He longs for us to humble ourselves and turn from our wicked ways so that he can heal us (2 Chr 7:14). He won't drag us, kicking and screaming, to an experience of his mercy and grace, but he will allow the justice of the consequences of our own poor choices to wear us down until we finally seek his face.

I'm afraid to imagine where the natural consequences of Emma's choices will ultimately take her. She remains in a state of hard-heartedness, and her pain tolerance is so high that it terrifies me to think of what it will take to break her heart. She's been willing in the past to use immorality to avoid facing painful truth, and I suspect that her anxiety will take her there again. As long as she remains more committed to an image than to the truth, she'll toy with the immoral rather than honestly appraise the foundations of her marriage covenant, which might lead her to a decision that, when sought for legitimate reasons, isn't immoral: separation or divorce.

A THEOLOGICAL REFLECTION

So what *does* the Bible say about "tying the knot" and about appropriate dynamics for the relationship afterwards?

Everything that we discovered in previous chapters about healthy, respectful relationship applies to the covenant partnership, *only more so*. Of all the people we should treat with respect, the primary object of our affection should be the person we promised to love the most, the one whom God has entrusted to us: our covenant companion. However, it seems clear from our divorce rate that partners treat one another *worse* than they do anyone else. You've probably picked up the phone in the middle of an argument with your spouse and noticed how kindly and with what consideration you spoke to the stranger on the other end. Why do we feel more shame about speaking unkindly to a stranger or a friend than we do about our lack of consideration for the feelings of our covenant companion?

Like the guidelines for general human relationships, the guidelines for the specific relationship of marriage come out of the first book of the Bible. In Genesis 2, we read that God made Eve to be a helper (the word is עזר or *ezer*, and it is mostly used of God, the helper of people) to Adam. God also created the exclusive relationship of covenant requiring the man to leave his father and mother in order to cleave to his wife.

This instruction may seem odd, given to a man who didn't have parents to leave in order to be free to love his wife. (I'm assuming, for the sake of this example, that Adam and Eve are historical figures, not merely symbolic ones, although I realize that this is debated.) However, this is the first mention of a marriage dynamic—the two have to "forsake all others," (including parents, old flames, even old ways of being) if they're to make a life of their own together.

Genesis 3, the very next chapter, records the tragic story of the dire consequences of our first parents' disregard of their covenant with God. The curse generated a war between the man and his wife that has been raging ever since. This tragic turn of events made it easier to lose sight of the image-bearing nature of our covenant companion, and we're in a constant battle to remember and practice this reverent view of the other. But to the extent that we remember the original design of humankind, we can live in covenant relationship that is respectful and intimate, however fallen.

The concept of covenant is clear enough on a plain reading, even if a complete cultural perspective is not so plainly clear. In Exodus, God establishes a relationship with the nation of Israel for which he often borrows the language of marriage, as we saw in chapter 3. For example, God calls himself a husband and Israel his bride, a covenant relationship established in Exodus 19 and then renewed in Exodus 23. When Israel disregards the terms of the covenant, he calls her unfaithful, adulterous, a whore: the language of a broken, exclusive relationship. Time and time again, God pleads with her to return to this exclusive relationship with him, but there's a limit to the hurt he'll take from her divided loyalty. So, as established when Israel agreed to the covenant, God delivers consequences for her unfaithfulness, time and time again. Remember, while his love is unconditional, relationship with him is not.

In his book, *Divorce and Remarriage in the Church*, David Instone-Brewer describes how biblical vows have survived from their origins in the book of Exodus, via ancient Jewish marriage contracts, through the book of Ephesians, and into early English marriage services, which have remained virtually unchanged for a thousand years.[14] As we've discussed, couples today make vows to 1) love, 2) honor, and 3) cherish their spouses; 4) to remain faithful to them; and 5) to do all of this "as long as they both shall live."

---

14. Instone-Brewer, *Divorce and Remarriage in the Church*, 139.

This final phrase and its equivalent wasn't part of wedding vows in the ancient world because it was understood that people don't always keep their agreements and that there are consequences for not doing so. When promises are broken frequently enough or to a high enough degree, covenants, including marriage covenants, can come to a legal end. Divorce is merely a legal acknowledgement of marriage agreements that have been irreparably broken.

The Song of Songs provides a beautiful counterpoint to marital breakdown. This ballad describes the passionate love of partners who honor each other and their covenant. If we all behaved in our marriages like the couple does in the Song of Songs, God wouldn't have needed to provide the saving grace of divorce, because there would be no couples who regarded one another contemptuously.

The passage in Ephesians 5:23–33 can be considered the Song of Songs of the New Testament as it beautifully addresses the covenant love of both human beings and of human beings and God:

> The husband provides leadership to his wife in the way Christ does to his church, not by domineering, but by cherishing. So, just as the church submits to Christ as he exercises such leadership, wives should likewise submit to their husbands. Husbands, go all out in your love for your wives, exactly as Christ did for the church—a love marked by giving, not getting. Christ's love makes the church whole. His words evoke her beauty. Everything he does and says is designed to bring the best out of her, dressing her in dazzling white silk, radiant with holiness. And that is how husbands ought to love their wives. They're really doing themselves a favor—since they're already "one" in marriage. No one abuses his own body, does he? No, he feeds and pampers it. That's how Christ treats us, the church, since we are part of his body. And this is why a man leaves father and mother and cherishes his wife. No longer two, they become "one flesh." This is a huge mystery, and I don't pretend to understand it all. What is clearest to me is the way Christ treats the church. And this provides a good picture of how each husband is to treat his wife, loving himself in loving her, and how each wife is to honor her husband.

If marriages operated like that, like healthy relationships, there wouldn't be a need for divorce. When the preacher who officiated our marriage ceremony referred to this passage in Ephesians using the word "institution" Chip and I should've questioned it. Marriage is a covenantal relationship, not an institution, and honoring our promises when we establish such a covenant is the best way to safeguard our covenant companionship.

SNEAK PREVIEW OF THE NEXT CHAPTER

The most intimate expression of connection between a man and a woman is the sexual relationship. Nothing has done more damage to the beauty of this intimate experience than sexual harm, both of children and of adults through abuse, insufficient guidance, pornography, trafficking, and other perversions. In the next chapter, we'll look specifically at sexual abuse because of the pervasiveness of this wound for both males and females. We'll also look at the intimate beauty that is possible for couples, what abuse steals from them, and how their sexual treasures can be restored.

6

Naked and Unashamed

I DIDN'T PLAN TO include this chapter in this book until I presented the material to a recent sexual abuse recovery group that I facilitate and saw the reactions. One woman was spellbound by the material and encouraged me to get it in print as soon as possible.

People are starving for information on meaningful human sexuality; our culture, with its erotica epidemic, is void of it. The oldest individual in my clientele right now is sixty-eight years old, and because she's taking to heart the material presented here, she's experiencing true sexual intimacy with her husband for the first time. How can we reach our golden years without understanding that human sexuality is designed to be about more than sensual pleasure, that human sexuality at its best is about intimacy?

Living in intimacy can be disarming; it's meant to be. The professor of one of my counseling classes in graduate school instructed us to gaze into the eyes of another classmate for twenty minutes. Or maybe it was only two and just felt like twenty. Many students dissolved into giggles. Some used the other's eyes to zone out. A few entered into the natural intimacy that eye contact induces, and some became curious about classmates with whom they had not had contact before.

When clients begin re-claiming their sexuality, one of the first assignments that I give them is to establish regular eye contact—what I call "face time"—with their partner. Face time includes being across from one another and sharing conversation, establishing regular eye contact, or positioning themselves comfortably so that they can gaze into one another's eyes without speaking.

If I told you some of the stories that I hear after such simple exercises, I might embarrass you. Many report that they are moved to tears when they realize that the last time they gazed into the eyes of another human being was either during breast feeding or during their dating experience. That should tell us something about the importance of eye contact for creating intimacy.

A THEOLOGICAL REFLECTION

Naked and Unashamed: It's About Intimacy

The Song of Songs provides a window into covenant sexuality from the human side. As we traced the communion of God, the Divine Lover, with his bride in chapter 3, we began to note the special intimacy that covenant sexuality is designed to reflect.

In *To Have and to Hold*, David Atkinson presents Barth's view that human sexuality is part of the divine image because it's a drive toward communion with another person.[1] In other words, human sexuality reflects the oneness of relationship within the Godhead. "Marriage is the context in which such interpersonal male-female relations find their most complete expression; it is a life-partnership of self-giving love, by which God's covenant pattern for life can (increasingly in time) be expressed."[2]

Although the phrase, "one flesh," in Genesis 2:24 doesn't specifically refer to sexual intercourse, it does include it. Covenant sexuality isn't merely about "flesh," not merely about bodies joining together. It involves the whole being and affects the personality at its deepest level. "It is the union of the entire man with the entire woman."[3]

Of course it's possible to engage in sexual activity without any personal encounter, even in marriage. A wedding doesn't necessarily establish that the couple will enter into the spiritual dimension that is possible and intended for human sexuality. The concept of "oneness" is the "promise of marriage that may be claimed. It is the meaning of marriage granted by God. His action in the total union of one man giving himself totally—in intention initially, and then increasingly as the covenant relationship deepens over time—to one woman, who gives herself totally in the same way in response. This union is first established by and finds growing physical expression in sexual intercourse. It grows to be

---

1. Atkinson, *To Have and To Hold*, 78.
2. Ibid., 79.
3. Ibid.

more and more in fact what it is in intention, as the relationship works out in time."[4]

Just as it's possible to engage in sex without intimacy, it's also possible to refrain from sexual expression in a misguided effort to increase intimacy with God. Paul addresses this problem of forced asceticism in 1 Corinthians 7. Sex was rampant in the city of Corinth, and as a reaction to the immorality of their culture, some of the Corinthian believers were abstaining from sexual intercourse, believing that this would help them become more spiritually mature.[5] Paul corrected this misguided notion.

In our day, many have misused this passage to demand sex from their spouse, although this passage doesn't command couple to have sex. Because the oneness referred to in Genesis 2:24 refers to the closest possible personal relationship, any sexual relationship between people outside of a covenant relationship is immoral. This doesn't necessarily mean, however, that covenanted people are required to be sexual even if the relationship is characterized by contempt. In fact, some have suggested that to engage in sex when the relationship is defective is also immoral, and that any offspring of such a union would be unwelcome.[6]

A covenant of love, however, is the foundation of the family. God blessed Adam and Eve, saying, "Prosper! Reproduce! Fill the earth! Take charge!" (Gen 1:27–28), a statement that the Jews interpreted as a command. Children born of parents whose covenant *is* a reflection of the divine relationship are considered to be a blessing from the Lord. We'll briefly address the issue of covenant and parenting in chapter 10.

It's an honor to present a model of healthy sexuality to clients who haven't a clue about how the words *healthy* and *sexuality* can be appropriate bedfellows. It's a privilege to help people who've been sexually wounded—by abuse, by poor (or non-existent) teaching, and/or by poor modeling—begin to appreciate sexuality, particularly their own. This is no easy road for most people, but when they begin to realize that human sexuality is designed to be about intimacy, not merely about pleasure and procreation, they're able to start thinking about sex in a whole new way.

When I present a healthy understanding of sexuality in my counseling practice, I begin in the realm of theology, move into the realm of psychology, and finish in the realm of physiology. As Allender says:

4. Ibid.
5. Elwell and Comfort, "Sex, Sexuality," 1181.
6. Atkinson, *To Have and To Hold*, 108.

> God loves sex. And he intends for sexuality to be a naked experience of pleasure on behalf of one another. . . . To become a "one flesh" person with your spouse means that you have submitted to their pleasure and they to yours . . . it is indeed to be the context where we know something about communion with God. . . . Sex is all about communion with God. The Bible begins with sex; it ends with sex. The Wedding Feast of the Lamb is about sexual union that becomes a metaphor for our relationship with God. Even the phrase 'to know God' comes from the very notion of knowing one's spouse. Knowing one's spouse is not an intellectual process; it is a sensual, physical experience, and that experience is meant to take you both into a far deeper relationship with one another, and to praise, to glory, to worship the God who thought this up.[7]

As we noticed in chapter 3, God presents himself as an intimate lover to his people. In the Bible, healthy sexuality begins with knowing: "Adam *knew* Eve his wife; and she conceived" (Gen 4:1, KJV, emphasis added). To be deeply intimate with someone is to know what makes her tick, what motivates him, what she dreams about, what makes life meaningful to him, what her goals are in life, how he wants to be remembered. In other words, intimacy is about knowing and being known, about mutual vulnerability: about being naked and unashamed, emotionally and physically.

Many people refer to sex as intimacy, but true intimacy occurs long before sex, and it's possible to be intimate with someone without even being sexual. While sex can be the deepest possible intimacy we can share with another human being, it's also possible to have sex without being intimate at all. See the latest movie out of Hollywood, and you'll likely see this kind of sex. In my neck of the woods, it seems like an adult book/video store is on every corner, and those who frequent them are desperate for intimacy that they'll never find there.

Psychological Differences

Healthy sexuality includes our psyches, which, according to Genesis, are made in the image of God, representing him in different ways. "Men reveal (only to a small degree more) something about God's strength and righteousness. Women reveal (only to a small degree more) something about God's tenderness and mercy. Joined in redemption, they reveal

---

7. Allender, "Desire and Ecstasy."

both his strength and mercy; sinfully divided, they expose violence and enmeshment."[8]

When we consider the character qualities that we commonly attribute to the masculine and to the feminine, we come up with lists that often look something like this:

Masculine	Feminine
Strong	Tender
Protective	Vulnerable
Penetrating	Receiving
Initiating	Supporting
Leading	Following
Valiant	Nurturing
Hard	Soft
Majestic	Beautiful
Conquering	Connecting
Competitive	Relational

Let me be clear that by this chart, I'm not advocating a hierarchical structure for male-female relationships. Notice that I didn't title the columns "male," and "female," because men and women have both masculine and feminine qualities.

Place all of these qualities in one column and you get a picture of the heart of God—both masculine and feminine. Our job, then, is to appreciate the qualities of both masculine and feminine. I don't want to imagine a world that is either exclusively masculine or that is exclusively feminine. We need both to express the full character of God, and we need to grow up our children with an ability to tap into whatever "side" of us a particular moment demands.

Physiological Differences

Physiologically, our very bodies reflect our psycho-spiritual make-up as masculine and feminine. Little boys, for example, often show their independence in relationship very early in life as they play with other children: they tend toward competition. Little girls usually show their natural bent for connection as they play with their friends, tending toward cooperation and making conversation. These differences catch up

8. Allender and Longman, *Intimate Mystery*, 90.

to little boys and little girls by the age of six or seven, when they typically no longer have best friends of the opposite gender.[9]

The differences between boys and girls become especially obvious, of course, during puberty. Adolescent boys often show their strength by heading to the weight room to bulk up so they can display their muscles. Adolescent girls typically show their interest in beauty by heading to the department store to don the latest fashions and makeup.

Consider the psycho-spiritual event that we witness in these bodily changes. When a boy begins to notice girls, he takes note of their vulnerability. Though he may not have words to describe his experience, budding young Jack looks over at blossoming young Jill, sees that she is vulnerable and soft, and decides that she needs protection. So he goes to the weight room to get strong for her.

When a girl begins to notice boys, she takes note of their strength. Though she may not have words to describe her experience, blossoming young Jill looks over at budding young Jack and decides that he can protect her. Realizing her relative vulnerability, she is attracted to Jack's muscular physique, because her instincts tell her that he can protect her with his strength. To attract him, she accentuates her beauty, knowing somehow deep inside that Jack is drawn to her softness. Jack looks over at Jill's vulnerable, tender beauty, and Jill notices Jack's strong, firm protection, and when they make eye contact, intimacy begins to occur.

Over time, Jack, if he knows and appreciates his masculinity and the strength that he can offer Jill, and if he appreciates her feminine tenderness, will seek out Jill to connect with her on an interpersonal level. Jill, if she knows and appreciates her innate skills for building connection in relationship, will respond to Jack's pursuit, and they can begin to explore whether or not their distinctive qualities might mesh well in a covenantal relationship. As they embark on this discovery process, in an ideal world, Jack and Jill will cherish one another, appreciating the gifts of their respective genders, seeking out each other for their strengths, and protecting one another in their weaknesses.

Unfortunately, we don't live in an ideal world, and Jack and Jill have likely been wounded in life. If so, they've experienced this wounding as a male and as a female, respectively. Jack's wounds will penetrate to his masculine spirit, and he'll be weakened as a male. Jill's wounds will

---

9. Goleman, *Emotional Intelligence*, 130.

penetrate to her feminine spirit, and she'll be blemished as a female.[10] How this manifests in Jack and Jill's relationship will depend on the particular wounds they've incurred along the way, how those wounds have weakened and blemished them, and how their self-protective styles of relating intertwine. Generally speaking, we find in Genesis 3 that Jack and Jill will begin expecting and demanding that the other take life's painful wounds away—a job neither one was designed to do.

As a weakened man, Jack's greatest vulnerability is his sexuality—he's hard-wired to seek out relationship and connection through sexual union. If he's a wounded man, it's easy for him to confuse sex with intimacy—to lose sight of the need to protect and honor Jill with emotional intimacy before he gets to enjoy the pleasures of sexual intimacy. It's easy for Jack to give romance to get sex (for example, he may buy her gifts and write her poetry, expecting her to "pay" with sexual favors), only to find that sex without intimacy doesn't deliver the soul-connection that he most deeply desires. Without intimacy, he finds that sex never really satisfies.

As a blemished woman, Jill's greatest vulnerability is her desire for connection—her internal software seeks relationship and union through romance. It's easy for her to seek romance at all costs—to lose sight of the importance of protecting Jack's greatest area of vulnerability: his masculinity as expressed by his sexuality. It's easy for Jill to give sex to get romance (for example, she may dress provocatively to seduce him into a possessive relationship), only to find that romance without intimacy doesn't deliver the soul-connection that she most deeply desires. Without intimacy, she finds that romance never really satisfies.

When Jack and/or Jill decide that the other is untrustworthy and that they need to wrest their power back from the other, they neglect to protect the other's area of greatest vulnerability—they move from protecting one another to possessing one another for their own satisfaction. In doing so, they wound one another to the core—often without having words to describe the disillusionment, resentment and emptiness they feel inside.

Psychological Differences in the Bedroom

The differences between Jack and Jill's psyches also play out in the bedroom. Although both experience four sexual stages (desire, plateau, orgasm, and decline), their experiences of these phases are mirror

---

10. Crabb, *Inside Out*, 221–39.

opposites. Jack is aroused quickly, often through visual images; Jill is aroused slowly, often through words. His arousal builds rapidly and is intensely focused; hers takes time and is easily disrupted. His orgasm explodes; hers reverberates. His decline is fast, moving towards sleep and distance; hers is progressive, continuing to desire cuddling and conversation. Contempt for these differences often causes deep divisions between couples. Fortunately, it doesn't have to be this way, if couples are able to sacrifice for and surrender to each other. In fact, sacrifice and surrender, Allender and Longman contend, is the reason that God created these differences.[11] "It is meant to create a heart of service, a heart of surrender, really a heart of submission to one another, to honor the body that God has made for you, that is your spouse. And if you honor one another's body, and honor your own, what you'll begin to find is it requires you to be a servant in order for you to have good sex."[12]

Obstacles to Covenant Sexuality

The fact that Jack and Jill, and every other man and woman, have been wounded creates a variety of obstacles to overcome if couples are to experience the intimacy that covenant sexuality was designed to bring. Overcoming these sexual obstacles is difficult to the degree that we've failed to identify our wounds from the past and the ways of being that we've adopted to prevent ourselves from being wounded again. Allender and Longman identify fear, anger and disgust[13] as the great killers of covenant sexuality.

Fear, Allender and Longman explain, stems mostly from comparison, either to a specific person or to a whole gender, and makes us afraid that we may not have our spouse's exclusive loyalty. Anger also kills covenant sexuality because it prevents intimacy between the couple. Conflicts need to be engaged and resolved together in order for the couple to maintain the kind of trust that is required for surrender and submission to one another. Disgust is a result of self-contempt or shame that a person feels toward him or herself, often due to past sexual abuse, promiscuity, or use of pornography. All of these obstacles can be overcome if the couple is willing to face the ghosts that prevent uninhibited covenant sexuality.

---

11. Allender and Longman, *Intimate Mystery*, 89–98.
12. Allender, "Different Bodies."
13. Allender and Longman, *Intimate Mystery*, 77–87.

When they do so, which often requires professional help and always requires honesty and time, sexual healing can occur, and they can be restored to the freedom and innocence of God's design. Restoring or discovering the gift and joy of sex "is an assault against all the powers and principalities that would divide and devour the glory of intimacy."[14]

(Allender and Longman's *The Intimate Mystery* is an excellent resource regarding covenant sexuality. Also, the two fables in Appendix E provide a picture of healthy sexuality destroyed and then redeemed.)

A THERAPEUTIC REFLECTION

Regardless of how our sexual woundedness manifests itself—whether through the impact of sexual abuse, through the damage of poor teaching about sexuality, or through sexually compulsive behavior—sexual wounds are laden with deep shame, making the healing journey especially difficult. Sexual healing is the most difficult work that many clients ever do. Consequently, many try to avoid it.

Lilly, however, entered her sexual healing work with gusto. She wanted to reclaim her feminine sexuality so that she could engage in sexual intimacy with her husband without reservation. Lilly had come to me in her mid-forties after working sporadically with various counselors over several years, and our work progressed quickly. We'd been working for over a year on the impact of various losses in her life, including the impact of sexual abuse, when she was ready to address matters of her own sexuality directly.

I had Lilly create a body map, a life-sized sketch of her body, on which she wrote all the messages, both positive and negative, that she'd received about her body parts throughout her life. As many clients do, Lilly felt much of her shame centered around a single part. As we talked about her body from head to toe, grieving the pain of the wounds she'd received, the shame Lilly had held for her body began to dissipate.

Lilly also completed a sexual development chart[15] like the one below to help her understand what healthy sexual development looks like (row 1) compared to what her own experience had been (row 2). This assignment helped her identify what she had come to believe about herself and her sexuality (row 3), so that she could make connections between

---

14. Ibid., 87.
15. Kehler, "Sexual Development Chart."

what had happened in her past and the way she responded to sexual experiences in the present (row 4). She was also able to identify what she wanted her sex life with her husband to be like (row 5).

Healthy Sexual Development	*Affective, cognitive, and behavioral learning*
My Sexual Development	*Affective work*
Views/ Lessons	*Cognitive work*
Behaviors/ Functions/ Responses	*Behavioral work*
Hopes/ Desires/ Longings	*Affective, cognitive, and behavioral work*

The work of healing from the losses listed in the "My Sexual Development" section is *affective* work; it requires connecting with the feelings of those losses and then grieving them. The work of healing in the "Views/Lessons" section is *cognitive* work; it requires identifying and challenging those beliefs and lies that our experiences have taught us and replacing them with the truth. The work of healing in the "Behaviors/Functions/Responses" section is *behavioral*; it requires identifying and working through trauma responses in order to learn more adaptive ones. The work of healing in the "Hopes" section is a combination of all three areas; it requires identifying our desires and working with a covenant companion toward intimacy of both soul and body. Unfortunately, much of the table results from deficits of appropriate modeling and teaching of healthy gender and sexual development, starting very early in life. What we don't learn from healthy sources, we'll learn from unhealthy sources; for better or worse, this information creates our arousal template—the conditions which sexually stimulate us.

Outside of session, Lilly continued to connect with God about her sexuality, and he came through for her in dreams, events, music, a body reconciliation therapy group, her passions, and her fears. Like she had been with every other issue, Lilly was a bulldog, locking onto God and not letting go until she had answers. She was able to make connections between her past abuse and her current sexual behavior, and as she did, she was willing to engage in sexually intimate experiences with her husband that had been impossible for her before.

Lilly was able to move through her sexual healing journey without a sexual healing vacation. Most of my clients, however, find that they need to take a break from sex altogether in order to start over. Spouses who've been compassionately engaged in the healing journey of their partner can respect this need, and can trust that this purposeful moratorium on sexual activity will lead them to an even deeper level of intimacy.

Most of the exercises and assignments I give couples as they work through this process together arise out of our discussions in therapy sessions. I often refer clients to *The Sexual Healing Journey*,[16] which describes the impact of childhood sexual wounds, and offers practical exercises for those who are in the process of healing from such wounds. Helping people move from sex to sexual intimacy is slow work, and often begins with simple eye contact. As mentioned earlier, most couples stop looking into each other's eyes even before they get married, and many find re-establishing this intimate contact awkward at first (or even terrifying), and then powerful. Eye contact is part of knowing and being known, and it's unfortunate that we get so used to our partners that we stop looking into their eyes.

Although healing from sexual wounds often starts with simple physical and sensual exercises, it soon becomes difficult emotional work. Much of this work must be done in a safe relationship, in real-life emotional and sexual encounters with a safe partner, where fears can surface and then be worked through to resolution. For healing to occur, such a relationship must be one that honors and respects sexuality. It must be a relationship that experientially challenges, with firmness and compassion, the beliefs and feelings of a sexually wounded partner. To help a spouse heal from sexual wounds requires gentleness, patience, and support. Many spouses have too many unresolved issues of their own to be a strong but tender presence for the sexually wounded partner.

Because so many men and women were sexually abused as children, and because sex without intimacy has become readily available in our culture, covenant relationships are being tried in ways that they've never been tried before. Keeping the faith-bonds that we made with our covenant companions is more and more challenging, and it's all too easy for us to allow our loyalties to be divided by activities and attitudes that keep us from having to face our pain or deepen our intimacy with our partners. Those who choose to walk this path together are rare indeed, but they're rewarded with rare treasures and gifts.

Men and women who join together in an honest sexual healing journey always amaze me. There should be special recognition for such couples, because it's exhausting, slow, frustrating work, and it's easy to

---

16. Maltz, *Sexual Healing Journey*.

lose sight of the potential rewards. But if your partner is willing to do his or her part, and if you can stay the process, the intimacy that you can create together can be even deeper for you than for people who've never been wounded.

I have great hope for those who enter this work, and I feel privileged to be a part of the healing process of couples who commit to it. It's truly possible for some couples to heal from sexual woundedness, and when they do, it is a cause for awe.

A PERSONAL REFLECTION

My own story of sexual recovery is a pain-filled one. I share this story here to provide an example of how past wounds eventually impact our sexual relationships in our covenant unions.

My Sexual History—The Setting (Covert Abuse)

Mom tells me that I was a gift from God when I was born because I became the reason why my parents' relationship took a brief respite from its downward trajectory. I'm told that Dad treasured, cherished, adored, and even favored me over my two older siblings. Too bad that all of this treasuring took place before I can remember it. I only remember *longing* to be treasured, *longing* to be cherished, *longing* to be valued... particularly by my father. But my family and my church esteemed females very little, practicing strict gender roles. Women were forbidden to speak in church gatherings. We were required to have long hair and wear head coverings to demonstrate our submission to the "headship of men" (as a lesson to the angels about God's economy of authority). We were forbidden to wear "immodest," or "masculine," clothing (such as shorts, jeans, or pants), and we were prohibited from wearing any accoutrements of beauty, such as jewelry and makeup, because inner beauty, as displayed by a "meek and quiet spirit," is "of great price"(1 Pet 3:4, KJV) in the sight of God. Women were valued in terms of their duty to serve, to submit, to meet the needs of others—in a word, to be *useful*. Men, on the other hand, were to be heard and obeyed. Their spiritual responsibility was to be "exercised" to participate in the meetings of the "assembly." Men were to be valued and respected simply because Adam was created before Eve, and men represented the original design for humanity.

It wasn't long before I, a tomboy, butted up against these rules and roles, but because I so desired my dad to value me, I tried to comply as best I could. This submission meant I had to hide my pain, too, since being honest about it would have been too much for my already strained family to handle. My power to engender friendliness between my parents had dissipated as quickly as it had sprung to life, and my compliance seemed to me to be the best way to keep the fragile peace. But no matter how well I behaved, I couldn't get my dad to delight in me, so I sought the attention of my brother instead, who was four years older than I. I admired Davie, idolized him, and felt honored when he chose to play with me. I felt special to Davie, who seemed to adore me.

Davie, on the other hand, was special to my mother—in her eyes, he could do no wrong. Mom protected Davie from my father, and sadly, Davie likely ended up in an emotionally incestuous relationship with my mother. Ken Adams, in *Silently Seduced*, says that emotional incest, or covert incest,

> occurs when a child becomes the object of a parent's affection, love, passion, and preoccupation. The parent, motivated by the loneliness and emptiness created by a chronically troubled marriage or relationship makes the child the surrogate partner. The boundary between caring and incestuous love is crossed when the relationship with the child exists to meet the needs of the parent rather than those of the child. As the deterioration in the marriage progresses, the dependency on the child grows and the opposite-sex parent's response to the child becomes increasingly characterized by desperation, jealousy, and a disregard for personal boundaries. The child becomes an object to be manipulated and used so the parent can avoid the pain and reality of a troubled marriage. The child feels used and trapped, the same feelings overt incest victims experience. . . . Over time, the child becomes preoccupied with the parent's needs and feels protective and concerned. A psychological marriage between parent and child results. The child becomes the parent's surrogate spouse.[17]

When Davie left home at the age of sixteen, protecting the fragile emotions of my mother fell solely to me, a role I had assumed long before, but which became much more intense at this time. Consequently, I, too, carried the effects of emotional incest for many years, particularly

---

17. Adams, *Silently Seduced*, 9.

with the loss of my own identity.[18] In describing the impact of emotional abuse on children, Adams says, "if the oldest boy is in a psychological marriage with his mother, he may act out the covert sexualized energy with a younger sister in an overt sexual way."[19] Certainly, this is how I understand my own story.

As a child, my relationship with Davie provided me with a little bit of life in a mostly dead world. Davie and I played cars; we climbed trees; we played baseball; Davie and I were inseparable. Eventually, though, Davie began to develop relationships outside of the family as he made friends at school. But I was always loyal to Davie, my ultimate hero, even (or perhaps *especially*) when he did disobedient things—such as when he stole cigarettes, when he drove the car to the convenience store when he was fourteen years old, when he introduced me to a game called "post office" with his friends, or when he taught me how to French kiss. In fact, being privy to, and sometimes being a participant in Davie's disobedience and rebellion made me feel special—Davie and I shared secrets. My relationship with Davie assuaged the loneliness of isolation from friends my own age (I wasn't allowed to associate closely with kids who weren't a part of our denomination), and I felt sophisticated hanging out with my big brother. In my heart, Davie and I were best buddies.

The Sexual Abuse Proper (Overt Abuse)

So, it wasn't unusual when Davie led my sister and me over to the James' house one summer day. The James' lived about three miles from our house, and the roads to get from our place to theirs were hardly safe for three children, approximately thirteen, eleven, and nine years old, to travel on foot—one reason why we weren't allowed to go. But we did anyway.

I remember being bored playing dolls with Betty James in her bedroom when Davie came to her doorway and invited me to come with him. I was flattered. He took me across the hall to Eddie James' windowless room, decorated with cheap posters of rock stars and scantily clad supermodels. Loud rock music filled the air, and Davie suggested that I engage in a particular sexual act with Eddie. It seemed a strange way to receive the attention of these older boys, but out of the flattery of being "chosen," and out of obedience to "male headship," I complied.

18. Ibid., 53.
19. Ibid., 13.

I don't know how long I engaged in this act, but my mind was elsewhere. I thought, *What's the point of this? It'll be over in just a few minutes. Just a little while longer. Hang in there. If you do exactly what he says and even do it well, it'll be over soon. It'll all be over soon.* Eventually, they simply dismissed me; I went downstairs to smoke cigarettes and watch TV with Betty. That first invasive sexual experience wedded sexuality in me with betrayal, servitude, and dissociation (splitting mind from body). In addition, being enjoyed became merged with suspicion and distrust.

After my experience with Eddie, Davie's friends used me for sexual favors countless times. I don't specifically remember each time, but I do distinctly remember that first time and two others because they completely changed me and my view of sexuality.

My next distinct memory with one of Davie's friends from church was so vulgar that I won't describe it here. However, as is most common with victims of sexual abuse, *I* took on the shame of it, instead of leaving the shame with the offender. In my view, this event made my ignorance about sexual things painfully obvious and exposed me as a naïve little girl instead of Davie's sophisticated kid sister. That incident formed in me the conviction that sexuality was disgusting, repulsive, and dirty, and it engendered in me a deep sense of being stained.

The summer between my seventh and eighth grade school years marked my third distinct memory of sexual experiences with Davie's friends. Preceding this unforgettable experience, my own puberty had been awakening, and I had developed a crush on my brother's best friend, Ryan Roosevelt. I could feel this crush all over my body, and I was both embarrassed and flattered when Davie and Ryan commented on my developing feminine form. They told me that I was going to be prettier than Suzie (my sister); nothing could have penetrated my heart more directly. I had longed to be pretty and noticeable since I was five years old, and I had even prayed that God would make me so. I didn't have much hope that he would, however, because girls in my world were supposed to be plain, not pretty. But Ryan said that I was, and his words ignited hope in my heart. *Did Ryan, with his big, white, charming smile really think I had potential? Could it be that this eighteen-year-old young man actually liked me, a thirteen-year-old kid?* I wasn't sure, but I yearned for it to be true.

When Ryan began kissing and caressing me, every cell in my body responded to his touch. Against all logic, I allowed myself to hope that

Ryan actually cared about me. None of Davie's other friends had ever kissed or caressed me, and for the first time, I didn't dissociate from the experience. Instead, my pubescent body responded deeply to Ryan's touch. None of the other boys had suggested, tried, or even seemed to realize that I might have desires, too, and until that time, I never had.

But Ryan.... My mind reeled with the possibility that Ryan might really care about me. Even though my head told me that an eighteen-year-old could never be interested in thirteen-year-old me, my body said otherwise, and my heart hoped for at least a secret relationship with him, if nothing else. At some point, Ryan's kissing and caressing became more insistent, his breathing became heavier, and we ended up on the dining room floor with all of our clothes off (as usual, Davie was keeping watch somewhere, in case Mom or Dad came home). I began to panic. *If we have sex, I could become pregnant!* I thought. *I'll have to confess this before the church, and I'll be shamed before everyone I know. Dad will kill Davie and me, and our already unstable family will fall apart in disgrace. All because of me. But I can't stop this now. It would be cruel to Ryan. Besides, I've been doing this for years. People count on me for this. What reason do I have for suddenly stopping now?*

Finally, the fear of exposure and humiliation won out, and I pushed Ryan off of me. "I'm sorry," I said, getting up off the floor. "I just can't do this anymore. I'm sorry. I'm so sorry." And I gathered my clothing and escaped to the bathroom. Neither Ryan nor Davie followed me, neither got angry with me, neither apologized, and neither sought me out again. You would think I would have been relieved, but all I felt was an aching loneliness. Suddenly, it was painfully clear that I'd been used for years. Not one of those boys had desired to be in relationship with me. Not one of them had any idea, or any care, about who I was or what I was feeling. Not even Ryan, who had pretended so well. I had allowed myself to be convinced, to be hopeful, and I was a fool. This experience wedded danger, abandonment, and betrayal to the confused and tormented mess that was my sexuality.

How I Acted Out What I Learned

That day I decided that I would never trust or need anyone again. I had been toyed with, played for a fool, and no one would get that chance again. I had no one with whom I could talk about sexuality, especially because I held *so many* sexual secrets by that time, so I just carried on. I became mechanical, burying my shame and releasing my anxiety through academic and athletic performance, and any other activity that required enough intense concentration or that provided enough physical or emotional intensity to overwhelm the level of extreme anxiety in my spirit.

How I Acted Out with Chip

My romance with Chip was both tumultuous and sexual, and it was intense enough to distract me from my pain. We mistook intensity for intimacy, as so many do. Although we had not had intercourse together by the time we got married, we were involved in many other sexual activities. Even the very beginning of our relationship was sexual. In fact, the first time I knew Chip was interested in me was the weekend of my father's funeral when he broke a date with another girl and traveled ten hours to be with me. That weekend, we spent a lot of time making out, and it wasn't long before our relationship was based solely on the physical.

Chip and I were married eighteen months later, and the wedding night was one of the worst of my life. The jokes that I heard Chip's friends cracking at our wedding concerning the wedding night were arrows to my heart. But they were right: we *were* supposed to have sex that night, weren't we? Chip was *supposed* to "get laid." By the time the wedding was over, the last thing I wanted was to have sex. But we left the reception and went off to celebrate our first night as newlyweds.

My first experience with sexual intercourse was physically and emotionally painful, and I couldn't stop the tears streaming down my face. When Chip asked why I was crying, I replied, "Because I'm so happy." How this lie ever convinced Chip (or me) I'll never know, but that was the end of the conversation. I was empty and confused. *What have I done? Is this what marriage is all about?* I wondered. There was no tenderness or mutuality, and I felt used as I had so many times before. I had no idea what to do, and I was too ashamed to talk to anyone about it, so I just carried on.

Chip, who had come into the marriage with his own sexual baggage, had no better idea than I about the sacredness of sex. About five years into our marriage, Chip revealed that he struggled with sexual addiction, and that he had married me, in part, because he thought that having a constant sex partner would cure it.

The Beginning of Healing

After six years of extreme marital tension, I finally sought counsel and began to deal with my own sexual history. I had never considered my experiences to be sexually abusive, but when my counselor asked if I would consider it abusive if what had happened to me had happened to his children, I had to acknowledge that I would. He spoke kindly to me and treated me with the delicacy a wounded person needs. His words, "It's not your fault," and "I don't see you as a prostitute," were almost too good to be true. When facing the pain of my abuse led me into a spiritual awakening, my hope for my marriage changed dramatically for a time, but my disgust for sex was still beyond my understanding, so I just carried on.

At one point, Chip began to explore his own sexual issues, and for a while, his compulsive Bible study replaced his compulsive masturbation, and he described experiencing freedom from the power of the addiction. Years later, Chip joined a men's group at church specifically for men struggling with sexual addiction. In this group, he found community and good reading material on the subject for the first time. Although he learned a lot about sexual compulsion, he continued to make sexually compulsive choices, and he remained critical and contemptuous toward me. Still, there was no tenderness.

At the same time, I was taking a "Marriage and Family" class in seminary, which provided Patti (my commuting buddy) and me with endless material to discuss. On the night of class when Dr. Templeton outlined the differences between the sexual cycles in males and females, I mentioned to Patti that it was hard for me to work on sexual issues with Chip because I felt guilty that meeting my needs demanded that his be sacrificed. "It always reminds me of the time when I left Ryan on our dining room floor, fully aroused," I confessed. "I felt so guilty that I had allowed him to get all excited and then just dropped him like a hot potato."

Patti's response rocked my world: "How is that different than what you have experienced for the last fifteen years? In terms of the feminine sexual cycle, your own sexual needs have *never* been met." *Wow!* What an epiphany for me to realize that for my entire married life, I had been sacrificing the way I, as a woman, experience arousal (emotional intimacy) for Chip's style of arousal, and that my experience with him was tantamount to being fully aroused and then left completely unsatisfied. I had never connected before that *I* was sexually deprived.

With this realization, I initiated a discussion with Chip about our sex life. We'd been having several over the previous weeks, so Chip wasn't surprised. When I explained that having no heart-to-heart connection with him for the last fifteen years was comparable to bringing him to full arousal only to stop the sexual experience, Chip seemed to understand. We decided to make a plan: Chip would be in charge of initiating romantic times, with the expectation that such moments *wouldn't lead to intercourse*. My job was to initiate sexual intercourse at least once a week, as long as the romance was occurring. This plan required that both Chip and I relinquish to each other the control of our deepest longings, even though both of us had a pathetically poor track record of meeting each other's need for true intimacy. It was a terrifying proposition, but it was so contrary to our natural ideas that it felt to me like the paradox of the gospel: life through death. "The plan" called for us to trust each other to be committed to the good of the other, even if it meant self-sacrifice.

It turned out that Chip and I had a miscommunication about this plan: Chip thought that *I* was going to be in charge of romance, and that *he* was going to be in charge of initiating sex—just the opposite of what I had thought, and just the way it had been for our entire fifteen-year marriage. Chip wasn't willing to switch roles, and I didn't know what else to do, so nothing changed.

Redeeming Sexual Desire

I continued to search for the meaning of human sexuality, which at thirty-something still eluded me. I couldn't figure out how human sex was any different than animal sex, but after much soul searching and reading, I finally realized the beautiful distinction: human sex is personal, intimate, sacred—a *reflection*, on the physical level, of what we can have with God on a spiritual level. Animal sex is a mere *reflex*, a biological drive. Animals can't have intimate personal encounters when they're having sex; people can. Because I had never had a personal, intimate sexual encounter, this difference, which may be obvious to many, had eluded me. The two words, *personal encounter*, revolutionized my whole outlook on sex. Sexual abuse and sexual intimacy began to differentiate themselves in my understanding.

This was the beginning of appreciating the beauty of sexual desire, which had always seemed treacherous to me because it took me back to the scene with Ryan in the dining room. Then, my desire for intimacy, and ultimately sexual connection, had been stirred. I'd been completely caught up in the moment . . . I'd been present to myself like never before; I'd felt alive; I'd abandoned myself to the moment. I'd given myself over to my longing, and before long, I'd lain naked on the floor. I'd lain my desire bare, and my body had followed close behind. Then, Instead of honoring my desire as a holy thing, a thing that defined my very soul in that moment, Ryan had exploited it and took advantage of it. From that moment with Ryan, I became terrified of sexual desire in any form because I learned that my desire leaves me naked, and that when I'm naked, someone will use my vulnerability to his own advantage. When he doesn't honor the holiness of sexual desire, his own and mine, he'll see my nakedness as an opportunity to strip me and steal from me.

I remember the night that I finally faced what it felt like to have my desire exploited. I was lying in bed after a sexual experience with Chip. Chip had gone downstairs, and the memory of Ryan and I on the dining room floor flooded my mind and my body. I sat up in bed, hugged my knees to my chest, and watched that horrible scene unfold in my mind's eye, moment by moment. I didn't resist feeling my desire, my terror, or the betrayal of exploitation. I allowed myself to feel fully the horror that my desire had left me wide open, raw, naked, exposed. As I allowed myself to feel the panic and the pleasure of those moments with Ryan, I sobbed with fear and with sorrow for my wounded thirteen-year-old soul.

It felt good and right to recognize with tears both the terror and the desire. It felt like I finally honored what should have been honored back then. I honored my soul, laid bare. I had never really felt my sexual desire to be good, but now I realized that, even in that moment when it was exploited, it was an expression of my very being. Over twenty years after the event, I finally wept for the lack of reverence that was paid to my soul's desire that day. It had become safer for me not to desire at all, which had been a source of great disappointment in my marriage. I had never been able to recover my desire, and sex always required strenuous mental and emotional work for me. I had asked God to restore my desire, but my fear of it being exploited for someone else's pleasure had seemed insurmountable.[20]

But, I had to be brutally honest with myself: I had wanted to reclaim my sexuality without the pain of a fundamental change of heart. Something in me sensed that this possible change was profound, and that it was likely to cost dearly to recover a healthy experience of it. I had to ask myself, *How badly do I want to change? How much am I willing to invest in this change? How much am I willing to pay? Am I willing to give all I have to change for the sake of loving well?*

It just so happened that, as I was pondering these questions, I was also reading *The Awakened Heart*, by Gerald May; it proved to be a tremendous book to read with the issue of sexual desire on my heart. In this book, May explains how desire is fundamental to our identity. I had never thought of desire in that way. I pondered all the desires that I had followed throughout my life. I couldn't think of any desire that I hadn't pursued, other than sexual desire. My desires to accomplish various things in life had defined me. I'd always felt that those desires were pure, that they were a large part of my identity, and I'd been true to them (academics and sports, for example), despite my family's and my church's opposition to them. I had become less and less willing to allow what I thought others might think to steal my desires from me. I may not have had all of them fulfilled, but they were mine, and I was most alive when I felt them and lived them out.

It was a powerful moment when I realized that my sexual desire is pure, too. It's how I am designed as a human being. My sexuality is a *gift* from God, and it's just another way in which I can feel alive. I realized that, when I cut off those desires, I re-abuse myself, in that I treat my desire as an unholy thing—the enemy. In fact, my desire *is* me in those moments, and when I don't allow myself to feel it and abandon myself to it, I don't allow myself to live—I murder myself—and I didn't want to do that anymore. Every time I did, it replayed the abuse scenario, except that now *I* was the perpetrator, violating myself.

I'd read it in Allender's material many times: sexual abuse victims wrongly believe that it's their desire (not necessarily sexual desire, but

---

20. See the final footnote in chapter 9 for the amazing and rare conclusion of this part of the story.

certainly desire for relationship) that's the problem, and so they decide never to desire again.[21]

Taking My Desire into Covenant

But trusting Chip with my desire seemed nearly impossible, and I wasn't even sure whether it was wise, given his history with sexual compulsion and his disdain for me. I couldn't measure up to his fantasies. I had to ask Chip and myself some hard questions: Would Chip protect me if I gave myself over to my own desire, at which time I would be completely powerless to protect myself? Could I allow myself to follow the desire, if I knew that Chip wouldn't take advantage of it?

I needed to ask Chip if he would be able to protect my desire like a treasured possession and treat it tenderly, like an innocent, vulnerable child. I needed him to promise that he'd guard my desire, that he'd cherish it as my very soul, that he'd regard it with great reverence. I needed him to promise not to use my vulnerability in order to get what he wanted or needed. I needed him to hold my desire with the utmost care and recognize it as spiritual, sacred. I needed him to revere my desire as holy ground.

One evening, I expressed to Chip that, in our relationship I was no longer willing to settle for ground beef when we were meant for steak. I assured Chip that I wanted the best for us, that I wanted *us*. I told Chip that I was no longer able to believe that our difficulties were all about my sexual abuse. Chip had always insisted that his issues were minor in comparison to mine, and I was unwilling to accept that anymore. Everything I saw said otherwise. Betrayal bonding indicated that both of us had acted out our trauma on each other. People who have no trauma, or little of it, don't develop sexual compulsions, and they don't treat their wives with disdain. So I shared with Chip my conviction that until he stayed the entire process of recovery, the two of us would be stunted in our marriage. I had come to realize that a large part of my perpetuating the trauma bond had been about my own lack of willingness to place Chip's responsibility to be a man on his shoulders, rather than taking it on mine. Chip was responsible for his own recovery, for his own life, and for his own choices. I would no longer, as much as I could understand, suffer under what was Chip's to carry.

Chip didn't understand what I was trying to communicate, so I explained that I was unwilling to settle for second best in our relation-

---

21. Allender, *Wounded Heart*, 59.

ship. I could no longer have a sexual relationship that was devoid of intimacy. I explained to him that I'd like to enjoy initiating lovemaking, that I wanted it to occur more frequently, but only if it were a result of intimacy in our relationship in general. I explained that there'd been no affection toward or interest in me personally for quite some time, that I was the only one showing affection. Without emotional intimacy between us, making love just couldn't and wouldn't happen. I was doing my part, but Chip wasn't doing his. I explained that it had been no favor to Chip that I'd been settling for a sexual relationship that required so little of each of us. The way Chip and I had been relating sexually called neither one of us to be all that God had designed us to be, and I couldn't settle for anything less than the best anymore. We'd been content with crumbs when God had made for us a banquet.

Chip was confused by my explanation. He didn't understand what his part was, what I was looking for, what I wanted. Though I desired that Chip treasure me for my sake, I mostly wanted Chip to be happy with himself, as a solid individual, for *his* sake. In the end, I hoped that this stability would spill out into our relationship as a by-product that we could both enjoy. This was no different than what Chip had said he wanted, as well, and yet he hadn't worked through his issues enough to be able to offer intimacy. He still struggled with poor self-esteem, passivity, angry outbursts, and a lack of basic convictions about the significance and value of human beings and of the sacredness of relationships. Chip still saw his problems as outside of himself. If he just had a job, if we could just tickle each other and play, if we just had some money.... Until his focus turned inward, he would continually fall into funks that never really resolved.

I explained to him what I wanted for me. I wanted to be cherished, respected, loved, and treated with kindness and consideration. My healing process had left me feeling worthy of respectful treatment, and Chip had to learn the same thing. The only way he would be able to offer respect and love to me was when he was filled up with respect and love in his own heart, so he could have overflow to spill into me. Chip wasn't there yet.

I began to imagine how our relationship could begin anew. I envisioned both of us having an opportunity to go back in time, establishing who we would have been if we hadn't gotten sidetracked by our own woundedness and poor choices. I realized that if I had gotten help much earlier, I'd be doing exactly what I was doing: pursuing a career in counseling, a desire I'd had since junior high school. Chip, too, could take the opportunity to find himself, to find employment and recreation that he enjoyed and in which he could find satisfaction. If we both did this, we'd spend less time with each other, but the time we did spend would be of highest quality. We wouldn't be looking to each other to fill ourselves up. We'd come together full and be able to spill over into each other.

Starting Over

To break our trauma bond, we'd have to start over, as suggested in *The Betrayal Bond*.[22] I realized that, as wounded as our relationship was, we'd need to separate and establish a formal dating time where our emotional and sexual relationship could be pursued in a new way. I needed Chip to pursue emotional intimacy with me and refuse to settle for second best in our sexual relationship. I needed him to respect and protect me as a woman. The time to break our trauma bond was long overdue.

Starting over would mean that Chip and I lived separately. With hindsight, it's easy to see that finding separate residences might have helped us to sort through our issues more effectively. However, we chose an in-house separation so as to limit financial difficulty. (I now realize that the *goals* of the separation should have driven whether or not we cohabitated during this re-evaluation time; finances should have been secondary.) I wondered if it would also help to have a re-marriage date, a date when we could begin physical involvement that slowly led to making love.

Chip didn't seem to envision what starting over would look like, but I was sure that we would have to establish a friendship first, without expectations or attachments to particular outcomes. We'd need to go on regular dates, something we hadn't done for fifteen years. We'd need to communicate clearly whenever we were ready for the relationship to go to a deeper level.

Both Chip and I would have to be in the process of healing as individuals, for *ourselves*, even if our relationship couldn't be put back together again. Chip would have to demonstrate his desire to connect with his masculinity, in part, by finding a job (I had been the only one working while the two of us were pursuing our education). Chip would have to connect with his masculine soul and become the preserver and protector of his own sexual healing. I'd have to stop rescuing Chip, and he'd have to stop looking for me to rescue him. I'd have to focus solely on my own healing, whether or not Chip focused on his. We'd have to honor

---

22. Carnes, *Betrayal Bond*, 145–70.

the differences in one another, without role expectations and assumptions. We'd need to be differentiated from each other, so that each of us felt free both apart and together. Differentiation could include each of us having friends that were not necessarily mutual ones. Honor, respect and acceptance would have to replace control, contempt, and criticism. We'd have to learn to communicate through our conflicts, and to do whatever it took to be honest and healthy.

To resolve old wounds between us, we'd also have to be in counseling together, since working through our issues alone had proven futile. One of our first counseling assignments was to do a little dreaming about what the ideal marriage would look like. Here's some of what was important to me:

- We share a camaraderie in regards to dealing with and healing from past hurts
- We've recognized and worked through the hurts that we've caused each other in our relationship, past and present.
- I feel that Chip cherishes and treasures me.
- We're secure that each will empathize with the other.
- Chip feels tenderly toward himself regarding his own past hurts and toward me regarding mine, and vice versa.
- I can admire my husband because he's not afraid of life, of his own pain, and of honest appraisal of past and present hurt (family of origin issues, ways he's hurt me, ways I've hurt him).
- I can admire my husband because he's proactive, not passive, toward life.
- I can admire my husband because he's both strong and tender.
- When we talk about our relationship, sex is not the first thing we discuss.
- Sex is a natural expression of a whole relationship; emotional intercourse comes first.
- Sex is not merely a way to regulate affect; it's an expression of intimacy.
- I'm no longer deprived of what "turns me on"—intimacy (as described by all these bullet points).

- Chip is willing to do whatever it takes to work through sexual compulsion issues.
- Each of us takes responsibility for our contribution to our relational brokenness.
- We each assume the best in each other, not the worst.
- Chip honors the uniqueness of women and fights to protect it; he's willing to take a hit for me or go to bat for me. I can rest in his protection of my heart.
- Chip has a clear picture of manhood and takes pride in representing that picture. Because he is secure in himself, I feel secure in Chip's leadership.
- I have a clear picture of womanhood and I take pride in representing that picture. Because I'm secure in myself, Chip feels secure in my support.
- We take pride in each other as we represent true femininity and true masculinity.
- We share a deep affection for one another.

I'm sorry to say that Chip didn't complete this assignment, and we never did compare or discuss our lists. I include this list to encourage you to define what's important to you with regard to covenant communion. If you can't agree on your emotional needs in the relationship, your sexual relationship will reflect the division between you, and one or both of you will continually get hurt. Covenant relationship always begins in the heart, and whatever is there eventually makes it into the bedroom.

Obstacles to Covenant Sexuality with Chip

Chip and I were unable to come to a heart-to-heart understanding of how his sexual issues and mine interacted with one another. After we divorced, however, I still wanted to discover as much as I could about what had gone wrong within me and between us sexually, so I remained in therapy for another year, working on my body image and other issues regarding sexuality.

Over several months, my counselor and I discussed the issues that arose when I completed a body map. What we discussed led to writing a prayer about my body that reflects my gratitude for each of my body parts, from head to toe, in the specific way that each can give and receive love.

HEALTHY SEXUAL DEVELOPMENT	*0–2 yrs.*—mom and dad modeling masculine/feminine
2–4 yrs.—same as above; plus, learn body parts; privacy issues; read *A Very Touching Book*,[23] or equivalent
4–6 yrs.—same as above; plus, age appropriate discussion about sexuality (where babies come from); anticipate and answer child's questions; take kids on dates (modeling); build strong relationship with your child
6–8 yrs.—same as above; plus, more sophisticated explanations
8–10 yrs.—same as above; plus, discuss puberty
10–12 yrs.—same as above; plus, prepare to celebrate child's entry into manhood or womanhood
12–14 yrs.—build on above; parents initiate increasingly sophisticated and honest instruction about sex and gender; negotiate dating rules
14–16 yrs.—build on above
16–18 yrs.—encourage more independence; keep communication lines open; spend one-on-one time, as young adult allows
18+ yrs.—be open to give *solicited* advice; let them fail, then pick them up

The work: identify (cognitive) |

---

23. Hindman, *A Very Touching Book*.

My Sexual Development	Dad controlling; Mom accommodating; modeling *broken* masculine and feminine
	Dad disrespects Mom; Mom does nothing about the injustice
	Mixed messages about beauty and strength, male and female; confusion
	Gender and sexuality is confusing, not purely enjoyable within responsible limits
	Preaching/teaching on the "impurity of women"
	Preaching/teaching on female submission, obedience to men
	Mom protected Davie; likely enlisted him as a surrogate spouse
	Mom enlisted me as a surrogate spouse
	Uninformed by the right people; no age-appropriate guidance
	Over-informed by the wrong people
	Brother's betrayal into sexual abuse
	Early stimulation
	Stolen discovery
	Sense of wonder lost
	Loss of innocence
	Boys dominate sexual interaction
	Sexual favors gave me "friends"
	No protection of sexual boundaries
	Exploitation of innocence and admiration
	Pain is covered up
	The work: identify and grieve (affective)
Views/ Lessons	Men are powerful; woman are weak
	Female (my) needs or desires are not important
	Sex must be secret
	Sex and sexual pleasure is perverted, dirty, exploitive
	Femininity is dangerous, alluring, seductive
	Men have no self-control/should not be expected to have it; this is the sole duty of the woman

VIEWS/ LESSONS -CONTINUED-	Females must do as males want
	Female sexual desire is perverted
	Sex is power; if you don't use it, you lose it (battle of the sexes mentality); somebody will inevitably get hurt
	To be desirable and have sexual power, I must be thin
	Sex is an obligation/duty
	Sexual Feelings = Acts (no choice); sexual feelings are uncontrollable
	Celebration vs. Seduction—no understanding of the difference
	Men want sex without relationship; sex is for males; males dominate; all guys want is sex
	The attention of a man is critical for self-esteem; it's better to be with an abusive man than to be alone
	I must be in control so as not to be exploited
	Sex is a way to say, "thanks for being my friend"
	Submission (defined as *obedience*) to males is godly
	Masculinity is about power and control—loss of appreciation for masculinity and strength
	Femininity is about fragility and weakness; loss of appreciation for femininity (beauty and vulnerability)
	You can't trust anyone
	Not knowing makes you a fool
	It's up to me to survive
	Males are more important to God than females
	Christians aren't supposed to have pain
	Image is more important than truth; justice isn't important
	The work: identify and challenge (cognitive)

Behaviors/ Functions/ Responsiveness	I accommodate others; I don't know my needs or desires; can't speak them	
	Arousal leads to shame	
	Selection of harmful partner	
	No *or* only male friendships	
	Dissociation; lack of presence	
	Not active participant; sex as obligation of woman to her man	
	Arousal cycle is extended	
	Seduction; sexuality as power	
	Avoidance (e.g., not wanting to be seen naked; staying busy)	
	Aversions vs. Preferences	
	Compulsive masturbation	
	Addictions—food, work, education, busyness, exercise, image—anything to avoid intense loneliness	
	Flashback management—sex is too much work	
	Desire dysfunction/ disorder	
	Shame about sexual passion or any sexual feelings	
	Loss of passionate sexual expression; inhibition	
	Focus only on bodily pleasure, no intimacy	
	Tough Girl, Good Girl, and Party Girl styles of relating, as needed	
	The work: identify and work through (behavioral)	
Hopes/ Desires	(I haven't included my responses for the last column, because I want to save what I desire in a sexual relationship to share with a covenant partner. However, I encourage you to complete this column for yourself.)	
	The work: identify, challenge, grieve and work through (affective, cognitive, behavioral)	

Two Parables

After completing this chart for myself, I decided to write my story and Chip's story in fable form, which turned out to be a particularly healing exercise for me. (See Appendix E.) The first fable shows a girl's sexual journey from abuse to healing and freedom. The second shows how a boy found healing and freedom after a non-sexual wound manifested itself in sexual confusion. I hope that you'll brew a cup of tea and sit back to enjoy these twin parables that paint a picture of what's possible for couples when they work through sexual wounds and ignorance to see innocence restored. I tell the same story in narrative non-fiction form in the Personal Reflection of the next chapter.

My Wish for You

As a therapist, I get to help courageous couples reach new places of intimacy in their lives together. If your wounds have impacted your sexual understanding, I hope that you, too, will commit to a process of brutal honesty with yourself so that you can enjoy a sexual awe and gratitude that gives you a, "foretaste of heavenly worship."[24]

SNEAK PREVIEW OF THE NEXT CHAPTER

If you've ever been involved in a divorce—as a child, as an adult, or as a friend of someone who has—you probably hate it as much as God does. The only reason sensible people seek to dissolve a marriage is if the dynamic of the relationship is more painful than the prospect of ending it. Even God reaches his limit in the face of continual unfaithfulness, and we can learn from what he eventually did to terminate his covenant with Israel. These are the hard realities of the next chapter.

---

24. Allender and Longman, *Intimate Mystery*, 97.

7

A Decalogue to Diagnose Hardening of the Heartery

A Toxic Condition

When I was in the third grade, my little African American buddy, Wes Brown, stole my heart. He wasn't the cutest boy in my class, but he was a lot more fun than blonde heartthrob, Jim Docker. I remember writing love messages into the condensation on the bus windows: "Jade + Wes 4ever." I was embarrassed to admit to Wes that he was number one on my long list of boys that I liked because I was pretty sure he liked Kim Hall better, so at nine years old, I already felt the sting of unrequited love. Was it possible that love didn't last forever after all?

In sixth grade, after puberty had hit and my appearance was more important to me than ever, I fell in love with another less-than-beautiful boy, Bailey Green, who had enrolled in my school a little late in the year. I remember that when he entered the class, I decided not to become friends with him because I thought he wasn't very good looking. Several months later, after I had gotten to know sweet, quiet, lost Bailey, I found again that appearance was less important to me than true connection. (With the clarity of hindsight, I can see that at the age of eleven, I was already drawn to boys who seemed like they needed to be rescued. And I found that as I got to know him, Bailey grew to be more attractive to me. I committed our love to paper—the brown, paper bags that covered my textbooks—"Jade Green 4ever."

One day I found out that Bailey was in danger of being held back in sixth grade. I felt the sting of abandonment, so I met him at his bus at the end of the school day and warned him that our relationship was in jeopardy if he didn't pass. "I can't wait for you, you know," I told him. "You'd better pass." He didn't.

It turns out that "4ever" lasted only until the last day of school that year, although the little girl in me will always love the little boy in Bailey. As adults, we still long for the security of "4ever" love, and we rarely stop to consider what we will do if our lover's heart becomes hard and turns away from us?

God uses the same word when he declares his forever *love* for Israel, but he's careful to include stipulations that put conditions on forever *relationship*, as we've seen. Though he has great patience for and compassion on us, if we harden our hearts and abandon him for long enough without responding to his attempts to draw us back to him, we can expect to feel a lack of intimacy with him. When that happens, God hopes that the pain of our failures will drive us to turn back to him again (Deut 31:17–20). We also know that God is merciful, compassionate, and understanding of our frailty—we're but creatures made of dust—and humble, contrite hearts move him. We find mercy by simply admitting our sins and leaving them (Prov 28:13); this restores us to relationship with God. (More on the cure for hardheartedness, repentance, in the next chapter.)

In chapter 5, we took a close look at the meaning of marriage vows, and we tried to imagine what our vows might sound like if we promised what we ended up living out. If we wrote the vows between God and hardhearted Israel the way she ended up living them out, I imagine they would sound something like this:

Do you YHWH, Creator of Israel, take Israel to be your treasured possession? To live with her, love her, protect her, and remain loyal to her regardless of her disloyalty to you? To endure her stubborn insistence that she be allowed to engage with impunity in emotional and sexual affairs with other lovers—lovers like money, sex, power, greed, handmade idols, other ideologies? Do you promise to remain in relationship with her even when she incessantly demands her freedom, when she uses your gifts to entice other lovers and to create a life without you? And do you promise to do this forever?

Would God agree to such an arrangement? We know from previous chapters that he didn't. Intimate relationship with him is conditional, even if his love is not. Like Bailey, who, it seemed to me at the time, didn't love me enough to heed my warning and pass sixth grade, Israel ignored God's warnings and developed a toxic condition: hardness of heart. Despite repeated warnings about how hardheartedness would ruin her and her relationship with her Husband, Israel refused to go under the knife of the Heart Surgeon and cut out the cancer. After many periods of separation, plague, famine, and war in hopes of bringing her back to him forever, God finally drafted the divorce decree (Jer 3:6–11; Hos 2:1–2).

A THEOLOGICAL REFLECTION

As we noticed in previous chapters, the scriptures provide broad outlines of the way human beings ought to treat each other as fellow image-bearers, but there's little additional instruction regarding the specific covenant of marriage. In chapter 1, we noticed that the Torah provides a primer for human behavior and a basic law code for violations of respect. In chapter 2, we noticed that any covenant can be broken, and *broken* covenants may result in *cancelled* covenants. In chapter 3, we noticed that God has his limits with regard to violations of his covenant of love with Israel, although what he wanted most was for Israel to genuinely repent so that he could be reconciled to her.

In all of these broad strokes, the scriptures don't describe the process of *how* to end a marriage covenant when its vows are broken without the genuine effort of both parties to repair the breach. The only extended example we really have is husband-God with wife-Israel. In this example, we see a husband who is *almost* infinitely patient with his wife, while she is only marginally committed to him. Of wife-Israel, husband-God says,

> "These people make a big show of saying the right thing,
>   but their hearts aren't in it.
> Because they act like they're worshipping me
>   but don't mean it,
> I'm going to step in and shock them awake,
>   astonish them, stand them on their ears.
> The wise ones who had it all figured out
>   will be exposed as fools.
> The smart people who thought they knew everything
>   will turn out to know nothing."
>   (Isa 29:13–14)

Wife-Israel's hypocritical lip-service, pretentiousness, and presenting a false image eventually got old for husband-God. In the meantime, Israel received warning after warning, discipline after discipline, while *YHWH* hoped that his wife would care about his hurting heart and repent of her covenant violations.

In the end, God wrote her a certificate of divorce and sent her away, but not until he'd done everything in his power to prevent this drastic measure. *How* did he arrive at this decision? What was his process? The first thing he did was at the beginning of the relationship, when *he established clear covenants and conditions before he entered into the union* (Exod 19 and 23; Deut 27–30). He would love, provide for, and protect the nation of Israel, and she would choose him as her God. If she chose to renege on the deal, *YHWH* would discipline her by withdrawing his provision and protection. If Israel refused to return to the covenant promises even after this, God would separate himself from her. If she still refused to soften her heart, God would divorce her.

Second, when Israel became unfaithful (within a week of the covenant signing), *God followed through with the covenant consequences.* Through the prophets, he warned her of the coming repercussions if she refused to return to the promises of the covenant agreement. Third, *he employed creative attempts to win her back,* including the object lesson of the prophet Hosea, who exemplified in his marriage to a prostitute the covenant of God with Israel. Fourth, when she continued in her unfaithfulness, *God withdrew from her,* allowing her enemies to pummel her, in the hope that she would still turn back. Occasionally, Israel returned to God in repentance, and a whole generation would enjoy the blessings of the covenant agreement. But it was never long before her loyalties became divided again, and God followed through on his promises to do whatever it took to win her heart back. Finally, after too many of these cycles, God's heart was too broken to suffer another cycle of abuse, and he repeated his ultimate warning: return to him or be cut off. Israel chose not to heed the warning and found in her hand a *certificate of divorce.*

From *YHWH*'s example, we can learn several things about the marriage covenant. First, a couple needs to come to a joint agreement on the covenant conditions and what they mean before they enter into the union. Second, the marriage vows should include an understanding that the relationship is conditional regarding keeping those promises. Third, when marriage vows are broken, as they will certainly be, the erring spouse should have an opportunity to genuinely repent and sincerely repair the damage. Fourth, too many cycles of broken vows eventually wear on a person. Not even God chose to withstand a constant emotional roller coaster. If God has limited capacity for divided loyalty and establishes consequences for it when he establishes covenant, marriage partners should do the same. Marriage relationships need to be characterized more by loyalty to their spouse than by loyalty to anything or anyone else. Any breach in primary loyalty needs to be wholly repaired.

If it's not, the offending partner should expect to suffer appropriate consequences, while the offended party hopes that his or her spouse's pride will not be greater than the desire for restoration.

Hardheartness Defined

When Israel's loyalty was divided between Adonai and other gods (both literal and attitudinal idols), God did whatever he could to encourage her to soften her hard heart. As we've noted, this sometimes meant dire consequences for his bride. When God gave the original law of divorce to Moses, he made provisions for hardness of heart.

The Bible refers to the concept of hardheartedness many times and in many different contexts. "Hardness of heart" is often interpreted to mean "sinfulness," but in the Old Testament, hardheartedness refers to "stubbornness."[1] For example, Pharaoh's hardness of heart refers to his resolve to refuse God's command to set Israel free. The passage in Psalm 95:7–8 contrasts hardening one's heart with hearing God's voice. A hardened heart sometimes refers to a lack of understanding about God's redemptive work in the world, as in Mark 3:5, when the Pharisees tried to find a reason to accuse Jesus of breaking the law, and as in Mark 6:52, when the disciples failed to understand who Jesus was. (See also John 12:40, 2 Cor 3:14, and Eph 4:18.)

Israel is also called hardhearted on many occasions and for a variety of reasons, including such obstinacy as idolatry, half-hearted worship, failing to tithe, false teaching, practicing religion for the sake of image, performing what was required without emotional engagement, adopting the pagan religion of the nations around them. Romans 11 can be understood as a description of the consequences of a perpetually obstinate heart: God's rejection of one lover (Israel) in favor of another (Gentiles). This state of affairs is described as temporary (Rom 11:25), but the separation is sorely felt.

Several passages of scripture refer to different ways to make or break various kinds of covenants, such as the bond of faith (2 Thess 2:13), of friendship (1 Sam 20:42), of promises to God (Exod 20:37), of covenant with a nation (Josh 9), of a promise (Titus 1:2), of a treaty (Amos 1:9), of trust (Col 1:23), of one's word (Jer 34:15–16), of one's vow (Num 30:2). Breaking faith, or disloyalty of any kind, represents a hardness of one's

---

1. Instone-Brewer, *Divorce and Remarriage in the Bible*, 144.

heart, and it is accompanied by consequences. Leviticus 26:26 promises plague, famine, and war upon Israel for breaking the covenant. Numbers 5:5 refers to *any* sin as a broken trust with God, and details various consequences for different breaches of that bond. Deuteronomy 17:2 declares death as the consequence for breaking the covenant through idolatry. Deuteronomy 32:50–52 records God's judgment upon Moses and Aaron for breaking faith with God before the whole nation of Israel at the waters of Meribah Kadesh. In Joshua 7:10–14, we read of God's condemnation of Israel for breaking the covenant with him by taking forbidden plunder—a sin that needed to be purged from the camp if they were going to win the battle over their enemies. In Judges 2:1–3, God condemns Israel for making a covenant with Egypt, which would become a thorn in their side. Ezra condemns Israel for breaking trust with God by marrying foreign women, and then God requires that they divorce them (Ezra 10:10). Jeremiah 34:11–15 refers to Israel's broken promise to free its slaves every seven years and promises that Israel will suffer for neglect through plague, famine, and war. Ezekiel 16 condemns Israel for breaking the covenant with God in ways that made Sodom seem righteous. Ezekiel 17 describes a king of Israel who tried to skirt God's judgment. "Does anyone break a covenant and get off scot-free?" God asks (18). In chapter 44, Ezekiel indicts Israel for breaking covenant by putting foreigners, uncircumcised in heart or flesh, in charge of the sanctuary. Hosea 6:4 chronicles Adam's broken covenant with God, the consequences of which have been reverberating through the ages. Hosea 8:1 names Israel's practice of breaking covenant by saying they know God but not acting like it.

No matter how you do it, breaking loyalty belies a hard heart, but confession, sincere change of heart and repair, can restore right relationship. The opposite of a hard heart is, of course, a soft one. Pliability toward God means to be "enlightened by God's truth, obedient to God's commands and compliant with God's will."[2] Such a soft, receptive, humble heart can be a way of being or it can be the result of a humbling process by which God leads us to repentance, the focus of chapter 8.

Jesus, when calling ancient Israel stubborn, alluded to the passage in Deuteronomy 4, which describes Moses giving the original divorce law to the Israelites. This passage is unclear about whether their stubbornness 1) is sufficient grounds for divorce, 2) refers to the heart of the

2. Ryken, "Hard, Harden, Hardness," 364.

one who initiated the divorce, 3) concerns the obstinacy of the Israelites who insisted that Moses allow them to divorce, or 4) is in regards to the problem of their unbending refusal to give divorce certificates to former wives. Because wives would find it impossible to remarry without such a certificate, Instone-Brewer suggests that the fourth interpretation squares best with the original context of the law. However, because the phrase "hardness of heart" is an invention of the Septuagint, it would have been unlikely that Jesus' audience would have known this context, and would have more likely thought of Jeremiah 3 as they listened to him, which refers to God as the indignant, jilted lover, and to Israel as the unfaithful partner who refused to repent.[3]

In *Grace and Divorce*, Carter puts it this way:

> When Moses gave the original law of divorce, he was issuing the words given to him by God. Clarifying this pronouncement, Jesus explained that God (through Moses) allowed divorce because there were some instances where spouses were so hardened in attitude that a reasonable marital life could not proceed. In this respect, Jesus gave an answer to their question about the motives behind divorce. People can sometimes be so stubborn, so entrenched in ungodly ways of living that they refuse to bend, or they refuse to live with the mind of love that is essential for a thriving relationship. It is an unflattering truth, but hardened hearts, according to Jesus, cause divorce. He was not saying that He liked the idea of divorce; rather, He was acknowledging the prideful, painful state of mind that leads to a broken marriage.[4]

Just as there are many ways to break the spirit and the letter of our bond of faith with our heavenly husband, so there are many ways to break the bond of faith with our human covenant partners. As Atkinson notes in *To Have and To Hold*, Jesus addressed the *spirit* of the law on adultery, not just the *letter*. Jesus taught that, "any unfaithfulness, which cuts against the principle of 'one flesh' marriage—of heart as much as of deed—is a breach of the commandment against adultery. . . . [T]o focus only on physical infidelity may hide many of the real causes of marital breakdown of which adulterous intercourse may be a symptom rather

---

3. Instone-Brewer, *Divorce and Remarriage in the Bible*, 144.
4. Carter, *Grace and Divorce*, 64–65.

than the cause."[5] It is by upholding the *spirit* of the law that we avoid the legalism of the Pharisees.

Physical adultery and desertion are the traditional grounds for divorce in the church community, but if we interpret marital breakdown only literally, we ignore all of the other ways that a marriage covenant can be broken, ways that are addressed by a variety of other scriptures on relationship.

The Tradition of the Church Fathers

Some like to believe that a plain reading of scripture would land everyone in agreement in regard to marriage and divorce. However, a peek down the corridor of history shows that even the church fathers haven't agreed regarding these subjects. Prior to the first century, divorce was accepted as part of reality, and divorced persons were *expected* to remarry. They weren't automatically treated as morally corrupt and deficient in God's eyes.

However, when passages from New Testament scriptures became separated from their cultural and social contexts, debate was stirred up, as we noticed in chapter 2. What we didn't address in chapter 2 was the tradition of the church fathers. Let's do so here by considering the positions of some of the most prominent theologians of centuries gone by. (In *To Have and To Hold*,[6] David Atkinson presents a more complete discussion of the history of the theology of marriage and divorce in the church. The information I include here is from this source.)

Although there is debate about how to interpret Origen (ca. 185–ca. 254) and Basil (ca. 330–ca. 379), some say that, for these two church fathers, remarriage was sometimes considered the lesser of two evils, although contrary to the ideal for marriage.

St. Augustine's (ca. 354–ca. 430) point of view represents one end of a spectrum in regard to marriage and divorce as he supported the idea of the absolute indissolubility of the marriage bond, meaning that it wasn't permissible to dissolve a marriage. Some have interpreted Augustine to have meant that what he called the *sacrament* of marriage created an ontological bond. However, this medieval sense of the word *sacrament* came into being long after Augustine's time in history. In Augustine's

---

5. Atkinson, *To Have and To Hold*, 141–57.
6. Ibid., 36–69.

day, *sacramentum* was a technical Latin term for a Roman soldier's oath of obligation, and Augustine used this term in the sense of moral obligation and sacred sign. The question for Augustine wasn't whether unbelievers *could* divorce, but whether believers *should*, given that their marriage was a sign of Christ's relationship with the church.

After the fifth century, the Greek and Latin churches diverged on this issue. At this time, the Eastern church began to accept civil law regarding divorce, which was considered by some to be a lax and inexcusable departure from what was considered the divine law of the indissolubility of marriage. Today, the Eastern church seeks to uphold what it believes has been the tradition of the centuries: to hold a strict view of marriage as a sacrament, and to practice loving care toward believers who get divorced and who desire to remarry. In this tradition, both divorce and remarriage are permitted for a variety of causes as concessions to human beings' hardness of heart.

The church of England currently upholds six civil grounds upon which marriage may be voidable: 1) non-consummation, due to incapacity for whatever reason; 2) willful refusal to consummate; 3) lack of valid consent because of duress, mistake, emotional incapacity for the responsibilities of marriage; 4) mental disorder at the time of marriage; 5) venereal disease at the time of marriage; and 6) pregnancy by another at the time of marriage.

In the Roman tradition, the church held more and more firmly to the indissolubility of marriage, eventually adopting the idea that marriage between baptized believers with consummated marriages *could not* be broken, even with a legal divorce decree. However, during medieval times, the practices of dispensation and annulment came into being for various "impediments."

During the Reformation period, many church fathers protested the sacramental nature of the marriage bond and sought scriptural support for the lawfulness of divorce and remarriage in certain cases. The Council of Trent (ca. 1545–ca. 1563) concluded that marriage could be dissolved by heresy, "irksome cohabitation," desertion, and adultery—although the ruling wasn't unanimous. The Roman Catholic church today officially maintains the indissolubility of marriage, but still practices annulment for a variety of reasons (some of which are noted below and were mentioned in chapter 2).

Although the Reformers attempted to return the church to biblical principles, there was much debate among them. Luther (ca. 1483–ca.

1586) flatly disagreed with the interpretation of Augustine's view of marriage as a sacrament for three reasons: 1) it contained no particular sign to make it such, and scripture doesn't promise grace simply by getting married; 2) even unbelievers get married; and 3) the Vulgate translation of the word *musterion* (mystery) as *sacramentum* (sacrament) is not a solid translation of the word. The idea that marriage wasn't a sacrament had the effect of passing the jurisdiction of marriage from the church to the state. With regard to divorce, Luther accepted adultery and desertion as appropriate scriptural grounds for divorce, and he allowed the state the right to decide on even wider grounds for divorce, such as cruelty.

Calvin (ca. 1509–ca. 1564) agreed with Luther that marriage was the jurisdiction of the state, but disagreed that the state had the right to administer a wider ruling on divorce than he saw prescribed in scripture, namely for adultery, desertion, "incorrigible vagabondage" on the part of the husband, and a strong presumption of adultery on the part of the wife.

Bucer (ca. 1491–ca. 1551) accepted divorce and remarriage on broader grounds than either Luther or Calvin, saying that Moses had permitted it, and that Christ had not come to destroy the law. He argued that marriage was intended to be a "one flesh" union, and that such a union could be absent due to obstinate malevolence, deep inbred weakness of mind, or incurable impotence of the body. Based on his interpretation of the concept of "one flesh," Bucer expanded appropriate grounds for divorce to include serious crime, impotence, leprosy, and insanity.

Peter Martyr (ca. 1499–ca. 1562), a most highly esteemed church teacher, became one of the most influential fathers in regard to the doctrines of marriage, divorce, and remarriage when he directly addressed the subject in his book *Commonplaces*. Martyr was clear about the divine intention for the permanence of marriage but permitted divorce for adultery and desertion, maintaining the right of remarriage afterwards.

Currently, the Roman Catholic church upholds three elements of an indissoluble union, namely validity, sacramentality, and consummation, and if any of these three elements does not exist, the union may be nonexistent or null. Since the Second Vatican Council, there has been much debate concerning what constitutes a valid "community of life and love," with some proposing that personality disorders render a person unfit for married life, and that half-hearted or inadequate consent may be grounds for nullity.[7]

This summary hardly does justice to the divisions in church history with regard to the topics of marriage, divorce, and remarriage, so I encourage those who consult the tradition of the church fathers for help in understanding God's intention for us today to study more widely on these subjects.

A plain reading of scripture through the ages of the Common Era has yielded no more clear understanding of these difficult topics than it does today. The sources we have to understand and interpret the scriptures in their grammatical and historical contexts can provide deeper insight into the passages of scripture that have caused division in the church over the centuries regarding these issues. (See chapter 2 and Appendix F.)

A THERAPEUTIC REFLECTION

As already mentioned, *how* to go about evaluating, and possibly ending, a covenantal bond of marriage is not explicitly recorded in the scriptures. Although we have the example of God with Israel, we don't have specific instructions to follow. In Bible times, both the covenant of marriage and the dissolution of it were recorded orally, mostly. The stipulations upon which a couple established a marriage or divorce were uniformly understood. Though God commanded that a husband provide a wife with a divorce certificate, mostly to protect the wife's right to remarry, few words were recorded in this document. In ancient times, the common phrasing for a divorce certificate was: "You are free to marry any man you wish."[8] *How* individual people in crisis should decide when enough is enough, however, is not the domain of the Bible.

That the scriptures are virtually silent on what constitutes a healthy process of evaluating and possibly ending a marriage covenant is disconcerting to some. However, the Bible was never meant to be a manual on every subject. For example, we would never expect the Bible to instruct us on how to milk a cow, replace a wagon wheel, or treat leprosy. In the same way, the Bible isn't a step-by-step manual for relationship processing. While it does contain helpful principles to consult if we want to evaluate our relationships honestly, it doesn't tell us exactly what to do

---

7. Ibid., 167.
8. Instone-Brewer, *Divorce and Remarriage in the Bible*, 30.

to determine whether our marriage covenant has been violated enough to constitute grounds for divorce.

As I've worked with couples in my counseling practice, I've noticed that few couples commit to evaluating their relationship with 100 percent honesty. Many come to my office alone because only one of the partners is willing to acknowledge that he or she can't resolve his or her issues without professional help. This in itself is diagnostic of a lack of partnership, which is to be expected when couples are in crisis.

I've also noticed that individuals who seek counseling to address relational breakdown often come hoping that the therapist will perform a miracle. After avoiding dealing with the cancerous tumors in their relationships for years, they want the therapist to fix the problem quickly, painlessly, and without cutting out the tumors. When it becomes clear that each individual must take responsibility for his or her own healing and then also need to subject their relationship to emotional surgery with little or no anesthesia, many drop out of therapy, choosing an easier "fix," such as more avoidance, indulging in addictive behavior, having an affair, or committing suicide or homicide. Also, if they choose to self-evaluate, but they do so only out of conscious or unconscious motivation to force the other spouse to change, the process breaks down, and the individual is left to decide whether to commit to his or her own healing or to drop out of therapy.

The Idol of Image

Most of my clients come from the evangelical Christian sub-culture, and I find that the single greatest barrier to their honest evaluation of themselves and of their relationships is the idol of image. Somewhere along the line, Christians have come to believe that they aren't supposed to have problems and that acknowledging failure is a shameful thing. Most would rather do something immoral (as noted in the previous paragraph) than honestly evaluate their relationship, for fear that this evaluation might lead them to divorce.

The fear of admitting marital failure in the church is completely understandable given the stigma that the church has often perpetuated about divorce and divorcees. How we've treated people during one of the most difficult crises that they can experience is unconscionable and embarrassing. Les Carter, in *Grace and Divorce*, offers a Christ-like way to interact with people during this most painful time of their lives.

When a client does indicate a readiness to honestly appraise their relationship no matter what anyone else will think, I discuss with them my "Decalogue of Honest Appraisal and Personal Responsibility." The word "Decalogue," literally "Ten Words," is the Hebrew title for the Ten Commandments. I've borrowed the term, and like the Law of Moses, the whole list is one package. If you violate one principle, you violate the whole thing. When we commit to honestly appraise ourselves and our relationships, we can't pick and choose what principles in this tool we'll follow. Each point relies on the others in order to serve its purpose, and failure in one point prevents the instrument from yielding honest results.

This evaluation tool is the result of my own processing when I finally acknowledged that truth, no matter what it cost me or how much it hurt, was more important than image. The following list comprises the principles that I established for myself during the two years prior to the official dissolution of my own marriage. (Note that this Decalogue defines the "*letter* of the law" in italics, and then offers an explanation of the "*spirit* of the law" in regular print. Also note, that because the English language has no neutral human pronoun, male and female pronouns are used interchangeably in this tool. See Appendix D for a reproducible version of this tool.)

The Decalogue (Ten Commandments) of Honest Appraisal and Personal Responsibility

1. *Take personal ownership of anything and everything that you've contributed to the breakdown of the relationship.* Don't demand that your spouse take ownership of his or her contribution in order for you to take ownership of yours. This process may require the help of a counselor, pastor, or honest friend who isn't afraid to help you identify your own contribution to the marital breakdown, but who recognizes that marital breakdown takes two.

2. *Commit not to engage in arguments, but to simply collect data and come to reasonable conclusions based on the behavior you witness.* Use this time to collect data about yourself and your own harmful style of relating, as well as about your spouse and about his or her style of relating. Use your journal, prayer, meditation, and other soul-searching techniques to find comfort as you absorb the criticism, contempt, entitlement, dependence, avoidance, passivity, denial, insensitivity, rejection, passive aggression, defensiveness,

stonewalling, blame-shifting, incessant worry, negativity, lack of compassion, lies, disregard, inattention, carelessness, distance, coldness, indifference, obsessions, or whatever other attitudes or behaviors are toxic in the relationship. Again, third party help is often invaluable here. Absorbing the pain of the relationship isn't intended to be permanent, but it is necessary for the evaluation period. Who knows, your spouse may even respond positively to the change in your demeanor. If not, I must warn you that he or she may become even harder toward you, because we tend to become either softer or harder; we don't remain neutral.

3. *Refuse to cover your hurt with anger (or your anger with hurt), and stop holding your partner responsible for your emotions.* Commit to naming what is true (my spouse is being contemptuous, defensive, critical, insensitive, and I'm tempted to be passive aggressive toward him) with regard to the dynamics of the relationship, and allow yourself to feel whatever emotions are appropriate for every situation. (If you typically hide your hurt behind anger, allow yourself to feel hurt. If you typically hide your anger behind hurt, allow yourself to feel angry.) This is simply being honest about your pain, allowing yourself to feel your raw emotions.

4. *Refuse to dump your hurt or your anger with your partner onto others.* You've probably gotten into the habit of dumping your frustration with your spouse onto your friends who offer you sympathy and compassion. If you deny yourself a forum to receive this sympathy, you'll come face to face with your pain. Once you can no longer deny it, you'll have to deal with it instead of deflect it.

5. *Refuse to try to control your partner's healing process.* In order to love the other person well, you have to let her succeed or fail on her own. Completely let go of your over-functioning, your avoidance, or whatever your typical mode of operating in the relationship is. This principle requires that you relinquish any control, overt or covert, that you have over your spouse. You have to let go and allow the other to freely choose whether or not to be in relationship with you.

6. *Refuse to believe the lie that either you or your spouse is the only one contributing to the breakdown of the relationship.* You're probably

triggering each other. Even the most innocent party will be able to identify some contribution to the dysfunctional dynamic. Evading the issues, avoiding one's own pain, spiritualizing, enabling, and trying to be the savior are some of the toxic contributions of seemingly innocent parties.

7. *When the other person's behavior doesn't match his or her words, commit to reading and believing the* behavior, *no matter how painful the truth might be.* When we have competing desires, we pursue what we *most* want. If your spouse wants to change things, not just rearrange things, he or she will seek help on his or her own volition. This may be one way to gauge the level of commitment (or lack thereof) that your spouse has to you and to the relationship. Remember, the nation of Israel "honored God with their lips, but their hearts were far from him" (Isa 29:13, NIV). Their behavior belied their true feelings.

8. *Open your heart to feel the pain of the other, particularly the pain that keeps him or her bound to a way of being that comes from a wounded past.* "Hurt people hurt people." If you can't find compassion for your partner's bondage, without condescension, you're likely still holding him or her in contempt. If you want your partner to feel your pain, you have to be willing to feel your partner's. When you enter your own pain and allow God to minister to you in it, you'll begin to feel the pain of your spouse. Be aware that it's easy for an empathic person to set aside compassion for his or her own experience in favor of feeling for others, which is sometimes an unconscious way to avoid one's own pain. It's also easy for empathic people to not only feel compassion for someone but to take responsibility for making that person feel better. Refuse to fall into the trap of setting yourself up as your spouse's savior, which isn't compassionate at all in the long run. People need to have the freedom to choose for themselves, either poorly or well, and it's compassionate to let them do this. It may hurt, but severe mercy, administered with gracious confidence, is the best medicine in many circumstances.

9. *Be open to unconventional sources of revelation and epiphany* (i.e., dreams, your body's stress symptoms, someone you dislike, a collision of events, an old journal entry, an experience in ob-

servable nature, etc.). Be open to God's voice as he may speak in unexpected ways, being careful to listen with your heart, not just with your head. I'm always amazed by the myriad of ways that God communicates with people when they allow themselves to listen with their hearts. If you listen with your spirit, your core, which requires that you delve into the deepest pain in your spirit, you'll find God there, and his voice becomes clear. He's not a voice in your head. He's a spirit, and he communicates to your spirit through his spirit.

10. *Commit to sharing your heart with your spouse, even if he or she stomps all over it.* Become completely vulnerable to your spouse and open your heart to emotional intimacy with him or her. Understand, also, that you'll only be able to do this when your personal healing journey leaves you strong enough to hold onto yourself, even if your spouse doesn't receive you well. Give your partner one more chance to show genuine interest in the relationship. Of course, "one more chance" will eventually become "one last chance" for the offending party to join in a genuine repair process. (Note: If your spouse is abusive in any way or is emotionally checked out, I suggest that you only share your heart with your partner with third party help.)

Warnings about The Decalogue

When an individual or a couple commits to following this tool, they're on their way to either repairing and reconciling the relationship or to dissolving it, and there's no way to determine what the outcome will be before the process is followed through to its natural conclusion.

Sometimes couples are in counseling for months addressing their resistance to honest evaluation of themselves and of their relationships before they're ready to commit to not pretending anymore. It's at this point, and not before, that the "Decalogue" can be an effective tool. Once this shift takes place, however, people are able to see things in themselves, in their relationships, and in the scriptures that they've never been able to see before.

I must caution that it's possible to misuse this tool. If it doesn't ultimately soften your heart toward yourself and toward your spouse, it's not being used honestly, and your therapist should help you explore what the barrier is to total honesty and humility.

I must also caution that honest appraisal doesn't necessarily lead to reconciliation of a relationship. Both parties must simultaneously engage in this honest appraisal of themselves, first, and of the relationship, second, if they are to find the truth behind their issues. If only one partner commits, the relationship won't be reconciled. The individual can come to understand the dynamics that have led to the dysfunction, as understanding takes only one; however, reconciliation takes two.

Finally, I must caution that even if two people simultaneously engage in an honest appraisal of their relationship, there's no guarantee that they'll be able to engage in a true, covenantal relationship together. The couple may come to realize that they entered the relationship on the basis of trauma re-enactment, and they may come to acknowledge that while they and their spouse are not bad people, they entered a false covenant. I believe that it's possible for some trauma-bonded couples to work through their individual healing processes, separately, but as simultaneously as possible identifying who they are, to the point where they're ready to address the false covenant and then establish a true covenant.

I *have* seen trauma-bonded couples work through their individual healing processes and realize that they've forged a false covenant. From this standpoint, they're able to acknowledge that the best thing for both of them is to unhook the trauma bond and dissolve the marriage. This isn't an easy process for people who married with the intent to never divorce, but it's freeing for people who know that God forgives failure committed in ignorance if we're willing to face the truth and come to him with softened hearts. As we can be forgiven for other choices that we've made outside of his will—as David was forgiven for murder and forging a false covenant with Bathsheba—we can also be forgiven for trying to make life work on our own, even in the poor choice of marriage partner. Rather than force ourselves in our own willpower and arrogance to stay bound to a false covenant, God honors our willingness to humbly admit our mistake and move on from it. We don't have to be bound to covenants that God has neither established nor sanctioned, particularly when staying bound continues to harm one or both of the parties involved. What we do need to remain bound to is the truth, which includes humble confession, repentance, and restoration to God.

What Hardness of Heart Looks Like in a Marriage Covenant

As I mentioned in chapter 5, a grid that I often use to evaluate couples in crisis is presented by John Gottman in *The Seven Principles for Making Marriage Work*.[9] We've already explored marriage from a positive perspective: what makes marriage work. Let's now explore what *prevents* marriage from working: hardheartedness.

Gottman's research helps put skin on this skeleton called "hardness of heart," and he gives us a better understanding of what "stubbornness" looks like in a marriage. He describes six signs of hardheartedness in marriage.[10]

The first sign is *harsh start-ups* to discussions about difficult issues. When a discussion starts with criticism and/or sarcasm (two toxic forms of contempt), a discussion is almost certain to escalate to an unproductive argument. Expect nothing good to come from harsh start-ups.

The second sign of stubbornness is the presence of what Gottman calls the "Four Horseman of The Apocalypse." The first horseman is *criticism*. The difference between a complaint (a legitimate concern about a failure in the relationship) and a criticism is that a criticism adds negative words about your mate's character or personality. Expect nothing good to come from criticism.

The second "horseman" that destroys relationship is *contempt*, which takes many different forms, including sarcasm, cynicism, name-calling, eye-rolling, sneering, mockery, belligerence, passive aggression, passive resistance, hostile humor, and the like. Of the horsemen, *contempt* was found to be the most toxic of them all because it conveys disgust for one's partner. From this one characteristic, Gottman says that he's able to predict the outcome of a marriage with 91 percent accuracy.

The third "horsemen" is *defensiveness*, which is really a way of blaming your partner. Without clearly spelling it out, defensiveness says, "You're the problem, not me." In reality, it takes two to tango, although one can certainly step on more toes than the other. There's never any need for defensiveness, however, because if you're right, you need no defense; if you're wrong, you have none.

---

9. From THE SEVEN PRINCIPLES FOR MAKING MARRIAGE WORK by John M. Gottman, Ph.D. and Nan Silver, copyright © 1999 by John M. Gottman, Ph.D. and Nan Silver. Used by permission of Crown Publishers, a division of Random House, Inc.

10. Ibid.

The fourth "horseman," *stonewalling*, refers to the unilateral decision to disengage from the conflict. Such disengagement may be quiet and passive aggression, like the silent treatment, or it may be obvious and loud, such as a command to "talk to the hand." A stonewaller acts as if he couldn't care less about what you're saying, whether he hears it or not.

The third sign of hardheartedness is *flooding*. Every relationship will encounter conflict, but flooding indicates that your spouse's negativity (no matter which horseman she's using) is so suddenly overwhelming that it leaves you shell-shocked. When a person is flooded, the only thing he can think about is self-protection from the spouse's turbulence. Stonewalling, or disengagement, is often a sign that flooding has occurred, and flooding leads to divorce for two reasons: 1) it signals that at least one partner feels severe emotional distress when dealing with the other, and 2) the increased heart rate, sweating, and other physical sensations that accompany flooding prevent productive problem-solving.

The fourth sign of a hard heart, the *body's physiology*, flows from the third one. When flooding occurs, the male cardiovascular system is typically more reactive to stress and slower to recover than the female cardiovascular system. When heightened blood pressure and increased pulse are regular occurrences in the relationship due to stress reactivity, the ability to process information becomes more difficult. Over time, this process overtaxes the body and the relationship.

The fifth sign of hardheartedness in marriage is *failed repair attempts*. A genuine repair attempt, the secret weapon of emotionally intelligent couples, refers to any statement or action—silly or otherwise—that prevents negativity from escalating out of control. Individuals who send and receive successful repair attempts forge strong friendships, which is the strength of marital relationship.

The sixth sign that a marriage has been overrun by a hard heart is *bad memories*. Happy marriages look back on their early days with fondness, but when a marriage is on the rocks, previously fond memories get subsumed by negativity or forgotten altogether.

When one or both partners develop a hard, stubborn heart, they'll find themselves leaving their marriages, either literally (by divorcing) or emotionally (by leading parallel or separate lives). Gottman suggests that four signs indicate the final stages of a relationship: 1) when you see your marriage problems as severe; 2) when talking about things is fruitless, and you try to solve your problems on your own; 3) when you start leading parallel lives; and 4) when loneliness sets in.

Divorce-proofing or saving a marriage at this point, or at any other, takes couples who are willing to change their way of being with each other, not when they're fighting, but all the time. Couples must together commit to strengthening their friendship by honoring, from their hearts, the vows they made to each other when they first entered their covenant. If they're unwilling to commit to honoring their vows, the stubbornness—the hardheartedness—of one, the other, or both suggests that divorce is likely inevitable and, as Jesus reminded us, permissible. Carter says in *Grace and Divorce*, "Many divorcees do not want to be divorced at all. They find themselves in that situation from choices made by a spouse who would not cooperate in finding solutions to personal problems or marital needs."[11]

A PERSONAL REFLECTION

My History

Our histories set Chip and me up for this kind of relational breakdown. Let me try to paint a picture of how our stories interweaved. Your story may have comparable elements.

By the time I met Chip, I'd been searching for *anything* that would fill the voids in my heart for most of my life. My goal was freedom from the emotional pain left by a volatile and inconsistent home, an abusive father, a codependent mother, and the betrayal of my brother into sexual abuse. Eventually, I unconsciously demanded that my husband assuage my pain.

As a little girl, I longed for my father's affection and attention. I yearned for him to hold me and to tell me that he loved me. Instead, he spent as little time with the family as possible. This was a mixed blessing, for when he *was* home, he was either a smoldering volcano or an erupting one. Dad was emotionally abusive to my mother and to the three of us kids, and was physically abusive to my mother and to my brother, Davie.

Because Dad was unavailable, Davie took Dad's place in my life; Davie was my idol. However, Davie had his own father-wound, which was re-injured again and again in many ways, including what I've been told was Dad's favoritism of me. Davie's mother-wound, feeling smoth-

---

11. Carter, *Grace and Divorce*, 30.

ered by but emotionally wedded to our mother, may also have been deep. I suspect that Davie was full of anger and that he grew to despise me (a less formidable and more convenient target than Dad or Mom) for being Dad's favorite and for simply being female.

By the time I was thirteen years old, I knew something was gravely wrong. When I refused to be used any longer, Davie and his friends wouldn't have anything to do with me. This abandonment left me feeling very much a fool, very much prostituted, and very much alone.

Though I wasn't conscious of it at the time, my life became one great opportunity to prove to myself and to the world that I wasn't a fool, that I wasn't a prostitute, and that I didn't need anyone.

At this point, I began rejecting the God who'd been presented to me since birth, and my heart began to harden. Unconsciously, I reasoned, "If God were so powerful, why didn't he protect me?" And I set out to protect myself. I became self-sufficient, self-serving, and self-righteous. I was able to hide behind my accomplishments that I was empty and insecure.

When I left home to attend college, I met Chip, and after a rocky courtship, we were married. Unconsciously, I thought marriage would provide the love and security I had pursued and longed for all my life.

Chip's History

Chip thought that marriage would provide him a regular sexual diet that would cure him of sexual compulsivity. Moreover, Chip had brought his own set of luggage from his family into our relationship. He was born, the youngest of three, into a family that was emotionally distant. His father was openly critical of his mother, and his mother absorbed her husband's contempt without comment. Taking pride in being pleasant all the time, she choose to stifle her pain and ignore the impact that her avoidance might have on her children as she and her husband modeled a marriage relationship. Chip learned to avoid conflict at all costs, that there was no need to respect women, and that women weren't supposed to require that they be respected.

Furthermore, Chip learned that his emotions were unimportant and that he would have to ignore them in order to survive in a household that was void of meaningful engagement. Viewed from the outside, the home was pleasant, but on the inside, it was emotionally empty, and Chip longed for his parents to pursue him, to invite him into intimate conversations, and to guide him through the difficulties of life and relationships. He was a sensitive boy, a boy of deep emotion, but no one in his family seemed interested in emotions, so he learned that keeping up an image and the appearance of peace was more important then being emotionally honest.

Chip was lonely all the time, and he often rocked himself to sleep to the sound of radio music performed by people who, though he didn't know them, seemed to be as full of emotion as he. Without healthy guidance, either through direct teaching or indirect modeling, Chip was left on his own to figure out the most important things in life, especially how to treat himself and others with value. He was left with no self-confidence and few skills to help him engage in intimate relationship.

When Chip was an impressionable and lost eleven-year-old, his family moved to another state, and he was torn from everything he'd ever known—everything that felt secure in his life. Without guidance, he found himself in an unknown place with no idea how to make friends and with no one to talk to about it. He was dreadfully lonely, and he had no idea how to improve his situation.

Chip desperately needed his father to train him in the ways of true masculinity, but his dad was too busy for him. Before long, he began to seek guidance and value outside of his family; he talked to the new friends he had managed to make in his new school. Their biggest questions involved how to be in relationship with girls, but because they had never been taught (directly or indirectly) how to treat girls well, or even that girls were worthy of such respect, they were left to learn by trial and error . . . mostly error.

When he was old enough, but hardly wise enough, to be called a young man, Chip entered into a few relationships with young ladies in ways that didn't honor his or their status as image-bearers of their creator. Chip was especially curious about sex, and he sensed that girls could enchant his loneliness away, so he was drawn to them. But because he had not been taught about the value of the feminine, he hoped that sex with them would save him from himself.

Chip had no concept that sexuality was designed to occur within an emotionally intimate relationship, and because he didn't know how to engage in such a relationship—he had never seen a man cherish a woman, and he had no idea what was within him as a man to offer to a woman in relationship—he was a prime candidate for sexual compulsivity.

Chip engaged in relationships with girls and fantasies, hoping that they would complete him. When he met me, I became the next girl who he hoped would assuage his insatiable loneliness. My intelligence and drive also appealed to Chip who had no confidence in his own intelligence and who had no idea who he was or what direction he wanted his life to take.

Our Histories Come Together

On October 22, 1988, Chip and I each married an illusion of the other. We didn't marry each other, because neither of us had a sense of our own identities or of the identity of the other. The impact of our families of origin with regard to abuse and neglect created a trauma bond between Chip and me, the evidence of which was present even before we got married. Had either one of us been honest and aware, we would've broken off the relationship when we were dating.

Instead, we married, and our marriage hit the rocks immediately, starting with our wedding night. For me, sex suddenly became expected, compulsory, and the lack of choice that I felt with regard to our sex life triggered childhood sexual abuse memories. Chip, on the other hand, expected marriage to cure him of his sexual compulsions because he expected to engage in it any time he wanted. Dutifully, I gave my body as often as I could muster, knowing nothing of true intimacy, and I felt used with nearly every sexual encounter.

In our resolve not to fail, we kept our problems to ourselves, maintaining an appearance of togetherness, as we'd each been conditioned to do. I had naïvely hoped that when I had the title of Chip's *wife*, he'd suddenly begin treating me with more respect. I found just the opposite to be true, and if I'd been honest with myself, I would've acknowledged that, again, I felt like a fool. Instead of recognizing the truth, however, I grasped for an old pattern: stay busy in order not to feel. I enlisted my naturally curious and energetic spirit in an illegitimate way and, at any cost, became determined to succeed in a career. I filled my life with education and work.

Between my unresolved issues and Chip's, we had more baggage than our fragile bond could hold, and after six tumultuous years, we were all but ready to call it quits. I hadn't failed at anything I'd ever done before, but at the end of my rope, I finally humbled myself and sought counsel; I was ready to admit that I was failing, and my hard heart was ripe for softening. John King, my therapist, soon recommended that I read *Inside Out*,[12] which helped me to see how my self-protective style of relating was an arrogant commitment to make life work on my own terms. The book encouraged me to face and grieve the losses that kept me in bondage to compulsive self-protection.

John then suggested that I read *The Wounded Heart*,[13] a faith-based book for adult victims of childhood sexual abuse. Through the scripture in this book, Allender presented a God I could never have imagined. Instead of the raging, vengeful, unpredictable, Dad-in-the-sky whom I imagined God to be, Allender showed God to be so loving that he *willingly* tasted his own medicine. In the human body of Jesus, he experienced the pain and the suffering of the human condition, the curse brought on the earth by the rebellion of his own creatures.

Through Matthew 26–27, I learned that *Jesus* experienced powerlessness, ambivalence, shame, betrayal and the abandonment of his Father—all the emotional wounds that threatened to destroy *me* as I worked through my feelings about past abuses. I couldn't fathom the love it would require to *volunteer* to experience this pain so that I might know God's love, a love he gave despite my arrogant self-reliance. According to the gospel story, my self-sufficiency, my hardheartedness, had nailed Jesus to the cross, and God *still* loved me, even though I had hated him and had blamed him for things he hadn't even done. How could I resist a love like that? It broke, softened, and changed my willful heart.

I no longer had anger and self-hatred feeding my volatility, and the arguments in our marriage diminished immediately. However, Chip refused to join me in counseling to repair the foundational cracks in our relationship, and our relative peace was short-lived. Coming to this spiritual awakening didn't change my abusive past and I still struggled with the impact of it. Chip's relationship with God didn't change his past or his unresolved issues, either, and our marriage eventually fell back into old patterns.

Having been taught that divorce was just short of unforgivable, I couldn't allow myself to consider the option, for fear of the disapproval of others. My fear kept my heart closed to raw truth; I was still single-handedly trying to make change happen in the relationship rather than accept my powerlessness to do so. So the pain in our relationship contin-

12. Crabb, *Inside Out*.
13. Allender, *Wounded Heart*.

ued to mount, and the distance between us grew. I pled with Chip to go to counseling with me, and he still refused, saying that counseling had become my god.

My journal was my emotional outlet, and into it I poured the words of my partially-softened heart's brokenness, confusion and frustration. I longed for our relationship to be healed, but it continued to be characterized by contempt and neglect on both sides. We were slowly squeezing the life out of each other, and Chip still refused to get help with me.

After Fourteen Years

As I continued to make progress in my own healing process, Chip made no visible progress in his. He had acknowledged his sexual addiction about five years into our marriage, but he hadn't committed to a systematic healing process. Fourteen years into our marriage, my own healing journey took me to a unique seminary in Seattle, Washington, where intensive personal counseling is built into the seminary experience. While I continued to heal, I also earned a master's degree in counseling, a desire I'd had since junior high school.

This process led me to own the pain that I'd contributed in my relationship with Chip and to stop protecting Chip from having to own his contribution to the pain between us, as well. I finally realized that my over-functioning and Chip's avoidance were a toxic combination. Chip never had to own his own relational failures because I continued to take his responsibility along with my own.

This realization was the first event that created hope for our relationship. I was no longer grasping after control, and I was willing to let the whole relationship go if Chip didn't seek his own healing or the repair of our relationship. When I realized that I could no longer do the work for both of us, our trauma bond began to unknot itself, and it was up to Chip to accept his responsibility in his own healing and in the healing of our relationship. I abdicated that position, and I initiated an in-house separation, so that we could start over. We needed to establish ourselves as individuals and then we needed to establish a brand new foundation for our relationship. Our relationship was so far from how a marriage covenant is supposed to operate that we needed a complete "do over."

I didn't know if Chip would join the process, and I knew that our whole relationship was on the line if he didn't. However, I didn't have anything to lose at this point, and I had great confidence that we could get to the other side if we did it together. I also envisioned us becoming helpers together of other couples who were in similar need of a massive overhaul. I was hopeful.

I committed to another season of counseling on my own, and I made several choices about myself that carried me through the next couple of years. The plan I developed for myself is the "The Decalogue of Honest Appraisal and Personal Responsibility" presented earlier in this chapter. I took responsibility for my own poor attitudes and behaviors, and I claimed my own hurt. It was mine to heal. I accepted the reality that I had no control over Chip's contribution, only over mine. I stopped arguing with him and trying to get him to understand my thoughts and feelings. I continued to pursue my own healing, and as I faced and worked through old wounds, I developed compassion for Chip's old wounds and for his bondage to them. I found myself longing to see him freed of his bondage as much as I was being freed of mine. I often wept over Chip's childhood pain, and I longed for him to connect with it and to share his heart with me. I longed for Chip's healing and wholeness for his own freedom's sake, and so that we could be intimate allies.

I didn't follow my "Decalogue" perfectly—hard hearts sometimes soften suddenly and other times they soften little by little—but over the next two years, I consciously tried to do nothing that would bring further harm to the relationship. The principles in the list became more and more like second nature to me, although it never got easier to see the wreckage of our relationship all around us.

Some Ugly, Personal Epiphanies

In my personal therapy, I continued to work through other issues that remained from my childhood, committing to be completely honest and nonresistant with Kyle, my new therapist. (I was no longer living in the state where I had counseled with John King.) As a counselor-in-training, I knew that resistance only prolongs the healing process, so I determined to face whatever was true—about myself first, and then about Chip and about our relationship. I also continued reading good materials and journaling about my process to help me heal on my own.

As I was completely honest with myself, I had to face some ugly realities. In my candid appraisal of the origin of my relationship with Chip, I had to acknowledge that I'd clasped onto Chip, demanding that he fill voids in my heart from my past. That I'd unconsciously set Chip up to heal my brother wound became clear to me after a fascinating interaction with one of my professors (as described in chapter 2).

When I realized that my attraction to Chip was largely an attempt to get Davie, to whom I'd been trauma bound to love me again, I also realized that if I wanted to have a relationship with Chip, I'd have to lose my childhood buddy. I'd have to let Davie go if Chip were going to have the chance to pursue me. Then I'd also have to let go of any control over whether Chip chose to pursue, which left me feeling vulnerable, frightened and powerless, but it was the right thing for my softening heart to do.

Without Help, We Won't Make It

As I healed more and more, my desire for emotional connection became an increasingly felt need, and I became more and more heartbroken about lacking it with Chip.

After fifteen years of marriage, I finally told Chip that he needed to get help, or I couldn't stay in the relationship. Chip finally went to counseling for the first time, and as a man without close friends, he seemed to enjoy having someone to talk to, at first. When counseling began to dig deeper into his soul, however, he started to complain about the process. He had difficulty completing his counseling homework assignments, and he seemed to despise introspection. He speculated that our therapist must not like working with men and that he must not know how to work with Chip's particular issues. Chip continued to define the problem as being something or someone other than himself, and it was becoming more and more clear to me that his resistance and defensiveness (in a word, hardheartedness) prevented his healing.

I didn't know whether Chip was *incapable of* or whether he was *unwilling to* change, but either way, the emotional distance was agonizing for me. If Chip were incapable of change, I had to acknowledge that my insistence on healing our relationship had to be frustrating for him. I'd learned in counselor training not to take away someone's defenses before I could offer something better, and I was afraid that I'd done just that.

But I still wasn't convinced that Chip was incapable of deep change, and it seemed more honoring to assume that he was. He paid lip service to desiring emotional intimacy, but he had no close friends, avoided emotional vulnerability, engaged in limited self-searching, and was resistant to honest appraisal of himself and his relationships. I failed to follow the seventh commitment in the "Decalogue," and believed his words about desiring intimacy with me over what he did (or didn't do) to secure it. To the degree that fear of the raw truth continued to drive some of my choices, my heart still had more softening to do.

Prior to this time, I wouldn't have described either Chip or me as hardhearted. I remember saying to my therapist, "It's been years since I've seen his tender side, but I know it's there somewhere. And I don't think I'm hardhearted, either." However, the honest appraisal of our relationship revealed to me the stubbornness of both of our hearts, and it was humbling.

SNEAK PREVIEW OF THE NEXT CHAPTER

There's only one cure for hardness of heart: softness of heart. And there's only one way to achieve it: brokenness of heart, or repentance. Perhaps the concept of *repentance* is confusing. It was for me, until life squeezed me so hard that I couldn't maintain my tough façade any more, and my heart couldn't help but break. What a relief it was to find out that repentance wasn't what I'd thought. The next chapter tells this story.

It also begins Part 3, which provides practical help on what to do when honest soul-searching has led to the conclusion that divorce is the best of bad options. Yes, repentance might even include the choice to end a dishonoring relationship.

Part 3

Decisions—The Spirit of Wholehearted Future

8

Repentance: Surprisingly Soft and Shame-Free

WHEN CHIP AND I married, my friends and family thought I was a Christian. I acted like one in that I didn't engage in immoral behavior, went to church, and engaged in various other spiritual disciplines like reading the Bible and praying. I even led various Bible studies and retreats. So when I announced six years into our marriage at age twenty-six that I'd just become a believer, Chip was dumbfounded, along with everyone else in my life who'd never questioned the profession of faith I'd made when I was thirteen years old. The difference between the occurrence that marked my profession of faith at age thirteen and the transformative encounter that occurred when I was twice that age is the experience of repentance.

When I was an adolescent, I couldn't comprehend what repentance was. I had heard the word often, and I was taught that it was required for spiritual awakening, but it just didn't make sense to me. When I finally did experience repentance for the first time, it was clear to me that my earlier profession of faith had been a false one. True repentance softens the heart, and this hadn't occurred at age thirteen.

Prior to my own experience of repentance, the word had always struck fear and confusion in my spirit. I thought it had something to do with feeling deeply guilty and ashamed, and I felt enough of that without adding more. After my heart had been changed by the unconditional love of a God who chose suffering to prove his love for me (as I briefly described in chapter 2), I found that repentance brings a soft humility and rest that is devoid of the humiliation and shame that I had expected. To this day, repentance is one of my favorite spiritual experiences, as it always leaves me at peace and at rest from whatever unnecessary, unproductive, and hurtful striving that has kept me bound. It also leaves me free to love others well.

A THEOLOGICAL REFLECTION

I began writing this chapter during the Days of Awe in the Jewish calendar, the ten days leading up to the Day of Atonement. Perhaps because my favorite novel, *My Name is Asher Lev*, featured a coming-of-age Jewish boy, perhaps because a dear high school friend was half-Jewish, or perhaps because I wanted to appreciate the "Judeo" part of the Judeo-Christian heritage, I was drawn to attend a Messianic Synagogue during the year after my divorce.

It was here, during the Ten Days of Awe, that I first heard, from the pulpit, repentance presented as necessary for restoring broken human relationships. In the church in which I was reared, repentance was described as a 180-degree turnaround, an about-face, a change of behavior, and whatever it was, it was absolutely necessary for salvation. In the Jewish tradition, however, ten days are set aside to reflect on our relationships, repent of the wrongs we've committed against others, and seek forgiveness and reconciliation with those whom we've hurt. This soul-searching and connecting are meant to restore the community to health. How unfortunate it is that the church has largely neglected this practice. Certainly, the church I attended in my family of origin observed no such practice at any time of the year. And no one ever said repentance was necessary to repair broken relationships.

In the Bible, repentance is most often associated with God's chosen people, the nation of Israel. The Hebrew word that expresses the concept of repentance is *sub*, meaning *to turn*, and given the covenantal context, is often expressed as "turning back" to God and to the covenant promises. The common job of the Hebrew prophets was to call for the people to allow their hearts to be broken as they considered how they'd turned away from their promise of undivided loyalty to God. They were promised that a "turning back" after a "turning away" would result in forgiveness and restored relationship with God.

When the people refused to turn back, God eventually turned away from them, allowing them to experience the consequences promised for covenant-breaking (Deut 4:15–28; 30:15–20; Dan 9:11–14). God intended these curses to move his people to repentance (Deut 4:29–30; 1 Kgs 8:33, 48), so that they might once again enjoy the blessings of the covenant. Severe mercy is sometimes the most loving and compassionate gift.

Psalm 51 contains probably the most prominent picture of repentance in the Old Testament. This Psalm expresses the cry of David's soul after the prophet, Nathan, confronted him concerning his affair with Bathsheba and his subsequent attempt to hide his sin by murdering Bathsheba's husband. In Psalm 51, we witness the profound evil our hearts are capable of and the confidence that a repentant individual can have in God's forgiveness and reconciliation. This Psalm demonstrates four characteristics of genuine repentance: 1) empathic understanding of wrong done; 2) sorrow for wrongdoing and desire for cleansing; 3) a renewed desire for the presence of God; and 4) behavioral change.

David recognizes his failure in a relational context. He recognizes how his choices have hurt people, namely Uriah (Bathsheba's husband), Bathsheba, himself, and the baby conceived as a result of the affair. In acknowledging all this harm done, he also acknowledges the justice of God's judgment against him (Ps 51:3–5).

The scriptures are replete with other examples of repentance. Job's repentance carries an understanding of wrongdoing; he confesses that he spoke untruthfully about God (Job 42:3). The Israelites, when Ezra reads the law to the nation after they return from exile (Neh 9:11), acknowledge their sin, as does Nineveh after Jonah delivers God's message to them (Jonah 3:5–6, 8). The crowd who hears Peter's message on the Day of Pentecost is "cut to the quick" (Acts 2:37), and the Prodigal Son is "brought to his senses" when the consequences of his poor choices catch up with him (Luke 15:17).

This awareness of harm done leads a repentant person to a sincere sorrow for the way his rebellion has obstructed his relationship with others and with God. Earnest prayer, fasting, tears, sackcloth, and ashes are among several biblical symbols of the heart's grief for the harm of broken promises (1 Kgs 20:31; 21:27; 2 Kgs 19:1; Job 16:15; Ps 69:11; Isa 32:11; 37:1–2; Jer 4:8; Joel 1:13; Dan 9:3; Jonah 3:5–6, 8), and represent a pliable agreement with the accuser along with a genuine desire for forgiveness and reconciliation.

This change in attitude about God, this inward emotional shift, this wholehearted return to the covenant promises is accompanied by the outward evidence of a soft face (Jer 5:3), a broken heart (Ps 51:17), and a humble tone (Ps 51:2, 7). These expressions demonstrate a desire to be back in full relationship with God and show a hunger and thirst for his presence. David's guilt over his self-centeredness had cost him both the "joy of God's salvation" and his "willingness of spirit" (Ps 51:12, NIV), and he longed to return to his old, unimpeded relationship with God. Such contrition of heart is marked by a renewed awareness of God's closeness (Isa 59:20; Jer 15:19; Luke 15:17; Acts 3:19), such as the prodigal son experiences upon his return to the father (Luke 15). When the woman who had had multiple affairs (John 4) and Zacchaeus (Luke 19) surrender to Jesus, they experience a glad and grateful change of heart. In each of these examples, the penitent person immediately and dramatically changes, resulting in personal circumstances that also profoundly change—to the shock, and sometimes the offense, of the audience. This is the nature of repentance: it "occurs in unlikely places and is always associated with a lavish measure of grace."[1]

Although God reads the heart, repentance also has an external, tangible expression: changed behavior. After he repents, David talks about his desire to teach truth, to lead others to repentance, and to praise God (Ps 51:13–15). "Turning from idols," is a most common prophetic expression of a call to repentance—an exhortation to return to the covenant promises. In the New Testament, the prodigal son demonstrates a change of heart by his change of plans, while Zacchaeus shows his repentance by returning fourfold what he had stolen. While people can make behavioral change without repentance, they cannot repent without behavioral change.

Behavioral change that is a result of true repentance is lasting because it is driven by an *internal* shift in motivation—a return to covenant love, purity, and obedience that comes from the heart. The benefits of such a change of heart are forgiveness and restoration of the covenant relationship (Deut 4: 30–31; 2 Chr 7:13–16; Ps 51:7–12; Isa 55:7; Jer 15:19–21; 32:37–41; Ezek 18:21–23; Hos 14:5–8; Mal 3:7, 10–12).

The call to repentance is common in both the Old and New Covenants, although one could make a case that the audience and the motivation of each Covenant are sometimes different. In the Old Covenant, God's most common focus is the *nation* of Israel (although individuals are not exempt), and he often seeks her repentance through reminders and demonstrations of the covenant curses. At times, he makes pleas for repentance based on reminders of his own keeping of the covenant promises (Mal 1:2), but his more frequent plea comes by warnings of impending doom. Although there is still a warning of ca-

---

1. Ryken, "Repentance," 705.

lamity for continued hardness of heart in the New Covenant (Luke 3:7, 9, 17; 13:1–5; Matt 11:20–24; 12:39–42; Acts 3:19–26; 8:20–24; 14:15; 17:30–31; Rev 2:5, 16; 3:3; 9:20–21; 16:9–11), God's most common focus seems to be *individuals* (although the church is not exempt), and grace seems to be the primary motivator for repentance (Rom 2:4). "Jesus' demand for repentance stresses God's covenantal grace, for he is its fulfillment and embodiment."[2] In keeping with this message of grace, Jesus associates with despised individuals and groups, such as prostitutes and tax collectors—people who were considered the outcasts of society. His mission is to those who know their need, not to those who are self-righteous (Luke 19:10; 15:4–32; Mark 2:17).

The New Testament word for repentance, *metanoeo*, emphasizes a change of mind and attitude that results in a change in the total direction of one's life.[3] Regret and mourning are internal and external evidences, respectively, of repentance (Luke 7:37–50; 15:17–20; 18:13–14), and heaven rejoices and celebrates this change of heart (Matt 13:44; 22:1–10; Luke 5:27–29; 19:6, 8; Acts 11:18).

It's important to recognize that the outward expression of repentance for one person may be the opposite of the outward expression of repentance for another. For example, a person who recognizes that she has been idolizing food as a comfort may demonstrate her change of heart by declining chocolate cake to cover emotional distress. However, the person who recognizes that she has been starving herself as a way to control her life may enjoy eating a piece of chocolate cake as an expression of her willingness to trust God that he will protect her soul, even while the battle rages around her.

As mentioned in previous chapters, *Grace and Divorce*[4] is an excellent resource to help us understand how to be with people who are making, or have made, choices regarding covenant betrayals of one form or another. For some, evidence of repentance may be to acknowledge that the marriage is already over—perhaps that it has been for a long time—and that a divorce decree would merely legalize this reality. For others, evidence of repentance may be to remain in, or to return to, the marriage to seek forgiveness and reconciliation, if possible. In sum, repentance begins with honesty and ends with a "shift in our perceived

---

2. Alexander et al., "Repentance," 727.
3. Richards, "Repentance," 522.
4. Carter, *Grace and Divorce*.

source of life. . . . It is a deep recognition that life comes only to the broken, desperate, dependent heart that longs for God. . . . It clears the senses in a way that exposes depravity and affirms dignity. It awakens our hunger for our Father's embrace and deepens our awareness of His kind involvement."[5] This, of course, requires that we are willing to feel our disappointment with the way things are and allow God into our pain to grieve our losses with us. Like the prodigal son, we have to look reality in the face and admit what is true. When we take such a risk, expecting and being willing to enter our shame, we find that we're not shamed at all. Convicted and humbled, yes, but not humiliated. "Repentance involves the response of humble hunger, bold movement, and wild celebration when faced with the reality of our fallen state and the grace of God."[6]

God welcomes the repentant hearts of all people: murderers, thieves, deceivers—people who harm others in every way. Is it too much to imagine that he welcomes the repentant hearts of people who have broken marriages, too? He waits for us until we are sick of our own polluted water, and then invites us to drink of the water of life when we come to his well.

A PERSONAL REFLECTION

The same is true of human relationships; repentance softens our hearts and opens the door to restored relationship. Allow me share a story of repentance in my relationship with Chip that softened and changed my heart forever.

About fifteen years into my marriage with Chip, as I continued to engage in raw and honest reflection about our way of relating, I began to realize what it would take to establish an emotional bond between us. One evening, I joined Chip in the living room where he was watching TV. I wanted us to connect somehow, but I felt the distance between us, and it seemed like the TV was always on, preventing intimacy for as long as we'd been married. So I asked Chip if I could talk to him for a few minutes when he got a chance.

When Chip turned off the TV, I expressed to him my sadness that it felt to me like the TV was more important than I was, and that I didn't

---

5. Allender, *Wounded Heart*, 217, 232–33.
6. Ibid., 219.

want to compete with it anymore. As I expressed my complaint, Chip's face reddened and his eyes welled up with tears. This wasn't his typical response in our disagreements, and I didn't know what to make of it, so I continued. Finally, Chip came unglued and interrupted me, exploding first with a string of male epithets. "You a*^#*$, you s*^#*$, you m*^#*$, you b*^#*$,! You've been neglecting me with your school and your work and all your busyness all these years, and you have the nerve to criticize me for watching TV. How dare you! You spend all your time in the office on the computer, and you have the guts to tell me not to watch TV. *For all these years, the television has been my closest friend.* How humiliating do you think that is? You..." And he finished his outburst with the epithets that he'd used to introduce it.

Chip wept, and the pain all over his face and body was raw and sharp. He'd never shared his feelings with this much vulnerability with me before, and I was stunned into silence. Typically, we didn't curse each other in our arguments, and his harsh epithets jarred me into reality. In an instant, I felt his pain, and I knew that I'd been kicking him in an old wound for sixteen years. Chip's Dad had done the same thing—had come home every night after work and holed himself up in his office at his computer to the neglect of the family—and Chip had felt the sting of that deeply. He'd come to hate when his Dad came home from work because it was a daily message to him of how little he mattered to his father. I realized that the male epithets he used were probably directed toward his father (which he later confirmed), but I had to acknowledge that I'd neglected Chip in the very same way. I'd neglected him in favor of my own ambitions and endeavors, sending him the same message he'd received from his father each day growing up.

I listened to Chip's explosion, knowing that I deserved every word of it. When he finished, my heart was broken for him. As I'd become more and more compassionate toward Chip's pain, I'd begun to understand how he must have experienced my constant busyness, but his raw pain helped me to connect with his hurt in a way that I'd never been able to before. I had wronged him, and I had no defense. I wanted to hold him tightly, to caress him, to say I was sorry over and over and over until he could believe me, and until his pain could melt away. But I knew the wound was so deep that nothing I could say would assuage it in that moment.

I remained glued to the couch where I sat, weeping for Chip's pain and with sorrow for having repeatedly kicked him in old, gaping, raw wounds. While it was painful to acknowledge my harm of him, I hoped that maybe this was the beginning of a deeper connection for us. My job now was to demonstrate my change of heart by a change of behavior, hoping to earn back Chip's trust over time.

That event starkly exposed my workaholism as one of the most harmful contributors to the breakdown of my relationship with Chip, and the sorrow I experienced as a result of coming to that understanding was so complete that I couldn't help but change; I could no longer use work to escape emotional distress.

Immediately I began leaving my weekends free for us to be together—to hike (one of our favorite activities) or to go to movies, museums, or wherever. We established a tradition of going to a little Greek restaurant for donuts on Saturday mornings, but the activity of choice for the rest of the weekend was watching television, which left me bored, restless, irritable, and disappointed.

I was also disappointed when Chip chose not to arrange his schedule to accommodate counseling anymore. Although he could have prioritized counseling, and later expressed regret for not having done so, he chose not to, and I took this to mean that our relationship was of marginal importance to him. After a year of sticking closely to my resolve to change my way of being in the relationship, I saw little change in Chip's demeanor toward me, and I knew that I couldn't go on any longer without a complete overhaul on the relationship. After sixteen years of marriage, I insisted that we go to counseling *together* or we'd have to split up.

Counseling Together for the First Time, Ever

Kyle was hopeful that Chip and I could be reconciled, and he began the work of trying to help us sort out the dynamics of our relationship. I knew this was our last chance, so I looked forward to these sessions each week. I was particularly hopeful when it came time to read the fables that I had written (see Appendix E), which describe, from my perspective, some of what had happened to make our relationship fail, and what needed to happen to get it back on track. With Kyle's help, Chip began to connect with my description of the harm I had caused him and the harm he had caused me. We shared moments of repentance.

For the first couple months of counseling, I was optimistic that this process could bring about change that could help us "start over." We'd never addressed our issues so openly before, and I was relieved to be able to do so with a facilitator. Soon, however, I began to dread our sessions. I continually felt like I had to fight to be seen in the relationship because I had to explain myself over and over again in various ways in order for Chip to understand me. No one had ever accused me of being inarticulate before, and I was weary from the new effort. It felt like we were recreating the dynamics of our relationship (Chip's passivity and my over-functioning) in the counseling office, which was maddening to me. Each week, new issues were surfacing, and none of them was getting resolved.

Once in a while, Chip and I were able to connect emotionally, and I'm grateful for every one of those moments, but they were few and far between, and they weren't sustained at home, which called into question the authenticity of the seeming change of heart in counseling sessions. I became exhausted with the process, and when Chip dropped out of counseling due to a work conflict that he could've resolved if he'd wanted to, I was all but completely spent. I felt unimportant, not chosen, and not pursued, but despite the disparity between Chip's words of understanding and the lack of behavioral change, I still wasn't sure if Chip understood the concept that we pursue what we most want. With hindsight, I realize that I didn't really *want* to believe that I was unwanted.

We Pursue What We Most Want

One day, Chip made a telling comment. He had an appointment to meet with a man who wanted to talk to him about a business deal, but the man called at the last minute and backed out, saying that Chip could call him the next week to reschedule. Chip was irritated about the last minute cancellation, but what he said concerning the man was enlightening to me: "I'm not going to call him back. If he wants to talk business, he can call me. *If he really wants it, he'll pursue it.*" I knew at that moment that I couldn't excuse Chip's passive approach to our relationship anymore, because it was clear that he *did* understand that when people want something, they go after it. The only reason he'd ever pursued me was for sex. If he'd wanted our relationship, he would've pursued it, and he would've made our healing his highest priority.

Kyle continued to encourage me to describe my heart's longings to Chip in various ways, but when Chip consistently responded with frustration or blankness, my dread and despair deepened. During this time, I relied heavily on journaling and prayer for comfort and spiritual discernment about what I needed to do, and my answers often came through my body. Anguish speaks, and I began listening to my aching chest, my chronically upset stomach, my persistent insomnia, and my throbbing head. I learned that if I tried not to cry when I needed to express my despair, I developed a migraine headache, and the only thing that brought relief was migraine medicine or crying out the pain of my soul, sometimes both. I learned to hear God through the body that he'd designed for me, which told the truth about my relationship with Chip being far from the way covenant is supposed to be.

I felt carried along by God during this time, because I'd often pose a question to God at night as I prayed and cried myself to sleep, only to read the answer to my question in a book the next morning. This happened so many times that I began to expect it, and I felt God taking care of me daily.

As my spiritual sensitivities continued to develop, Chip and I grew more distant. Chip's regard of me seemed unchanged by our counseling experiences, and I became frustrated with the process. The day came when I needed to share the final draft of the letter that I'd begun eight months before, detailing from my perspective what had gone wrong between us. (See Appendix C.) I didn't want to hurt him, but over the months that we'd been in counseling, I came to realize that not vulnerably sharing my perspective of our problems only protected Chip's ability to hurt me. If there were to be any healing in our relationship, I'd have to be as honest with him as I'd been with myself. The truth had often hurt, but the pain had been necessary because it had led me to soft-heartedness time after time. I had to give Chip the same opportunity.

With hindsight, I can see that beneath my desire not to hurt Chip was a more subtle motive: at a pre-conscious level, I sensed that reading the letter would make our mess even more real than when we talked about it in counseling or at home. If I clearly and specifically named my failure and his, there would be no going back. A final decision would have to be made, and that frightened me to the core. Plus, I didn't want to abandon Chip like others had. In the end, I had to realize that we'd abandoned each other long before, and addressing our issues honestly and directly was the only way that might allow true connection to replace the old patterns of emotional and physical abandonment. Sharing my heart with Chip without malice, resentment, or manipulation was one of the most compassionate things I could do for both of us.

It took three sessions to read my letter to Chip with sessions in between to discuss it. (We'd been encouraged not to discuss our relationship between sessions because our discussions only seemed to more deeply divide us.) The day I finished reading the letter was a Valentine's Day, the last one we'd ever spend together, and the last day we'd ever spend in counseling together. Chip decided that he needed to concentrate on his job, and that counseling would have to wait.

Counseling Alone Again

I continued to go to counseling alone, which was my only hope, even though I was completely frustrated with our lack of progress. Our marriage had a disease that had turned terminal from neglect. I considered that perhaps the most loving thing to do would be to amputate—to sever the relationship. It was a tragedy that might've been avoided if we'd treated the toxic conditions earlier, although Chip and I were different enough that we might've met an impasse even if we'd sought counsel early on.

Although our issues weren't merely personality clashes, I began to consider what it must be like for someone like Chip to be in relationship with someone like me. I imagined what it must be like for someone who was a dreamer to be married to someone who engaged life purposefully. I imagined what it must be like for someone who was laid back to a fault to be married to someone who was self-motivated to a fault. I imagined what it must be like for someone who sought a simple and uncomplicated life to be married to someone who sought out matters of philosophy, psychology, and spirituality. I imagined what it must be like for someone who avoided pain to be married to someone who pursued reality at all costs, for someone who avoided emotion to be married to someone who saw emotion as an important language, for someone who was sexually compulsive to be married to someone who insisted on emotional intimacy before sexual intimacy. *My very presence must be exasperating to Chip, just as his way of being is frustrating to me,* I thought. I started to understand that Chip and I might be able to think clearly if we didn't have to be around each other all the time.

It seemed more and more evident that neither one of us could change who we were at core, and, sadly, who we were caused pain to the other. Trying to force each other to change at this level would be like trying to get a dog to meow or a cat to bark: it would only set us up for more failure, increase our pain, and prolong the inevitable. It had become clear to me that Chip was either unwilling or incapable of sustainable fundamental change, and I had to acknowledge that I couldn't live with emotional disconnection.

It was all too obvious that we'd recreated some of the most destructive dynamics of our parents' marriages, and this realization left me nauseated. As I faced more and more truth about our reality, I allowed myself to feel the pain of my heart breaking and softening more and more. By this time, I was crying myself to sleep most nights, and then waking up in the middle of the night to cry and journal some more, sometimes for hours. My digestive system continued to break down from the stress of trying to maintain the integrity of honest relationship appraisal without Chip's partnership in it. My body couldn't continue in this stressed state forever, and the physical pain of my body forced me to listen to Chip's behavior, not just to his words.

By this time, my once-clear vision for our healing had become cloudy, and another quandary overtook me. How could I explain to my loved ones in my faith community what had happened if Chip and I separated? This was the question that was foremost in my mind as I read *Will and Spirit*,[7] a book that helped me face my need to let my public image crumble. I'd been living by some beliefs about myself that I had to release. I had to let go of the images that I craved to uphold, such as: *everything I do is successful*; *I have it all together*; and *I can, single-handedly, save this marriage, if I just do everything the "right" way*.

It occurred to me at this point that God might actually approve more of a divorce between believers who didn't exemplify a godly covenant than he did of keeping up a covenant in name only. It was a shocking thought, one that I'd never have considered on my own, which added to my confidence that I wasn't simply coming up with an idea that would make me feel better. In fact, the idea made me feel worse because I knew how much criticism I would face if I followed through on it. But the thought was in keeping with honesty and integrity, and it left me feeling more open and soft, though scared.

7. May, *Will and Spirit*.

An Experience of Malachi

As much as my heart was aching, I couldn't close the door on my relationship with Chip when I still had questions about what the scriptures say about divorce. My seminary training and my own study on covenants had given me an understanding of the conditional covenant that God had made with Israel, so I came to the text knowing that such treaties feature blessings for keeping the terms and consequences for breaking them. With this awareness, I committed to reading through the prophecy of Malachi, the book in which God declares his hatred of divorce.

I knew that I couldn't pursue divorce if doing so was contrary to scripture, and I was willing to die in my marriage if that's what God said I should do. Although it no longer made sense to me that a covenantal God would demand someone's emotional and physical health as payment for a poor choice of marriage partner, particularly when the choice was made in ignorance, I was willing to find out that I was wrong. It was becoming clear that a choice made due to betrayal bonding was more like a false treaty, signed with the ink of ignorance, than a true covenant of love. I understood God to desire being *well* over being *right* in non-moral issues, when the two seemed to be at odds—which was why he'd allowed divorce in the first place. By this time, I'd learned what hard-heartedness really was, and it was clear to me that God required humble acknowledgment of harm done and genuine repentance as conditions for forgiveness when we make poor choices. Did he treat marriage mistakes differently, I wondered?

My conditioning about divorce and God's judgment was so ingrained that I came to the text expecting to be condemned and required to "lie in the bed that we had made," experiencing the natural consequences for our poor, ignorant choice forever, as if we hadn't experienced them enough already. But I was willing to surrender to this understanding of God if that was what reading the prophecy of Malachi led me to do.

As I read through Malachi, the first thing I noticed was that God's love for Israel had compelled him to protect her from her enemies. Tears came immediately. I'd never felt protected by Chip, and I'd longed for his loving shelter as I'd processed through my healing journey. Instead, I'd fought my battles alone.

Secondly, God indicted Israel for giving him leftovers in worship, instead of her best. Her priorities were out of kilter, her loyalties divided. Chip and I were both guilty of this—of taking the other for granted and of making everything but our relationship a priority. As I'd been going to our joint counseling appointments alone for the previous three months, I felt the sting of this reality keenly. I'd wanted Chip to arrange his schedule to make counseling a priority, to make *us* a priority, but he hadn't. It was painful to consider the reality that I wanted the relationship more than he did.

Thirdly, God indicted the religious leaders, who were supposed to be teaching truth so that the people could look up to them as his representatives. Instead, they were messing up people's lives with their false teaching. In doing so, God said, they had corrupted the covenant with him. When I considered our marriage, it seemed that our entire relationship was built on faulty motivations and lies, and that conventional fundamentalist church teaching about "grounds for divorce" kept us in bondage to a false covenant.

Finally, God turned his attention to the men of Israel, and he accused them of breaking the vows that they'd made to their wives, the covenant companions of their youth. Some of them were even cheating on their wives, and God was disgusted.

It was in this context that God made the declaration:

> You fill the place of worship with your whining and sniveling because you don't get what you want from God. Do you know why? Simple. Because God was there as a witness when you spoke your marriage vows to your young bride, and now you've broken those vows, broken the faith-bond with your vowed companion, your covenant wife. God, not you, made marriage. His Spirit inhabits even the smallest details of marriage. And what does he want from marriage? Children of God, that's what. So guard the spirit of marriage within you. Don't cheat on your spouse. "I hate divorce," says the God of Israel. God-of-the-Angel-Armies says, "I hate the violent dismembering of the 'one flesh' of marriage." So watch yourselves. Don't let your guard down. Don't cheat.
> (Mal 2:13–15)

By the time I'd gotten to this verse, I could only say, "Yeah. I hate divorce, too." It was clear to me that it's the breakdown of covenant treaties—the broken promises to love, honor, cherish and be faithful to one another—that grieves God. In the whole context of Malachi's prophecy, God describes hating the breakdown of relationship. Divorce is merely the evidence of a break in covenant that happens long before the signing of legal dissolution documents.

Repentance: Surprisingly Soft and Shame-Free 183

I also allowed myself to connect for the first time to the pain of being cheated on by my husband. I don't believe Chip slept with another woman after we were married, but his heart was certainly divided. He struggled with sexual compulsivity, and it had been clear to me within the first few months of our marriage—when he told me that I was undesirable to him in comparison to the women on TV—that his heart wasn't mine. I'd wondered whether pornography constituted cheating, and my pain told me that day that it certainly does. Chip had been unfaithful to me, time and time again, and I could no longer fend off the truth or the pain of that. I'd been competing with airbrushed woman and other illusions for our entire relationship, and I'd never be able to measure up. Facing that reality hurt me to the core of my feminine soul.

I read Malachi many times in the next several days, and every time, I wept as I identified with the text. I'd never truly had Chip's heart. He'd come into the marriage with his fantasies of other women, real and imagined, and he'd never been satisfied with me—something he later acknowledged. I had owned my own divided loyalty (my career had been more important to me than Chip), but I'd never allowed myself to fully acknowledge and feel Chip's disloyalty toward me.

My reading of Malachi left me with no spiritual reason to stay in the marriage. I'd expected to feel condemned by the reading of it, but instead I had more clarity about what constitutes grounds for marriage and divorce. I found the book to be a miniature treatise on what it looks like to honor a covenant companion, and our marriage fell far short. Furthermore, there seemed to be no hope that Chip would ever understand and live out the concept of honor. We hadn't kept our vows to love, honor, cherish, and be faithful to one another since our first year of marriage, let alone "'til death do us part." We'd broken all of our promises far more than we'd kept them, and we hadn't genuinely repaired even one breach.

Reading Malachi also left me with deep sorrow for the way my wounded history and Chip's had come together to create a predictably damaging union.[8] I had to take responsibility for my own poor choices,

---

8. In *Facing Love Addiction*, Pia Mellody describes the interplay between an Avoidance Addict and a Love Addict. Love Addicts will tolerate almost anything to avoid being abandoned and Avoidance Addicts will try to avoid commitment and healthy intimacy. This text describes the dynamic of many trauma bonds between codependents and addicts.

and I wept with bitter remorse for having failed to treat one of God's image-bearers with the reverence and awe that are due his highest creation. I deeply regretted stomping on the sacred ground of Chip's soul for half of his life. "I'm so sorry, God," I cried over and over and over again, "I'm so sorry . . ."

However, I had no reason to believe that Chip would suddenly (or even gradually) begin to treat me as a fellow bearer of God's insignia, and I could no longer allow myself to be treated poorly; I had a responsibility to take good care of, protect, and treasure what God had created, including myself. Knowing that Chip's poor treatment of me came from a wounded place in him, I was able to let Chip off the hook for his harm of me. I hoped that someday Chip would be able to forgive me for my harm of him, as well. In the meantime, it was clear to me that staying together would only inflict more harm on both of us.

At that point, the two years that it had taken me to reach this conclusion had been the hardest two years of my life, both emotionally and physically, and my life has had its share of hurts. It had been a lonely time of sharing my tears mostly with God and with my therapist, and only rarely with my husband who didn't value them. I'd been driven into a desert where God could woo me into a relationship with him that was more intimate than any I've ever known. In that dark season of my soul, I experienced God's *checed* in a way that transformed my understanding of him and my relationship with him. In the end, my reading of Malachi removed my last spiritual reason to stay in the marriage.

A THERAPEUTIC REFLECTION

This is the dilemma in which many people of faith find themselves when facing their pain-filled covenants. Staying in a marriage, or returning to it, may represent repentance for one person, while acknowledging the marriage is already over and letting it go may represent repentance for another. What I find in my practice is that people who stay in a relationship are more often motivated by *fear* than by a heart-felt commitment to their covenant partner—fear of what others would say if they knew about the problems in the marriage; fear of what others would say if they separated or divorced; fear of what they would do economically if they had the courage to remove themselves or their children from harm's way; fear that God or their children would hate them if they divorce.

Emily

Such was Emily's story.

Emily came to me in a deep depression. She described how her husband controlled nearly every move she made. His words were cruel, his hatred palpable. But Emily continued to allow herself to be treated with indignity after indignity. As we talked, Emily revealed to me that she had felt God release her from her marriage to Ken long before, but that she was too afraid to follow through. What would people think of her? How would she survive without a man to take care of her? How could she explain it to her kids?

I don't know what Emily chose to do—she dropped out of therapy before we completed treatment, and she was still living with Ken at the time. My heart went out to her children who were the innocent witnesses of Ken's cruelty and Emily's passivity, and who were learning deeply damaging lessons about how to conduct themselves in relationship.

What would repentance look like for someone like Emily?

Elizabeth

Elizabeth also came to me describing a controlling husband, but by the time she came to counseling, she was already in an affair, and it wasn't her first. During her fifteen-year marriage to Josh, she'd been with two other men. Her two teenage boys felt deeply betrayed by their mother and had cut off all communication with her. Elizabeth wanted me to help her restore that communication, but she was unwilling to break off her current affair, with Erik, or explore the meaning of the pattern of her unfaithfulness throughout her marriage. Eventually, Elizabeth began missing her appointments, and she dropped out of therapy when she became engaged to Erik.

How different it could've been if Elizabeth had committed to seeking truth at any cost. Instead, she chose to continue in an old pattern, indicative of the hardness of her heart. I have no doubt that this stubbornness was fueled by old wounds that felt too painful to explore, so I understand Elizabeth's reticence. However, her choice not to deal with these old wounds will continue to hurt her and others, particularly her boys. She may have to live with the permanent consequences of their rejection if she continues to choose one man after another over the privilege and responsibility of teaching her children about true intimacy.

What would it look like for someone like Elizabeth to repent?

Both Emily and Elizabeth continue to live in denial of their pain, as many of us do. To avoid our pain, we tend to seek comforting idols: compulsive use of alcohol, food, sex, television, spiritualizing, education, achievement, money, exercise, possessions, virtuous causes, ideas, people, things—we can elevate anything to the level of idol, demanding that it assuage the pain in our hearts. Until we're willing to deal with our proclivity to seek relief from pain in illegitimate ways, we'll continue to make one poor choice after another. It's severe mercy, a gift of desperation, when the consequences of our poor choices finally catch up with us and squeeze us into repentance.

Merry

Merry finally was squeezed enough to seek truth at any cost. Merry and Aaron were high school sweethearts, and after almost 20 years together, Merry was content to be the mother of their three children. Their marriage had never been perfect, but it had been far from poor, and they'd been able to weather the storms of life together in defined roles. Aaron was the stereotypical dominant male and Merry the submissive female.

About fifteen years into their marriage, Merry discovered that Aaron was having an affair with a business colleague, Kelly. She insisted that it end, and Aaron agreed. But, despite his promises, his relationship with Kelly continued, and his contempt for Merry grew. Within two years, Aaron was a different person. His demeanor changed from cordial to cruel, and his harshness escalated. By the time Merry came to therapy, she had engaged in pleading, threatening, cajoling, and trying to bargain Aaron back into relationship with her. My work with Merry centered around helping her take responsibility for her own contribution to the failure of the relationship (not for Aaron's affair), and in helping her to let Aaron own and carry his contribution to the failure of the relationship. As Merry's heart softened toward her own and Aaron's emotional bondage, she was able to approach him with confidence, without engaging in passive aggression or other manipulative tactics.

When Aaron continued to refuse to engage in a healing process with Merry, Merry warned him that she couldn't endure his disengagement forever, and that he would need to choose whether or not he wanted to be in the marriage. Over several months, Aaron made no change, and Merry's sorrow eventually overwhelmed her hope. After coming to terms with her fear of being alone, Merry sought a divorce.

Anyone who witnessed the emotional toll that the relationship took on Merry would be cruel to suggest that she'd sought the easy way out. To the contrary, Merry fought hard to save the relationship and to repent from any attitudes of her own heart that had contributed to its breakdown. It grieves me to know that there are many believers who care nothing for such stories of sincere soul-searching and restorative efforts. Those who come by the decision to divorce honestly know that the journey often includes resisting this choice for many years longer than is healthy.

(For more examples of what repentance might look like in various case scenarios, see *Intimate Allies*.[9])

Paul and Kim

A few days ago, I had the extraordinary privilege of meeting a courageous couple, Paul and Kim, who gave me permission to tell their story of healing. Perhaps you've read Paul's novel, *The Shack*,[10] a parable that is helping millions of people see and connect with God in ways they never knew were possible. In this parable, the shack represents our broken lives, into which God comes to live and make things new. Paul wrote this parable after his own broken life had driven him to God in a whole new way.

Many years ago, Paul received a phone call from his wife: "Paul, I know, and I'm waiting for you," Kim said. What Kim had learned was that Paul had been in an affair for the previous three months with her best friend. And Kim was waiting for Paul to come home so that she could read him the riot act.

Which is exactly what she did . . . for the next two years. Kim never worried about whether it was wrong to be angry. She didn't try to avoid emotions that other believers consider sinful. She never took responsibility for having somehow driven Paul into the arms of another woman, and she required that he take full responsibility for his own poor choices.

---

9. Allender and Longman, *Intimate Allies*.
10. Young, *The Shack*.

And he did. Paul immediately found a counselor who assured him that he could take Paul through a healing process to the other side. Paul surrendered himself to his God, to his counselor, and to his process.

Over the next two years, Kim required Paul to be brutally honest about everything, and he was. He knew that Kim had a hard choice to make about whether or not to remain married to him, and that he had no right to ask for her forgiveness. If she was going to offer it, he was ready to receive it, but he knew that Kim wasn't obligated to make such a choice. If she did, it would be by grace alone.

As it became clear to Kim over time that Paul's heart had truly changed, her anger with him began to subside. His humility convinced her that he was trustworthy again. She could tell that he was seeking healing for himself, motivated internally, not just to save his marriage.

Kim is one of the most non-codependent women I have ever met, and her requirement that Paul take full responsibility for his choices contributed to saving their marriage. So did Paul's complete surrender. A heart that has admitted that it cannot force life to do its will is a beautiful thing, and this contributed to restoring the Young's covenant. That these two critical factors occurred simultaneously is remarkable.

What is more common is resistance on the part of the offender to take full responsibility for the harm done and resistance on the part of the offended to let their partner do so. I hope the Young's story will help you envision what needs to happen in you and in your marriage if you and your relationship are in crisis.

SNEAK PREVIEW OF THE NEXT CHAPTER

Sometimes, however, quitting is a healthier option than continuing in a dishonoring relationship. In such cases, it's possible to end well. The next chapter offers practical help on how to do this for those whose covenants are irreparably broken.

9

To Have and to Fold

WHEN MY SISTER WAS thirty-six years old, she finally decided to throw in the towel in her fight against diabetes. Suzie had been diagnosed with the disease when she was four years old, and its complications raced to catch up with her in her late twenties and early thirties. By then she'd had a heart attack, had lost an eye, had received a kidney from our mother, had had two sections of one leg amputated due to gangrene, was about to lose another, experienced painful neuropathy daily, and was dependent on kidney dialysis. It seemed like she woke up every day with another ailment to fight.

During the months before she died, Suzie spent more time in hospitals and nursing homes than she did in her own home. She'd spent more time in such institutions in her thirty-six years than most do in their entire lifetime.

One day, Suzie learned that she needed yet another operation to amputate more of a gangrenous leg, and it wasn't long before I got a phone call from her. "I'm thinking about going off dialysis, and I wanted to get your input on that decision." She had arranged for the whole family to be on a conference call to help her decide what to do.

What do you say to your sister when you know that you may be assisting her death? I had just completed research on end of life decisions in terminal cases for a school assignment, and I told Suzie about the paper I'd written. She wanted to read it, so I faxed it to her right away. A few days later, she chose to accept only two more weeks of dialysis treatments. She never said so, but I hope my paper helped her find peace about her choice. Certainly, once she made it, she was at peace. Suzie wasn't a quitter, but I was proud of her for being so brave. Imagine how much pain a woman like Suzie would have to be in to choose to die to escape from it.

Fewer than two days after she received her last dialysis treatment, Suzie quietly conceded the fight she'd waged for over thirty years. According to Kenny Rogers, one of Suzie's favorite country music artists, "Ya' gotta know when to hold 'em, / know when to fold 'em / know when to walk away / know when to run." Gangrene had sucked from her the last shred of her will to live, and Suzie knew it was time to fold.

When gangrene has overtaken a relationship, couples need to do the same. It's merciful to acknowledge when a relationship has died and can't be revived. Sometimes letting go is the only way for each individual to heal and become whole again.

As I write this paragraph, the muted television bathes the room with images of the 2008 Summer Olympics. Last night's opening ceremony was beyond spectacular. I wish my sister could have seen it. It'll be nearly impossible for future Olympic cities to match the splendor and extravagance of this event, part of which emphasized the complementarity and harmony of life's opposites—the yin and the yang—or in this case, the complementarity and harmony of tenacity and of letting go. Knowing when to continue and when to quit takes great courage. Knowing how to do it with dignity is an art.

The athletes who compete at the Olympic games know about enduring pain. They're not quitters. We teach our children, Olympians or not, to persist through tough tasks in the interest of developing character and stamina. We teach them to delay gratification because, as we noticed in chapter 4, the ability to do so predicts life-long success more accurately than IQ. However, it's important to know when to quit, as well. Sometimes letting go of a dishonoring relationship is more difficult than hanging onto it, and sometimes it even takes our bodies breaking down before we listen to the wisdom of our souls.

Coming to the decision to quit is often complicated by not knowing how to end well. For this reason, marriages often end badly when they don't need to. Believe it or not, the approach that can facilitate genuine repair is the same one that can facilitate a peaceful end: firm, gentle, and honest confrontation. I hope that this chapter will help facilitate amicable endings for those who, after carefully considering the circumstances, decide that separation or divorce is the best option.

A THERAPEUTIC REFLECTION

Confronting a Spouse

Charlie Brown could have used some counsel to help him learn from his mistakes and confront Lucy. Remember Charlie's foolish behavior regarding Lucy's trickery? Though Lucy withdrew the football *every* time, Charlie kept trying to kick it, *every* time. What Charlie needed to do was kindly but firmly confront Lucy about her maliciousness and give her a chance to repent and to prove that she cared about her harm of him, establishing appropriate boundaries if Lucy remained unmoved.

When I work with spouses traveling this journey to confrontation, or "care-frontation," as Augsberger calls it in *Caring Enough to Confront*, I'm careful not to encourage confrontation of partners until my clients have confronted themselves with their own contribution to the failure of the relationship. This calls for identifying one's self-protective style of relating and how it has impacted the marriage. The therapist's work is to help clients connect with the pain of their wounds so that they're also able to connect with how they've harmed others. This recognition also helps them appreciate God's forgiveness in a way they may never have before. As Allender writes in *The Wounded Heart*, "When we are gripped by the good news that a just God has spared us death and condemnation and restored us to eternal relationship, we will discover the motivation to love."[1] When people come to this point, it's not uncommon for them to want even the people who've harmed them to experience the gift of forgiveness. If those who've perpetrated harm are ever to experience forgiveness, they'll need to be confronted with their harm in hopes that they'll allow their hearts to be softened.

The evidence of wounded individuals being softened, redeemed, and healed is when they're able to imagine their offender's potential if the offender repented and was redeemed. From this point, it isn't long before the redeemed victim wants to participate, in whatever way he or she can, in the restoration process of another. To love well means to "do whatever it takes (apart from sin) to bring health (salvation) to the abuser."[2]

---

1. Allender, *Wounded Heart*, 237.
2. Ibid., 241.

Loving well often means confronting the guilty party, even if it means risk of personal sacrifice and loss. Depending on the situation, such a rebuke may be direct (Luke 17:3) or patient and slow (Eph 4:32). Either way, the desire is for restoration. As clients repent from their own harm of their spouse, their demeanor softens toward their partner, and their confidence in telling the truth about the relationship begins to grow. In so doing, they develop a genuine, non-codependent compassion for the other party, as well as a desire to see that person healed and whole.

They also begin to be able to clearly name, without malice, how their spouse has been harmful. While they may not realize it right away, they've begun to forgive—to let go of harm done so that they can move into the future without believing that the other person owes them anything.

If the "letting go" for one spouse occurs prior to the other spouse joining a healing process, it's likely that the relationship will end in divorce. Jesus tells to us "forgive, if he repents" (Luke 17:3), making reconciliation conditional on the response of the offender. If only one of the parties agrees to surrender to a healing process, it's likely that the couple won't achieve reconciliation. They may continue to live together, but the relationship will likely retain whatever destructive dynamics it's always had. However, even if only one individual is willing to commit to an honest process of soul-searching, a counselor can help that person discover his or her own contribution to the failure of the relationship and to identify the partner's contribution, as well. At this point, confrontation may occur, and a process of forgiveness and reconciliation may begin.

If confrontation produces no interest in change in the second party, the counselor is left to help the first find forgiveness of themselves and of their partner. Since forgiveness takes only one party, an individual can come to understand and name the injury, grieve the losses associated with it, and begin to practice freedom from those hurts. In doing so, they can move from resentment to peace, not necessarily with the other party, but within themselves. This leaves the person with a known and felt sense of forgiveness, of letting go, after time and lots of effort.

In order to achieve peace *with* the offending party, the offending party must be willing to acknowledge and sorrow over harm done, and to make changes reflecting a softened heart. However, like the peace of forgiveness, restoration doesn't happen overnight. Reconciliation can occur only after trust has been re-established over time, as the offended party sees that the offender's humility and changed behavior lasts. (If the destructive behavior continues to come and go, it's likely that the appearance of repentance is merely the shame phase of an addictive cycle, rather than the sorrow of repentance that produces a softened heart.)

A Helpful Formula

It's important to confront only when the motive is right. When clients are able to identify their motive in confrontation as a desire to simply tell the truth, with no expectation of receiving anything from the guilty party, they're likely ready to follow through with the confrontation. To get to this point usually takes several months or years, as it usually occurs near the end of a personal healing process. Often, it takes several drafts of letter writing to prepare an individual for the event.

The first few drafts of a confrontational letter tend to reflect a latent desire for revenge, which expresses itself in destructive rage. Such anger is necessary and exhibits justice, but it leaves no room for natural consequences, which are far more effective than our puny, manipulative attempts to get others to behave as we want them to. Such fury leaves no room for restoration, either, and belies a need for further exploration of the motives of the victim.

As clients prepare to confront those who have harmed them, it's important for them to express several issues. First, they must clearly identify the other's harm in an effort to simply tell the truth, to expose the deeds of darkness (1 Cor 4:5), to hate what is evil, and to cling to what is good (Rom 12:9), in effect saying: "This is what you did." Second, they must clearly transfer the responsibility of the harm back to the offending party: "I hold you responsible." Third, they must describe the impact of the harm upon their lives: "This is how it hurt me." And finally, they must warn the offending party that they will no longer keep secrets about the offense: "I will no longer be silent."[3]

Allender describes a logical sequence of five steps to such a rebuke, and instructs that the rebuke should only continue as the offender complies with the requirements of each step.[4] First, when the victim addresses what the offenses were or are, the perpetrator must agree that the harm occurred. Second, the offending party must accept full responsibility for the harm, without defensiveness of any kind. Third, when the victim

---

3. Kehler, "Confronting an Offender."
4. Allender, *Wounded Heart*, 252.

describes the damage caused by the offenses, the offending person must express grief for the harm done. Fourth, the offending party must be willing to consider current relational failures that prevent reconciliation. And finally, when the victim describes the process for re-establishing relationship, the guilty party must be willing to pursue it, seeking additional help as necessary.

If the offender demonstrates sincere repentance, a deepening of intimacy may begin. If, however, repentance doesn't occur, the victim can still offer love by clarifying boundaries with kind firmness. If, over time, the guilty party continues to refuse to repent, the victim may need to sever relationship completely, letting the guilty party know that relationship is possible again whenever he or she chooses to commit to a sincere reconciliation process. Allender says, "This form of excommunication is actually a gift, a respectful choice to honor the abuser with the consequences of his own destructive choice, in hope that loneliness and shame will draw his cold heart back to the fire of relationship (2 Thess 3:14–15)."[5]

In cases where there is risk of danger, I recommend a waiting period after an initial confrontation before attempting to start a reconciliation process, even if there appears to be true repentance. True repentance will last regardless of how the offended party responds, so there's no need to rush into a reconciliation process. Also, confrontations are emotionally exhausting events, so taking a breather is wise for both parties. The process of moving toward reconciliation includes returning over and over again to each step, forgiving again and again, as long as there's evidence of genuine repentance, which manifests, not only in a sincere confession and apology, but in a lasting humility and a desire to make amends.

This is Hard Work

I'm a romantic at heart, and I hate to see marriages end in divorce. Unfortunately, marriage therapy doesn't have a good track record, particularly because most couples avail themselves of it only as a last resort. Marriage therapy has the most promise when couples seek help early and often.

Because most couples come to me in crisis, I deal with whatever reality they bring into my office. Typically, one party comes in first—often the wife—and the other comes in only when the spouse issues some sort

---

5. Ibid., 253.

of ultimatum: either we get help or we split up. If the second party is willing to join the process with his or her whole heart, it bodes well for reconciliation to occur in the relationship. At the least, the couple will be able to identify where they went wrong and decide whether or not they can salvage their relationship.

When couples are in crisis, it's not uncommon for them to embark on a trial separation, which can be a purposeful and intentional period of time during which both parties seek to understand what went wrong and what would need to change in order to re-instate the marriage covenant. (See Appendix B: Trial Separation Agreement Form.)

Options for Ending

When it becomes evident over time that reconciliation isn't going to occur, preferably after an intentional and purposeful trial separation period, there are several ways in which couples whose covenant has broken down can seek a legal end to it. The most preferable option, in my opinion, is the kitchen table agreement. When the divorce is uncontested, sometimes couples are able to sit down together and agree on how to split the assets and liabilities and how to continue parenting together. This kind of negotiation occurs only if there is a humble spirit of equitability on both sides.

The next best method of settlement is with the use of a professional mediator. If there are complicated assets and liabilities on which the couple must agree, having a mediator is an option for those who are non-adversarial.

Collaborative law is another amicable way to legalize the end of a marriage, particularly when there are children or other innocent victims involved. Collaborative lawyers only work with non-litigious couples, providing conflict management, guidance of negotiations, problem solving, and legal education. Collaborative lawyers help couples find mental heath practitioners, relationship coaches, and financial planners as needed. All of this takes place after the couple signs a contract not to litigate. If either party seeks litigation, the collaborative process is terminated.

The least desired method of legally dissolving a marriage is through litigation, which tends to be as adversarial as the relationship in crisis, and leaves valuable marital assets in the hands of lawyers. Although such a process feeds on the mistrust of its clients, this method is sometimes the only approach available to couples when one or both parties refuse to come to an agreement with humility and respect.

Stormie and Bob

Confrontation saved Stormie and Bob from such a bitter end.

Wisely, this couple sought help with their marriage after only three years. They had both been married and divorced before, and they wanted help with communication and blended family issues. Before long, it was evident that many of the couple's current conflicts stemmed from unresolved childhood traumas. Stormie's parents were alcoholics, and Bob's had been too self-absorbed to provide guidance. Stormie and Bob were also survivors of childhood sexual abuse.

The triggers in the relationship due to the mixing of all these issues seemed all but impossible to resolve. Complicating matters was Bob's alcoholism, which was especially provoking to Stormie, given her childhood history.

A colleague and I teamed up to provide individual therapy for both Stormie and Bob to help them focus on their personal recovery issues, and also to provide the opportunity for conjoint sessions in which we could all address the marriage problems together.

As Stormie grew stronger, she was able to let go of her fear of abandonment, which kept her bound to Bob and his alcoholism. As she let go, she was able to confront him on several issues regarding his endangering and neglect of the children. The more Stormie left Bob with his own responsibility to heal, refusing to give in to her codependent enabling of him, the more Bob felt free to pursue his own healing, although his continued drinking prevented lasting change.

Bob also began to confront Stormie on some issues he'd been too frightened to address. For example, Stormie sometimes had difficulty restraining her emotions when an issue between Bob and her seemed gridlocked, and at these times, she would be unconcerned about using unkind words toward Bob in the presence of the children. When Bob confronted Stormie on this issue, the two of them were able to work together to come up with "rules of engagement" so that they could fight fairly.

Eventually Bob's alcoholism threatened to destroy their family, and it came time for Stormie to arrange an intervention. Without even one objection, Bob agreed to go to treatment, and he chose to stay for almost three consecutive cycles at the treatment facility. Although he had been to in-patient treatment facilities twice before, something shifted in Bob this time; his will began to break. He is now humbly grateful to Stormie for the strength that it took to insist that he overcome his addiction or say goodbye to the relationship.

Bob and Stormie have a long way to go, but I anticipate that their willingness to confront and be confronted will continue to increase the intimacy between them. If they stay on this healing journey *together*, I have great hope for their future. As of this writing, Stormie and Bob continue in the afterglow of shedding addictions.

(For more on confrontation and forgiveness, see *Forgiving the Unforgivable*, by Beverly Flanigan; *Bold Love*, by Dan Allender; and *Caring Enough to Confront*, by David Augsburger.)

Best-Case Scenario

Although the best-case scenario ends in the softened hearts of both individuals and reconciliation of the relationship, this process takes two and can never be guaranteed. I've had the honor of helping couples, such as Stormie and Bob, walk this path, and it's gratifying for everyone involved.

I've also had the privilege of helping other individuals and couples commit to an honest process of appraisal that eventually led them to choose the lesser of two evils—divorce instead of a harmful marriage. At this point, couples who continue to care for the other can end their relationship well, before they inflict more pain. In these cases, couples usually say that they wish they had ended the relationship earlier. It's easier for them to see the hopelessness of their relationship when they've distanced themselves from it.

Unfortunately, I've also helplessly watched marriages end badly when one or both of the partners failed to take a fearless inventory of the relationship. As a therapist, this process is painful to watch, particularly when children are involved. Children whose parents don't commit to genuinely repair or maturely dissolve their relationship become innocent casualties of their parents' resentment, getting caught (or lost) in the crossfire of unnecessary, bitter relational dynamics.

If your marriage needs an honest appraisal, I hope that you'll have the courage to commit to one—for your sake and for the sake of all your relationships—trusting yourself that you'll find the strength to see it through. If you'll allow your heart to remain soft throughout the process, you'll arrive on the other side more liberated, either in your marriage or apart from it.

A THEOLOGICAL REFLECTION

Confrontation in the scriptures—also called discipline, rebuke, reproof, warning, and correction—was intimately connected with God's covenant with Israel. In the Old Testament it was understood mostly in corporate terms, although confrontation of individuals also occurred.

The first recorded confrontation in the Bible was between God and Adam in Genesis 3, after the Garden couple broke the single rule that God had established for them. God simply faced them with the truth of their disobedience and then allowed the natural consequences of their infraction to fall upon them. This provides a good principle for us to follow.

Other individuals who experienced the confrontation and discipline of God included Moses, who was forbidden to enter the Promised Land; Achan, who lied about taking forbidden plunder; Dathan, Abiram, Nadab, Abihu, and Uzzah, who disrespected God's instruction for worship; David, who lost the son he conceived in his affair with Bathsheba; and Job, who presumed to correct God and was reproved for his pretentiousness. Such examples are rampant throughout the scriptures.

A popular verse in Proverbs encourages us to appreciate God's discipline: "But don't, dear friend, resent God's discipline; / don't sulk under his loving correction. / It's the child he loves that God corrects; / a father's delight is behind all this" (3:11–12).

In the Pentateuch

The book of Deuteronomy presents God's discipline as a way that his people might know him as a father who wants their lives to go well: "Obediently live by his rules and commands, which I am giving you today so that you'll live well and your children after you . . . " (4:39). God wants to live in harmony with his people, so he tells them exactly what makes relationship work.

Should Israel not reciprocate his love, God promises discipline, not so much as a suzerain towards a vassal, but as a father towards his child (Deut 8:5). Lest the people forget God's ultimate power and sovereignty, however, the covenant curses listed in Deuteronomy 27 and 28 remind us that God's love is not so sentimental to prevent severe chastisement, which certainly did occur many times, such as during the wilderness period, the destruction of Jerusalem, and the Babylonian exile. If we follow God's example, our motives for confrontation will be intended to restore the covenant, as well. Keep in mind, however, that it's never the job of one partner to discipline or reprove the other since covenant companionship is a mutual relationship rather than a hierarchical one.

In the Wisdom Literature

Where the subject of discipline arises in the Psalms, its emphasis falls on the individual believer, who may pray to be spared discipline (6:1; 38:1), but who wisely recognizes discipline to be a blessing (94:12), even though it may be severe (118:18).

The book of Proverbs often refers to the concept of discipline, and, like Deuteronomy, sets this theme in the context of the parent-child relationship (e.g., Prov 1). Proverbs speaks of discipline as an act of love, however severe it may need to be, at times. Proverbs calls those who refuse such discipline "fools" (1:7), "scoffers" (9:7) and "wicked" (5:22–23). (See *Bold Love*[6] for an excellent treatment of these categories and how to respond to people whose behavior fits these descriptions.) Ultimately, the purpose of discipline is to shape godly character, and should not be excessive or administered in anger.

In the Prophets

As we noticed in chapter 1, the prophets were covenant enforcement mediators. When they warned the people of coming judgment, they were simply reminding Israel of the covenant curses for their disobedience to the covenant stipulations. Their message wasn't their own, but God's, and it wasn't original. The prophets just acted as God's representatives. Hosea and Jeremiah had particularly strong messages to deliver to Judah who repeatedly refused *YHWH*'s correction (Jer 5:3; 7:28; 17:23; 32:33). The end result of her stubbornness was exile, which, even with genuine repentance, couldn't be avoided. And as we've noted in previous chapters, Israel's broken covenant with God included the discipline of divorce (Hos 2:1; Jer 3:8). Broken covenants between human beings

---

6. Allender and Longman, *Bold Love*.

In the New Testament

As in the Old Testament, the purpose of correction in the New Testament is to bring about conviction and repentance (John 16:8; Jude 15). National discipline of Israel in the Old Testament corresponds to corporate discipline of the church in the New Testament (Matt 18:15–17; 1 Cor 5:1–5), although self-discipline, enabled by the Spirit, is also prominent.

Church discipline is intended to be corrective for believers whose behavior denies the truth (2 John 7–11; 1 Tim 1:20). Open and scandalous harm cannot be tolerated, and to protect the name of Messiah, severe action must be taken (1 Cor 5:1–5), always with the motive to bring about repentance (2 Tim 2:25). Excommunication, a sort of corporate divorce of a hurtful believer, may be the reluctant but necessary end of a disciplinary process (2 Thess 3:14–15), which depending on the offense, may begin with a rebuke that is personal, private and gentle (Gal 6:1–5).

In the Revelation, God refers to Proverbs 3:11–12 as he threatens severe discipline of an entire church (3:16), though his preference and plea is for repentance (3:19). Whatever discipline occurs, it should be in keeping with the entire body of scripture so that the punishment fits the crime. In the interest of protecting the innocent and powerless, severe infractions need to be met with severe consequences (perhaps legal ones), and less hurtful ones with less severe consequences. The hope should always be reconciliation, although this is dependent upon the sincere heart change of the offending party.

A PERSONAL REFLECTION

Care-frontation

Eventually, I came to realize that I needed to confront Chip, but not before I'd made significant progress in changing myself.

Fifteen years into our marriage, I finally decided to treat Chip with the dignity he deserved as someone made in the image of God. For the last two years of our marriage, I engaged in few arguments. There were times when I was tempted to give into old, contemptuous habits, but when I was feeling that way, I simply removed myself from the situation so that I could identify the hurt that I felt tempted to cover with anger.

During this time, I went to therapy regularly to help me evaluate my relationship with Chip honestly. After much processing of my own failure of the relationship and of coming to acknowledge Chip's failure of me, it was time to start the process of confrontation. I had written a couple of fables that represented my interpretation of the origin of our conflicts, and I read these to Chip in counseling (see Appendix E). With our counselor's assistance, Chip was able to connect with some of the pain that we had caused each other.

Still, nothing changed at home. Chip remained distant toward me and made little attempt to understand his own contribution to the failure of our relationship. After some time, it became clear to me that Chip wasn't able to connect with either his own heart or with mine, and I decided that it was time to read him a letter that I'd finished drafting eight months prior (see Appendix C). As mentioned in chapter 8, the day I was scheduled to read this letter in counseling, I was terrified. I didn't want to cause Chip any more pain than I already had, and I knew the letter would do just that. But our counselor, Kyle, reminded me how important it was to take this step.

It would be a tragedy if I sought a divorce without first giving Chip one, last, clear and direct chance to hear my heart and seek to renew our relationship. And with that, I purposed to show Chip the pain of my heart with complete vulnerability. If he understood and sought reconciliation, I would never regret giving this last chance my whole heart. If he didn't, I still would never regret giving it my whole heart.

It took three sessions to read my letter to Chip. When I began to write the letter, I found that I couldn't address Chip's failure of me before I had addressed my failure of him. For the next six weeks of counseling, we discussed this first part of the letter. With Kyle's gentle help, Chip seemed to understand and feel the harm that I'd done. After Kyle helped him grasp the weight of the opening section, Chip turned to me with anguish in his eyes, "You've dishonored me," he said. I acknowledged this truth sadly and without defense, and Chip wept; he had gotten it.

Two more sessions were required for me to address Chip's harm of me, with much less success in his understanding of my complaints. In the end, it turned out that after I read the last section of the letter to Chip in counseling (on a Valentine's Day, sadly enough), he never returned to counseling to complete the process of understanding.

Several months later, it became clear to me that reconciliation wasn't as important to him as it was to me. I finally had to face the fact that Chip and I were at different places with regard to our relationship. I had to let go.

The day that Chip commented that a business deal didn't go through because the other guy didn't want it badly enough to pursue it, I knew that Chip understood the concept that we pursue what we most want. It was never clearer to me that his lack of pursuit meant that he didn't want me. I couldn't *make* him want me, so for both of our sakes—to release Chip from a bond that he didn't want, and to release me from being bound to someone who didn't want me—I finally sought a divorce.

Ending Well

When I communicated to Chip that I didn't have any hope of reconciliation between us, we began the process of ending our relationship, which I was determined to do as peacefully as possible. I was committed to making the end of our marriage a good goodbye. Over the next six weeks, we shared some significant heartfelt connections—moments that I'll always cherish. With the end in sight, I was more vigilant to be sure that Chip knew that I considered him to be a good man, however broken, regardless of what had happened between us. We shared more moments of genuine apology and sorrow in those last weeks than we had in our entire marriage. I was particularly intent on staying fully present with my pain during this goodbye process, a commitment that was all but unbearable.

As I look back on those last couple months, I'm proud of the respectful way we ended our marriage. We were able to avoid litigation by coming to an agreement about splitting our assets and liabilities after just one mediation session, and a little work afterwards. The mediator made us aware of two issues that we hadn't been considering in a fair division of financial assets: Chip hadn't considered my advanced education, which in the eyes of the law translated into a higher income earning potential, and I hadn't considered Chip's pension fund.

Our discussion after the mediation session left us at an impasse, and it seemed that we'd have to involve lawyers, an adversarial process that I'd hoped to avoid in the interest of encouraging as positive an experience as possible. For the next twenty-four hours, I agonized in my spirit over what might constitute a fair division of assets, but, as I allowed myself to feel Chip's fear of financial instability, unfounded though it was, I was able to let go of the need for absolute equity. I finally decided that if Chip would be willing to pay off my car out of his assets, I'd be willing to leave his pension fund alone.

It wasn't an equal trade, because the amount in Chip's pension fund was about five times the balance on my car loan, but I was confident that I'd ultimately be fine financially. I knew that a lawyer wouldn't advise me to agree to such a financial loss, but this arrangement would buy me peace of mind, and that was worth it to me. I would take a loss if it would leave Chip feeling less anxious about his future, and if it would leave us able to retain a sense of care for one another through the process of legally ending our marriage. (I wouldn't recommend this for partners who aren't able to be financially independent.)

When I floated my proposal to Chip, he agreed, and the tension melted between us. We had successfully come to a resolution that felt satisfactory to both of us, and we could end our marriage on a congenial note, with nothing contested between us.

It was the most friendly divorce process that I had ever heard of, although it did come at a high emotional and physical price. I was willing to absorb these costs for a limited time if it meant that we could end our relationship in a way that retained our dignity. I'll never regret that.

Filing Papers

When the day came to file divorce papers, Chip and I met at the courthouse. On my way there, I focused on being present in my emotions. It was nearly impossible to hold back tears as the court clerk inspected our paperwork, and made casual small talk about her allergies and her "nonexistent" property on which she pays taxes. All I could think about was the weightiness of what we were about to do.

It took about thirty minutes to go over all the paperwork, and then the clerk turned us over to the cashier, who took our debit cards, charged $193 to each of them, and then stamped the case number on all the originals and on all the copies. I had never heard anything sound so loud and so final in all my life. Every stamp impression felt like a punch in my stomach. Somehow, I still managed to choke back my tears, and when all the copies were signed and stamped, we were dismissed.

On our way out of the family law offices, Chip made a joke advising me not to "go out and live it up right away," and the tears that I'd been barely holding back began spilling over. As soon as we were out of range of the family law area, the dam burst. The weight of our tragedy and the finality of filing divorce papers were beyond what my body could hold inside even a moment longer. It felt like my whole being was tearing apart. "I'm so sorry we've come to this," I managed through my sobs. "I'm so sorry." We embraced, and I gave Chip a card that I'd made for him, thanking him for the positive contributions he'd made to my life, and I asked him not to read it until he had some privacy.

We embraced, descended the stairs, and left the courthouse. After making small talk about where each of us was parked, we parted. It was the strangest thing. We'd been married for seventeen years, and suddenly we were going opposite directions while the world kept doing business as usual. I felt like all the world should stop and pay homage to the tragedy.

The shock and disbelief soon succumbed to a pain that was deeper and sharper than any pain I'd ever experienced before. I'd never felt such intense despair and overwhelming emotion, and I'd grieved many losses in my life. The pain of this relationship ending was greater than all of them combined. I cried so hard as I drove back home from the courthouse that I thought I might hyperventilate.

When I got home, I sat on my bed and cried some more. I wished I had taken the day off, but I hadn't, so I mechanically got ready for work. I got through the day somehow, probably due to the support of my colleagues during our staff meeting, through which I cried incessantly, and to our office administrator who could tell that something was wrong when I arrived at the office. When I told her, she wrapped me in a warm hug. I also remember being particularly connected to the pain of my clients that day, but dreaded having to go home and be alone with my reality afterwards.

A Final Heart-to-Heart

Shortly after I got home from work that evening, Chip called. I'll never forget the anguish in his voice. He said that he'd started to read my thank-you note, but he didn't think he could finish it. He wondered if we'd done the right thing, and I gently assured him that, from my perspective, the legal documents only reflected what had been true in the marriage for quite some time—or all along. He seemed to understand that, and between sobs, he offered words of deep regret about what he had and hadn't done in the relationship. He spoke words of understanding and apology that I'd longed to hear for seventeen years, and our tears mingled over the phone wires. I was especially pained by the torment Chip expressed as he spoke; my heart broke for him in his grief. I'd been processing my own regret and grief for the previous couple of years, but Chip was connecting with his all at once.

I didn't know if Chip's sorrow was about the pain his neglect had caused me, or if it was about his own loss of the familiarity of the relationship, or both, but it didn't seem to matter in the moment. Never had I wanted to rescue him more than I did that night, but I knew that if I did, I'd only be hurting him more. So I validated his pain and wept with him. It was all I could do.

I also expressed to him some sentiments that I'd never expressed so clearly before. I told him that I knew that he longed to be in an intimate relationship more than anything else, and that he'd been wounded in such a way that he was incapable of achieving such a relationship, at least at this time. He acknowledged that this was true. I assured him that I didn't hold him responsible for his lack of capacity, and that I harbored no resentment or hard feelings toward him, but I also acknowledged that I absolutely *despised* his parents for what they had done to him. Bitter sobbing broke up my speech, but it was the honest truth. Chip didn't express his usual defensiveness with regard to his parents, and he thanked me for having compassion for his story in a way that he hadn't had compassion for mine.

I told him how sorry I was that I'd been grieving this loss for the past two years and that he was just now beginning. He said that he regretted not joining me in the healing process.

I explained that there had been a window of time when my heart had been completely free to be captured, to be pursued, to be courted, to be chosen, and when he didn't take the opportunity to woo me, I had despaired of hope. He asked when it was that that window of time had occurred, and I explained that when I'd finally relinquished all attachment to my brother, I was free of my history and free to be in relationship with Chip exclusively. This sent Chip into another bout of tears, and he expressed sorrow for not having been aware of this opportunity.

Chip also expressed a desire to continue with counseling, although he agreed that he might have been talking out of raw emotion. I told him that it's never too late to pursue personal healing, and I encouraged him to do so.

I also explained to him that having unfinished business with my dad and with my sister before they died taught me how important it is to be purposeful about saying goodbye well. I'd learned that to grieve well, you have to be intentional about it, acknowledge the finality of the relationship as it was, honor the good and the bad, and you have to let it hurt. I had done this over the past couple of years with our relationship, and I told him that I hoped he'd be able to do the same thing. He said that he wished he already had, agreed that all of that was still ahead of him, and acknowledged that remembering our story hurt too much. He didn't think he could bear it.

It was a brutal conversation. I was brokenhearted for Chip, and the whole forty-five-minute conversation was unbearably painful. Much of the time we just wept together, and the deepest pain I felt was for Chip. He had few people to talk to, and although it was a situation of his own making, I realized that his unhealed wounds had prevented him from reaching out to people. His original wounds had occurred through no fault of his own, and never had I resented his parents more than I did that night. I know that their intention hadn't been to hurt their little boy, but because they hadn't been purposeful about their own need for healing, they'd severely harmed him (and they continued to do so by refusing to do any healing work in the present). Their lack of intent to harm made no difference in that moment to Chip who was deeply wounded and disadvantaged. Now he was desperate and despairing, on top of it all.

We ended the conversation saying, "I love you" (Chip initiating for the first time in years), and it was the first time I'd really meant it in a very long time. It wasn't a romantic love, but the love of friends who care for the well-being of each other. I loved Chip as a human being and I longed for his healing, and I knew that I had to let him go into the care of God.

After that conversation, I was afraid that Chip would continue to seek me out to comfort him, without him considering how hard it was for me to be constantly confronted with his lack of fundamental change. I hated that I might have to ask him what he thought it was like for me to desire his healing deeply but know that I was powerless to bring it about, and that he may have been, too. I knew that I might have to tell him that if he really cared about me, he'd try to understand that nothing would make me happier than if he were to make healing his number one priority, for his own sake. It had been too much pressure for me to be called on to be his savior, as I'd allowed myself to be, and that it hadn't been fair to either one of us. I would love to have rescued him, and there was still something in me that really wanted to comfort and nurture him like a wife would comfort her wounded husband, but that was no longer my job.

I had longed for Chip to be absolutely trusting and vulnerable with me as the norm in our relationship—not as an exception to the rule. Because this hadn't happened and because I no longer had reason to believe that Chip had the introspective capacity to know himself and to be known by me, it was best that we not be together. Other than more pain, I couldn't think of what I could receive from maintaining contact with Chip.

My fears proved to be unfounded; Chip didn't call on me to comfort him. We didn't have much contact after that, but the contact that we did have was friendly. I attribute this to the commitment to end well, even though that had meant front-loading the pain by being present to the ache of every moment when ending the relationship. I'd witnessed many relationships that had ended badly because of an unfortunate commitment to avoid pain at all costs. In addition, I'd learned my own hard lessons from saying goodbye poorly, and I am glad that I was intentional to end well with Chip.

Since Then—My Perspective

I'm pleased to say that Chip's fears about being unable to support himself have proven to be unfounded. Since our divorce, Chip is doing better than ever financially, though his journey to this place came by way of pain—necessary pain from which, in my co-dependency, I would've tried to shelter him, had we remained together. This pain helped him identify and get into the kind of employment that fits him well. I'm pleased to say that I've done the same.

Although dissolving our marriage was the best choice for Chip and me, I would be lying to say that the pain stopped there. Prior to filing for dissolution, the journey of honest evaluation had often taken me into the presence of God with sorrowful apologies for my broken promises to love and honor Chip. After the divorce, my thinking became more and more clear about our relationship, and I found myself apologizing to

God again—this time for joining myself to a person who didn't represent God's best for me, and then for staying too long in a relationship that had caused lasting damage to both of us. I came to realize that my fear of facing the truth had only caused more hurt to two precious people. I'm thankful, however, that I found the courage, late as it was, to deal directly with the problems in our marriage.

So as not to repeat the same mistakes that I'd made in relationship with Chip, I committed to not dating for at least two years after my divorce was final, a suggestion Smoke makes in *Growing Through Divorce*.[7] This choice felt like a gift to myself and to any future partner, as it gave me a chance to grieve well, continue soul-searching, and make it more likely that I would take a minimal number of wounds into any future relationship.

This turned out to be a wise choice, as I found myself within six months of the divorce at a class reunion, regressing emotionally to the time before I met and married Chip. I noticed that I was interacting with an old boyfriend in the same ways I had when I was eighteen years old. Although I had no actual interest in this man, I found myself seeking his attention in an effort to determine my attractiveness. This required me to identify old trauma bond patterns, which were embarrassing and painful to recognize. In the end, I realized that I had to learn a whole new way of being with men, and that it wouldn't be easy.

Since Then—Chip's Perspective

As part of my growing process, it was important for me to respect Chip by personally telling him about this book. I didn't want him to hear of it from one of our mutual friends or in any other jarring way. So when the deadline approached to send in the final files, I phoned him. Our conversation was friendly, and Chip was congratulatory. We talked for about an hour, and as we caught up on our lives since the divorce, I could hardly believe I was talking to the same man I'd been married to for seventeen years.

I experienced Chip as substantial, not hollow; humble, not defensive; encouraging, not critical. I was so impressed by his open demeanor that I asked if he'd be interested in reading the manuscript and offering

---

7. Smoke, *Growing Through Divorce*, 16, 27.

his perspective on our marriage, its failure, and life after divorce. He said that he would like that opportunity.[8]

That conversation began a series of exchanges that helped us make sense together of what had happened between us. Chip first wanted to apologize for not knowing how to romance a woman and for the impact his ignorance had had on our relationship. From his perspective, this shortcoming was his greatest failure in our relationship, and he expressed sincere regret for not having met my needs for emotional intimacy.

He also wanted me to understand that his sexual compulsivity may have stemmed from our poor sex life. He's learned from relationships since our divorce that sex can be very different than it was with us. Chip also wanted to make it clear to me that he'd married me because I was fun, witty, and intelligent, not merely because I presented him with an easy opportunity to satisfy a compulsive sex drive.

Chip affirmed that couples who undertake a healing process are wisest to do it simultaneously. When one individual in a couple engages in healing and the other trails behind, the relational gap between them continues to widen, and it may become too great to span by the time the trailing partner embarks on a healing journey. Chip also expressed that it isn't enough to hope your partner will heal on his or her own. Both partners must engage in individual healing of old wounds and in healing the wounds of the relationship together.

Although we agreed to disagree on a few details regarding interpretation and perspective of each other, we did agree on the way I've presented the dynamics of our relationship in this book. We also agreed that a commitment to an honest appraisal of a faltering relationship and the resolve to do whatever action is healthiest, no matter how much it hurts in the short run, is the wisest choice in the long run, even if that commitment leads to dissolution of the covenant.

Chip described his post-divorce regression to his pre-marriage mind-set, which took him into several painful relationships. Fortunately, he has been able to learn from these relationships a new way of relating with women—a way of deeper awareness and engagement. Although these learning experiences have hurt, each one has taught him some-

---

8. I'm grateful for Chip's willingness to read the manuscript and offer his perspective. Without it, the story would have been incomplete, so I consider Chip's contribution a gift to my readers. I also consider it a gift to me, an unexpected fulfillment of my desire for reconciliation expressed in the dedication of this book.

thing about himself and about relationships that he may not have been able to learn in any other way.

In the end, we concluded that our relationship was a perfect storm for both of us. We each had entered the relationship with significant unresolved wounds, a lack of self-awareness about them, and a profound ignorance about how to work through them together so as to cultivate intimacy. Ours was a toxic relational cocktail, and we agreed that dissolving our union was the kindest option for both of us. Our divorce was necessary for us to get enough distance from our trauma bond to begin learning the art of loving well.[9]

SNEAK PREVIEW OF THE NEXT CHAPTER

No other single factor makes the decision to continue or to cancel a marriage more difficult than how either choice will impact the children. Trying to make clear choices when a parent's greatest fear is disappointing or harming the kids requires tremendous focus. The next chapter can help bring this difficult decision into perspective.

---

9. Like it had with Chip, the time came when I needed to inform Ryan (remember him from chapters 3 and 6?) that I'd written this book. As he had six years before when I'd confronted him about how he'd harmed me, Ryan responded with validation, kindness, compassion, sorrow, and without defensiveness. We had a powerful conversation in which we grieved together over the incident and the context in which it had happened, leaving Ryan and me fully reconciled. I'm amazed and joyful that Ryan and I engaged in separate healing processes, beginning in our twenties, that prepared us to achieve reconciliation in our forties. I include this note to provide hope that repair is possible when both parties are willing to be brutally honest, open, and vulnerable with themselves and each other. Ryan expressed joy, too, that reconciliation is possible when there's authenticity on both sides.

10

Grounds for Parenting: What about the Kids?

ONCE A PARENT, ALWAYS a parent. A parent's role changes with each developmental stage of the children, but parents always have the responsibility to model mature decision-making.

When I'm working with parents, I try to remember that parents typically want to do right by their kids, even though they don't always know how to do it. There are a lot of good parenting resources (see Appendix F), but applying the principles they provide to one's particular children often proves difficult.

I view parenting as the most sacred ground of a parent's soul. No other job is more challenging, and in no other area do parents usually feel more vulnerable or more doubtful of their adequacy.

This doubt is multiplied a thousand-fold when parents are faced with having to make responsible choices about continuing or dissolving their marriage. Because of the stress of trying to make good choices in a covenant crisis, parents often forget that they're still parents—they're still responsible for helping their children understand and navigate the murky and tumultuous waters that the parents have stirred.

My clients who experienced divorce as children usually report that they needed their parents to help them process their parents' split—before, during, and long after the event—more than they needed their parents to stay together. When I'm invited to do so, it's my privilege as a therapist to help parents help their children through the decision, the event, and the aftermath of divorce. It's possible, though difficult, for parents to do this well.

A THERAPEUTIC REFLECTION

Most parents want the best for their children. However, all parents make mistakes, despite their best efforts not to, and despite their vows to never hurt their children in the ways that their parents hurt them. Most of my clients have a history of being poorly parented, which leaves scars. These scars then manifest in poor styles of relating with others, including with their own children. People who've neither witnessed nor experienced what loving well looks like can hardly envision it, and if they can't envision it, they can't practice it. However, when they begin to connect with the pain of their own childhood wounds that resulted from unmet needs, they begin to understand and feel the pain of their children, and they can then begin to envision what their children need from them.

Many of my clients report that their parents only stayed together because of the children. One client told me, "My parents said that they stayed together because of me, and I thought, 'So it was because of me that you endured such contempt for each other.' The responsibility felt overwhelming. I didn't want it."

Gottman's research found that,

> it is *not* wise to stay in a bad marriage for the sake of your children. It is clearly harmful to raise kids in a home that is subsumed by hostility between the parents. A peaceful divorce is better than a warlike marriage. Unfortunately, divorces are rarely peaceful. The mutual hostility between parents usually continues after the breakup. For that reason, children of divorce often fare just as poorly as those caught in the crossfire of a miserable marriage.[1]

For the sake of the children, Constance Ahrons, in *The Good Divorce*,[2] suggests ways to keep the family together when the marriage comes apart. Her research identified five kinds of parenting styles among divorced families: perfect pals, cooperative colleagues, angry associates, fiery foes, and dissolved duos. Needless to say, the first two parenting styles carry the most promise of helping children weather the storm of their parents' breakup.

Because there are many good resources for helping parents help their children through this most difficult of transitions, I won't reinvent the wheel here (see Appendix F for an annotated list of resources). Suffice it to say that children aren't always better served when their parents stay

---

1. Gottman, *Seven Principles*, 6.
2. Ahrons, *The Good Divorce*, 6–7.

together, and that parents are responsible for keeping their children out of their own adult messes.

Andrea

Andrea came to see me *after* she had made the decision to divorce. I was immediately impressed with her inner strength and calm resolve. She felt like she had made the best decision possible, the lesser of two evils, because she couldn't continue to expose the children to the unfaithfulness of her husband, Jack.

Andrea's concern was not for herself—she knew that, while it would be hard, she'd be okay. Andrea's concern was for her children, ages ten and thirteen. What should she tell them? How could she help them express their feelings without disrespecting their father? How much of the truth of the situation did they need to know? How could she make sure that they knew that both she and Jack loved them, and that the divorce was in no way their fault? How could they go through a divorce process with minimal damage to the children?

As we worked together, it became clear to me that Andrea had a good sense of her need to parent her children carefully through this difficult time. Andrea found space for herself to process her feelings so that she could be available to help her kids process through theirs. She followed through on checking out resources for children whose parents divorce. She initiated conversations with her children about their feelings, and brought her kids to counseling to help them sort through feelings they didn't feel like they could share with their mom. Divorce is never easy on a child, but parents can make it easier if they have cultivated (or can cultivate) an environment of openness and non-manipulative concern.

Gabby

Gabby's situation was very different from Andrea's. (Perhaps you remember Gabby from chapter 4.) Her two teenage boys, Alex and Preston, were sent reeling by their parents' announcement to divorce. Gabby and Neil had presented a clean image to the world concerning their relationship, and because they fought so seemingly respectfully, it was hard to see the trouble boiling just below the surface.

During the process of honestly appraising her relationship with Neil, Gabby tried not to stuff her feelings as much as possible. There were times when she just didn't want to feel, but the heart that had been awakening in her for several years prior to the divorce wouldn't allow her to stay numb for long.

Having been reared in a home in which analytical thinking was the most righteous way of knowing anything, Alex and Preston blamed the divorce on their mom. Neil, who didn't understand Gabby's longing for emotional connection either, had no way of describing that the failure of their relationship was as much his responsibility as hers. In fact, he really couldn't understand what his contribution had been at all.

Gabby was torn between self-preservation and staying in her marriage for the boys' sake. In the end, she found that she just couldn't live in a dead environment and remain alive herself. She could only hope that someday the boys would come to value the feminine along with the masculine.

I wish I could say that Gabby's story ended with Neil coming to a heart-felt understanding of Gabby's needs as a woman, and that he was then able to communicate this to their boys. Unfortunately, Gabby may have to live with the knowledge that her abdication of the femininity of her spirit in favor of the masculine in her home for twenty years may cost the boys much more than she ever imagined.

Gabby came to realize that her relationship with Neil gave her boys a one-dimensional view of God. Certainly, God wants us to *think* about our faith; he wants us to appreciate masculine strength. But he also wants us to *feel* his presence, to embrace feminine strength, as well. Gabby's boys only saw half of God's character, and they've suffered for it. It's quite possible that, without coming to understand the feminine character of God, they'll marry women who acquiesce to the masculine as a spiritual duty, and who later find that they cannot live with the deadness of their existence. Only time will tell what impact Gabby and Neil's relationship will have on their boys.

When children are involved, the choice to remain married or to divorce is always more difficult than when the decision is between only two individuals. For children to be best served, however, parents who choose to remain married should make the healing of their marriage first priority. Without such a commitment, the children will be impacted by the detachment that they witness between their parents. Of course, there are always exceptions to every rule, and this short section isn't intended to be your only source of help in making such a consequential choice. It's difficult to have to choose between two disagreeable options, when both will have negative impact. Let me encourage you to consider both the short- and long-term impact of either choice on your children. An honest appraisal of their needs is as important as an honest appraisal of yours.

A PERSONAL REFLECTION

I find it interesting that parents who tell me that they feel that they should stay together for the children's sake rarely know what their children really want. My mom decided that it was best to find out how her three children felt about the possibility of divorce, so she sat us down one day and asked us. Twelve-year-old Davie said that he wanted Mom and Dad to stay together; ten-year-old Suzie, and I (at eight years old) wanted them to split up. What is a parent to do when the kids have conflicting answers to such questions?

Although it's important to know your children's feelings, I don't recommend that parents ask their kids whether or not they want their parents to divorce. Children in chaotic families have enough work just in trying to survive, let alone having to help make the adult choice about their parents' relationship. Certainly, it's valid to ask the kids how they feel about the disarray of the family system, but if a culture hasn't already been created in which feelings can be discussed openly, it's unlikely that a parent will get an honest answer from the children anyway. Such a question, if asked, should be asked for the *child's* benefit, not for the parent's.

Asking a child to help make adult decisions that are hard enough for adults forces the child to become an adult before he or she is ready. Instead, parents need to honestly evaluate the relationship for themselves, taking the children's needs into consideration, and then choose what seems best for everyone involved, staying engaged with the aftermath of such a choice on the children. This is the job of a parent, because it takes a depth of maturity that a child doesn't have. It's hard enough for adults to make this decision; it's cruel to ask a child to do so.

Parents who choose to divorce need to remember that grieving is a process for children just like it is for adults. It takes time, sometimes many years, for children to process their feelings about their parents' failed relationship, and just like adults, they need resources, such as trained professionals. See Appendix F for written resources for helping kids process divorce.

When my mother asked us whether she and my father should divorce, she got a mixed response, and then decided to stay with my dad.

I don't remember if Mom sat us down to share with us her decision, but I'm sure I was disappointed by her choice. I desperately wanted Mom and Dad to divorce—I just wanted the fighting to stop.

Dad Manhandles Mom

It seemed like Dad and Mom fought about anything and everything—from finances to parenting, from taking care of my diabetic sister to Mom's decision to go to work to help pay for Suzie's medical bills, from traffic laws to my brother's drug use, from school issues to theology. Some issues seemed important; others seemed trivial.

Several scenes stand out in my mind as representations of the constant contemptuous dynamic between my parents. The most memorable one for me occurred when I was about six years old. It was after dinner on a summer evening, and Davie and I were outside playing in the yard. I heard a commotion in the house, and my stomach churned with dread. Was someone I loved getting hurt?

Feeling powerless to do anything tangible about it, I put my energies to willing, in my mind, that the fighting would stop. Instead, it escalated, and my heart rate followed. My father kicked open the screen door, carrying my mother like a life-sized rag doll. I was panic-stricken.

What I'd always feared, that my father would physically harm my mother or one of us kids, was occurring right before my eyes. "And don't come back," he ordered, as he finished his tirade. There was no mistaking his insistence.

Obediently, Mom descended the porch steps, issuing firm orders to us kids. "Get in the car. Right now." Though I was torn about what to do, I was terrified to stay with my angry father, so I did as I was told. As we were loading up, Dad came out of the house and told my sister that she had to stay and do the dishes. Mom wouldn't leave one of us behind, so we all stayed.

I don't know what happened next. I only know that no one asked me what that experience was like for me. I desperately needed to be held and reassured that I was going to be okay, but I was left to deal with my terror alone. It was at that moment that I decided that I would have to survive on my own. I steeled myself and resolved not to cause the family more stress; I became compliant and invisible in the chaos. I also became protective of my mother, who seemed fragile and lost. And most of all, I became determined that one day I would figure it all out and that I would find peace and quiet. It was going to be a fight to survive my environment, I knew, but it was clear to me that no one was going to protect me but myself. I was on my own. If I were going to figure out how to do life, I'd have to find out for myself.

Who's to Blame?

Another fighting experience that I vividly remember occurred one evening when I was about twelve years old. I remember the bickering during that meal being especially cruel, and my normally healthy appetite had turned to nausea. I pushed the food around on my plate, trying to make it seem like I was busy with it. I didn't want anyone to notice that tears were threatening to spill onto my plate. As the fighting continued, I longed to cover my ears or to scream at my parents to "stop being mean to each other," or to run from the table, but I felt immobilized and mute.

I don't know how long I sat there with the tension building inside me, but it finally reached a climax. "I'm sorry, but I just can't take this anymore," I blurted, and I ran from the table. Dad came after me, caught me in the kitchen, and prevented me from leaving the house by folding me in his arms. I remember feeling like Dad's hug was tainted by a manipulative motive—I sensed that he wanted to be the "good guy," trying to one-up my mother by pursuing me. Dad rarely touched any of us, so his "crisis hug" had nowhere to land in my heart. I don't know how that situation ended, but nothing changed between my parents.

Sometime in my early teen years, my father started a used car business in another city with one of his brothers, and he was out of town for weeks at a time. It was a relief to have peace and quiet in the house. I dreaded Dad's return, which often occurred in time to attend church on Sundays. As the time would approach for Dad to come home, the tension would mount, and internally I would shift gears from calm to chaotic.

With all of my father's cruelty, it was still easier to blame my mother for the problems in the relationship. If only she would do whatever Dad wanted her to do, Dad would be drawn to her meek and quiet spirit, and he'd eventually be won over by her submissiveness. This is what I'd been taught from 1 Peter 3:1–6, and the reality of 1 Peter 3:7, which instructs men to honor and delight in their wives as equals, was inconceivable. Besides, no one ever mentioned that part. My fear of my father was greater than my fear of my mother, so she became most responsible in my mind for the problems between them.

I realize now that both my parents contributed to the harmful family dynamic—Dad was abusive and controlling and Mom did nothing meaningful to protect us from him, enlisting her children to help her manage her emotions. The teaching of our church culture also made a significant contribution. As I look back on our family, it would've been an incredible lesson to me if my mother had found the strength to defy her own upbringing, the church culture, and her husband's abuse in favor of truth and protection of innocent children. Had she done this with firm gentleness, taking care to teach us kids the importance of equitable and humane treatment, I might've learned that females deserve the same respect as males, and it may have saved me from making poor relationship choices later on. Instead, what I learned was that it was preferable to be in relationship with an abusive man than to not be in relationship at all.

I realize that my mother was up against almost insurmountable obstacles financially, emotionally, spiritually, culturally. But her inability to face the truth and to act on that awareness placed me and my siblings against incredible odds. Incidentally, all three of us *became* harmful marriage partners, who also *chose* harmful marriage partners. While we have to take responsibility for our own poor choices, we also need to recognize how we learned to make them. To this day, I believe that, if my parents had divorced, and if such an event had been accompanied by solid teaching over time about justice and mercy and covenant, my siblings and I would've been better served. The damage of abuse and neglect had already been done, but a divorce may have prevented the occurrence of more.

A THEOLOGICAL REFLECTION

As mentioned in chapter 5, the covenant of marriage provides the foundation for bearing and rearing children. Parents share the incredible privilege and responsibility of presenting the divine image, both masculine and feminine, to their children, which they do by partnering in love and respect.

Everything said about relationship in chapters 1, 4 and 5 regarding how we're to be in relationship with one another applies here. Parents have an obligation to treat one another as image-bearers—they owe it to their children as much as they owe it to one another. Such an environment creates the security that children need to mature into loving human beings who know their worth and the worth of others as divine image-bearers. If children have seen such care modeled in their homes, they'll likely take this care to their adult relationships, and they'll perpetuate the cycle of consideration.

On the other hand, children who witness a pattern of contempt between their parents fail to learn what it means to bear the mark of the creator. If they don't see their parents treasuring one another, they won't witness the meaning and purpose of human relationships: to represent God in and to the world. As Allender and Longman say, "Marriage is the human relationship that most reveals the being, character and purpose of God. This key human relationship is designed to make known who God is and how he relates to his world."[3]

Parents must model values, practices, and attitudes to their children, teaching them, directly and indirectly, about the care of God in every activity throughout the day (Deut 6:4–8), so that they have the best opportunity to mature into responsible and considerate individuals. The parental unit is also the first place in which children experience the concept and practice of discipline (Prov 13:24), although this should be done without "exasperating" them (Eph 6:4). The scriptures teach parents not to leave their children without instruction, guidance, and discipline, because an undisciplined child tends to become an unruly adult (Prov 4; 1 Sam 3:11–18).

Such effective parenting is most likely to occur between two individuals who love and respect one another first, and then all of humanity. Parents who've broken from their ways of being that resulted from a wounded past and who are secure in themselves are the most likely to provide a helpful context for children to learn about how to be in all kinds of relationships. On the other hand, parents who are insecure and who are still unconsciously living out unresolved wounds inadvertently set their children up for failure in relationships later in life.

All of this is to say that, if a couple has grounds for marriage, as described in previous chapters, they likely have grounds for parenting. Without this foundation, however, parents tend to leave their children at a loss regarding how to love and how to choose relationships.

My highest recommendations on parenting include *How Children Raise Parents*, by Dan Allender, which offers an overall perspective on this most difficult and rewarding of ministries, and *Growing Up Again*,

---

3. Allender and Longman, *Intimate Mystery*, 19.

by Jeanne Illsley-Clark and Connie Dawson, which offers practical suggestions on the craft of the job.

SNEAK PREVIEW OF THE EPILOGUE

When I facilitate therapy groups with this material, one of the most common comments I hear is along the lines of "Why wasn't I taught this material a long time ago? It would've saved me and my loved ones so much unnecessary pain." I relate to that anguish. As I sit with clients in distress, I'm deeply saddened that this information isn't readily available in the evangelical church, when it could prevent generations of pain and suffering. So, in the Epilogue, I express the cry of my soul for the community of faith. May we face the truth with courage and grieve our pain so that our softened hearts motivate us to love one another well.

Epilogue

Head and Heart: Reunited, and It Feels So Good

In the Introduction, I referred to the fire in my belly that forged this book. From what I can gather, the apostle Paul was motivated by a fire in his belly, too. He longed to see believers loving each other well, and his letters reflected this passion.

The letters from Paul to first century believers were written to specific individuals or to specific groups of people for a specific reason. Twenty centuries later, I want to address believers from a passionate place in me, as well, a longing to see believers loving each other well. I'm no apostle, but this letter expresses the cry of my soul to the church.

A THEOLOGICAL REFLECTION

Dear brothers and sisters in Messiah,

I write this letter to all of you who follow Jesus, including Jews and Gentiles in all denominations of the body of the Messiah, who love God with all your soul, heart, mind, and strength.

I have some hard things to say about believers, and I'm concerned that my tone may be misunderstood, simply because the printed page doesn't allow you to experience my sorrow as I write. So I want you to know that I write these words out of grief. I'm pleading with the body of Messiah to return to the covenant that is written on our hearts. I yearn for us to listen to our hearts, to hear with our spirits, and to love from our souls.

I'm not proud of the way we often treat one another. I'm not proud of how we try to protect truth but neglect to protect the hearts of people whom God has imprinted with his insignia. I'm not proud when we act like the Pharisees, majoring on minor issues and minoring on major ones. How is it that we fail to model our relationship with God through our relationship with other people? How is it that we fail to adequately address abuse and neglect and idolatry, which are immoral, but we condemn divorce, which, depending on the circumstances, may not be? If what we say we believe is true—that God thinks people are worth dying for—why do we treat each other the way we do? If what we say we believe is true, we should have exemplary relationships. Why don't we?

Focusing on the small issues while ignoring the larger ones has created despicable divisions between us. Jesus prayed that the world would know that we're believers by our love (John 13:34). He didn't forbid denominations, but he prayed that we'd be united (John 17). I, for one, am glad that there are a variety of different places to worship, with styles of worship that appeal to the various ways that God has designed us. I'm not interested in cookie-cutter churches and synagogues. But, why do we insist that our way is the *right* way to worship or to behave, while all of us claim to be reading the same scriptures?

I understand that our differing approaches to these scriptures accounts for many of our divisions. But I don't understand why those differences create divisions between us. Why is doctrine more important than relationship? Can we stop the debate and enter dialogue? Can we be curious instead of critical? Can we believe strongly enough in God's goodness and understanding of our human frailties and limitations that we don't have to insist that we're "right," and everyone else is "wrong?" Why do we pat ourselves on the back by comparing ourselves to one another in a way that leaves us feeling more enlightened than some other brother or sister or group? Do we have to insist that just about everything is a moral issue and that those who don't believe or practice exactly as we do are somehow morally deficient? Can we be humble enough to throw ourselves upon God's goodness and mercy, trusting him to accommodate our lack of knowing all the answers?

In claiming to know truth, we've taught people what to think, rather than offering them tools to help them think for themselves. Then when they don't think exactly as we've tried to make them, we employ all kinds of manipulative tactics to force them back in line: fear, guilt, shame, threats, promises, rewards. We treat our faith like a product to sell, and fellow image-bearers as objects to persuade. And we do all of this in the name of God, feeling self-righteous about it. I'm afraid that we've become like the false prophets so often condemned in the Old Testament. Malachi says, "It is the job of priests [religious leaders] to teach the truth. People

Head and Heart: Reunited, and It Feels So Good 223

are supposed to look up to them for guidance. The priest is the messenger of God-of-the-Angel-Armies. But you priests have abandoned the way of priests. Your teaching has messed up many lives" (2:7–8).

My grief over the confusion we've caused sometimes feels like more than I can bear. I long to prevent people from experiencing unnecessary pain, but I can't. Even if I had all the answers, which I don't, I'm too small to save the world. Romans 14 and 1 Corinthians 8 suggest that there's no such thing as having all the answers because there are non-moral issues in which one answer will be right for one person and the opposite answer may be right for another. Not every issue is a moral one, and some things have to be left up to individual consciences, which none of us has the right to dictate for anyone else. I ache for us to step aside sometimes and let God do his work. Perhaps we don't trust people to allow him to work with them, or we don't trust God to make people behave like we want them to, but we don't have the right to insist that either people or God conforms to our wishes.

I yearn for us to care as much about people as Jesus did, which may mean we err on the side of relationship over rules. I know that making such a statement will incriminate me to some and endear me to others. I'm sad about that fact because I don't think it has to be so. If we could hold tightly to our favorite doctrines without looking down our noses at others who hold tightly to their favorite doctrines, especially when we differ, our faith community would be alive and well. If we only loved one another as Jesus loved us . . .

We could even love people with breaking (or broken) covenants. God knows how desperately they need our care. If only we'd offer them both truth and solace. I think we can, and there are resources that can help us do so. Three texts have been particularly significant in helping me understand the scriptures regarding divorce, all of which I found *after* I'd already divorced my husband. What anguish I would've been spared if I'd found these texts earlier. For the primarily analytical thinker, I recommend David Instone-Brewer's *Divorce and Remarriage in the Bible*. For the thinker-first-feeler-second, I recommend David Instone-Brewer's *Divorce and Remarriage in the Church*. And for the feeler-first-thinker-second, I recommend Les Carter's *Grace and Divorce*. *To Have and To Hold*, by David Atkinson, is also a helpful text, although its age is evident in Atkinson's style of writing.

Atkinson's chapter on what we can do as a body of believers when we're in relationship with those who are in marriage crisis reminds us that "preparation for marriage begins at birth,"[1] and then continues in the family and in the ministry of the church to families—a community of people fostering the growth of the kind of character that pursues successful covenant-love. The body of Messiah should provide adequate marriage preparation, including counseling and other mentoring relationships that are healing and enduring.

Broken covenants are bound to occur, particularly with the unique pressures of contemporary society, so we need to learn to deal with these in a godly way. To this end, the church needs to establish itself as a ministry of reconciliation for those with damaged relationships. While outside counseling is often necessary for couples in crisis, providing a safe environment for people to seek help before their relationships are unsalvageable could provide healing for marital hurts.

Should all these methods fail, as they inevitably will in many cases, we need to accept the reality (and the necessity) of divorce, and offer practical and emotional help to those who are hurting. In *Grace and Divorce*, Carter says,

> The Law is most necessary because it gives humans a needed framework for living. But there is one thing that supersedes the Law: love. My approach to people in circumstances of divorce is that I try to be true to the Law so long as I am also true to the loving character of Christ. If following the letter of the Law would result in a judgmental spirit or suspension of common sense, I am willing to examine the path of grace.[2]

Following a divorce, there should be ministries, often parachurch ministries, to help the individuals heal from the hurts of the marriage and from the wounds that they initially brought into the marriage covenant. Without carefully tending to these wounds, people will likely find themselves in similar re-marriages. "It is by no means a straightforward assumption that a second marriage will necessarily be any more successful than the first, unless such personal needs have been explored and some personal help received."[3]

---

1. Atkinson, *To Have and to Hold*, 185.
2. Carter, *Grace and Divorce*, 43–44.
3. Atkinson, *To Have and To Hold*, 172.

We'd be loving well if we created safe communities of believers where people who were ashamed of their choices and failures could come and find healing in relationship. We get wounded in unsafe relationships, and we must be healed in safe relationships. I long for the body of the Messiah to be a safe, healing community for fallen and broken-hearted people.

A THERAPEUTIC REFLECTION

As a counselor who often works with people in the church, I frequently weep for the pain that we've caused people in our very own family of faith, not to mention the pain we've caused that has driven people away from ever wanting a relationship with God. I can't blame them. We claim to hold the truth, but we destroy people with our versions of it.

I get to see my clients for about one hour each week. Most of their time is spent outside of my office where they have to think, make choices, and wrestle with God on their own. I've come to depend on the spiritual work that people do outside of my office, not just in it. They often encounter object lessons that I could never concoct in a session. I'm amazed and awed by these spiritual awakenings, and I'm grateful to be a tiny part of it.

When I first entered counseling school, I didn't want to work with believers. I never imagined that I'd be working with people whose belief systems have been distorted by leaders in the faith. But my own history, along with my own spiritual journey, has prepared me to work with this very population. I know these people, I know the partial-truths they've been fed, I know their wounds, and I know an effective healing process. It's my highest privilege to introduce people, through my therapeutic relationship with them, to Abba, a loving father; to Yeshua HaMachiach, a lover of children (of all ages); and to the Ruach HaChodesh, the Holy Spirit, and then to help them develop an intimate relationship with a God who brings them into deeper and deeper awareness of themselves and love for others.

I love to introduce thirsty people to a variety of ways of knowing God. My special favorite is through prayer, simply sharing life with him, experience by experience, thought by thought, feeling by feeling. His name, Immanuel, reminds us that God is present with us, that he's very near to us (Deut 4:7). He's not distant from us, and I've discovered that it's possible to live life as a prayer. It's sweet.

During most of history, God's people didn't have access to the Bible like we do today, so they got to know him in other ways. We get to know God the same way we get to know other people: we have to experience him. We have to talk to him; listen to him with our hearts, our spirits; find out about others' experience of him, both in the Word and in the world. And we have to be able to feel his presence, which requires that we be able to feel in the first place. Our feelings are incredible sources of wisdom, if we'll listen to them, and if we're determined to understand their meanings.

We come to know our feelings as we come to listen to our bodies. For example, when my chest is heavy, I'm likely feeling sorrow; when it's tight, I am likely feeling fear or dread. I can then express these emotions to God and allow him to comfort me. When my stomach is churning, I'm likely feeling anxious, and I can invite God into my anxiety, seeking his solace, his peace, and his wisdom. When I'm tempted to travel at unsafe speeds, I am likely feeling shame. I can then ask God to look into my eyes and tell me that I'm lovely, even in my imperfections. Different people feel their emotions in their bodies in different ways, but God gave us our emotions, and we can connect with him through the feelings that our bodies store if we're willing to let ourselves, and him, into them.

Prophets often spoke out of their emotions—grief, sadness, sorrow, fear, despair, joy, relief, and longing. I don't know when we as a body of believers decided that we were supposed to separate our feelings from our faith, but many of us have. I realize that some have done just the opposite, teaching that we don't need to think in order to know what is true, that we only need to feel our emotions to know God. Either extreme limits God, and I ache for us to seek both an intelligent and a heartfelt intimacy with him.

A PERSONAL REFLECTION

It was through my feelings that I first came to know God intimately. Traumatic childhood experiences had disconnected me from my feelings, and I'd become tough and emotionally distant from myself and from others. But when I discovered—through some believers to whom I'll be indebted forever—that God is a feeling being, and that his main representative, Jesus, willingly experienced the emotional and physical pain of the human condition so that people might know him, I couldn't resist a God like that.

Prior to starting on my own spiritual journey, however, my experience of believers drove me away from the one in whom they claimed to believe. If God was anything like they were, I didn't want to be in relationship with him. It wasn't until I encountered believers who were real—believers who didn't avoid pain, who didn't claim that life was easy to figure out, who encouraged me to seek answers for myself—that I was able to entertain the idea that God might exist, and that he might allow me to be honest about my questions and about my failures and my shame. They didn't dress my wounds as if they weren't serious; they didn't name peace and then claim it when there obviously was none (Jer 6:14). I'll be forever grateful to believers like John King, Larry Crabb, Dan Allender, and Kyle Bishop.

I've also come to appreciate my intellect, something that wasn't encouraged in women in the denomination in which I was reared. In Isaiah, God expresses frustration, regret, or disbelief over the ignorance of his people: "Are their brains working at all?" he asks (44:19). Although the logical, analytical field of apologetics did nothing to change my heart, it did give me cause to consider that faith in God wasn't unreasonable. When I discovered apologetics, I thought, *If I do come to believe someday, at least I'll know that I didn't blindly accept the faith. And because it'll take so much to convince me, I know that if I ever believe, it'll be evidence that I've completely changed inside.* It was important for me to know that the faith of the saints of the Bible could stand up to rigorous testing and questioning.

I encourage all of us not to depend on our teachers to spoon-feed us answers. Let us seek truth for ourselves, checking our understanding with people whose humble walk with God compels us. Let us repent of the self-protective motivation in our hearts, seek healing for our pain, and allow our harmful behavior to be altered by devotion to our good God.

Because my own circumstances forced me to research the subject of marriage covenant, my thoughts throughout this book center on this issue. But there are a myriad of other issues that divide us that could be addressed. I can't help but wonder what God will say when we all meet in eternity and find that the particular "truth" about one issue or another that we held so staunchly was inconsequential to God, and that we didn't correctly understand it anyway. If we only worried about the doctrines that are clear, which are few, but vital (such as loving God, ourselves, and other people), I wonder if we could agree to love one another even as we disagreed on this or that issue. I wonder if we could be curious about the stories of how people come to this or that conviction. I wonder if our curiosity could lead us away from criticism and contempt for one another and move us toward caring and concern.

Perhaps this is too much to desire, but I'm inclined to think that even this desire is too small. What if we all lived this way for just one day? Would we like the results so much that we'd continue for one more day? Would the second day bleed into a third? A fourth? What harm would it do to experiment? Could we just try it and see?

I can't help but wonder, "What if?"

Love to you all, in Messiah,

Jade

Afterword

Happily Ever After?

Since the writing of this book, many circumstances in my life that apply directly to the content presented have changed, so, as I anticipate publication, I'm drawn to include one last personal story to illustrate that unknotting a trauma bond comes with no guarantee you'll find a compatible intimate partner, but that there's good reason to keep hope alive. Plus, unless you come to understand how you got into and remained in a harmful relationship, you'll likely repeat the same patterns again, and find yourself in another harmful relationship.

As mentioned in chapter 9, I committed to refrain from dating for at least two years following my divorce in order to give myself time to get my bearings on my identity as an individual. I wanted to take as few wounds as possible with me into the next relationship. When the two-year mark rolled around, I knew that I wasn't yet ready to date; I was still defining my identity. An experience I had two-and-a-half years after the divorce, however, left me feeling free enough from the trauma of my marriage to begin connecting out in the world again.

I joined several social groups through a social networking site, www.meetup.com (which is not a dating service), and began to develop new friendships, some of which were with men. I found that I was able to weed out interested men who didn't fit the most important aspects of my ideal relationship criteria. Eventually, I found myself in a romantic relationship with a man who fit most of my critical criteria. However, this man presented mixed messages about his availability, which should've been the first clue that the relationship would go nowhere. Unfortunately, it took about a year for me to accept that the vagueness and obscurity of his carefully chosen words actually communicated *unavailability*. My heart was broken in the process, but I learned lessons from that relationship that I don't think I could've learned in any other way.

The relationship ended, and I was alone again.

Then one day, the following message popped up in my inbox: "Bailey Green wants to be friends on Facebook." Yes, my sixth grade boyfriend, whom I mentioned in chapter 7, contacted me after thirty years! We had great fun catching up by phone on the twists and turns that our lives had taken for the past three decades.

Bailey and I continued to connect by phone, and as our friendship grew, I realized that I'd have to share with Bailey the story that I'd written about him in this book. I didn't relish admitting to him the mean things I'd thought about him when he first enrolled in my sixth grade class. However, when I read Bailey the story, he wasn't offended that I'd thought disparagingly about him at first. He seemed to understand that I'd seen him through my own wounded blinders, and that as I got to know him, I was able to see how attractive and adorable he really was.

Bailey remembered the story about our break-up just as I'd described it, and I asked him how it had felt when I'd told him that I couldn't wait for him if he didn't pass sixth grade. "It stung," he acknowledged. Sorrowful that I'd hurt his feelings, I took the opportunity, after thirty years, to apologize for being unkind to the boy whose memory had lived on in my heart ever since. Again, Bailey was forgiving. He expressed understanding that I hadn't intended to hurt him, but that I'd simply been desperate not to lose him to elementary school when I was advancing to middle school.

I also learned that Bailey hadn't willfully refused to pass sixth grade in order to spite me, but that it had been a difficult year for him personally in many ways, not the least of which was that even our advanced private school education bored him, so he was always in trouble for talking. Plus, he always felt more compelled to ride his dirt bike after school than he did to do his homework on subjects that he'd already mastered.

I relate this story to share some of the lessons I've learned in relationship with Bailey. First, I had no control over Bailey's remembering me and contacting me after thirty years, but I can tell you that it was one of the nicest surprises of my life when his Facebook invitation graced my inbox. Many wonderful surprises have happened to me since I began to relax my grip on trying to make life work on my own terms. I now look forward to the adventure of life, whatever it brings me. I've found that some of the best things in life happen by surprise, and my goal is to love well in all the relationships that life brings my way. I hope you can trust life to bring you wonderful surprises, too, as you let go of old patterns of relating.

Second, I've learned that it's much easier to define what you need in relationship *after* you define who you are. If you want to be *with* someone of integrity, you need to *be* a person of integrity first. If you enter a romantic relationship too soon, you set yourself and your partner up for preventable pain. (See also point number five below.)

Third, it may be hard to believe this when you're in the dying throws of a trauma bond, but there are many potential mates out there, so there's no need to force together puzzle pieces that don't match. Know the form of your puzzle piece so that you can determine the kind of puzzle piece that matches yours. A bit of flexibility is needed, but not on the criteria that are most essential to you.

Fourth, when you break a betrayal bound covenant, you'll find yourself back in the same psychological place in which you first made it, but with an opportunity to do it over—this time with knowledge that you didn't have before. In this way, you get a chance to heal old wounds. It's hard work, but it's worth it. Upon regressing to my eighteen-year-old mindset after the divorce, I found myself making familiar mistakes, but as I learned from them, I developed a whole new way of being with men. I learned that the true feminine has the power to draw out the true masculine, and vice versa. It took intentionality and awareness to learn this, but in doing so, I've established healthy friendships with men who have integrity, and I've removed myself from relationships with those who don't. I wish for you to be able to do the same; life is much sweeter and less dramatic when healthy people are in your life.

Fifth, if you have a traumatic history, you can expect that it will get triggered in intimate relationships. In fact, the more intimate the relationship is, the more triggers you will experience while you determine the safety of the relationship. When your emotion seems too intense for the situation, assume you're being triggered, and work to identify the original wounds. Then you can determine whether the current relationship follows the same pattern or whether you're projecting your old wounds onto it. Some of your triggers can be worked out in relationship; others will have to be worked through on your own. Professional help may be invaluable to help you sort out which is which. Remember that while harm occurs in relationship, healing occurs in relationship, too. It's simply how interpersonal neurobiology works. Safe intimate relationships give you the opportunity to find healing, but your old trauma scripts must be activated so that you can learn new scripts to live by in secure relationships.[1]

Sixth, your vulnerability is your strength. As my relationship with Bailey continued to develop, we found that the *Grounds for Marriage* material provided almost infinite opportunities for intimate conversations. Although some of the stories ignited old shame in me, Bailey's kind and compassionate responses provided a healing balm for some old wounds. I often felt vulnerable and exposed, but knowing and being known is so important to me that I had to let him in to see the most vulnerable parts of my soul. Sharing at this level was scary because I didn't know if Bailey would respond with understanding, but it gave me an opportunity to find out fairly early in our developing relationship if he was going to be repelled by who I am and what I've experienced. It also challenged Bailey to share on levels that he had never been challenged to share on before.

The timing of our reconnection meant that Bailey bore witness to and provided invaluable support for the reconciliation processes that occurred between Chip and me and between Ryan and me. These processes, along with reading this manuscript over the phone together, left Bailey with several impressions. Mostly, he expressed a profound respect for the perseverance and dedication it requires to heal from traumatic wounds. He also expressed relief that help is available for those who are tenacious enough to seek fundamental change no matter the cost, and he's hopeful that those who read this book will experience healing within themselves that eventually results in reconciliation in their core relationships. Finally, Bailey expressed that even those who haven't experienced childhood trauma can benefit from the concepts presented here. For example, Bailey has begun to understand himself better as a result of this book and our relationship, he said.

Because Bailey and I live on opposite coasts, our friendship has developed mostly over the phone, and our conversations have helped us to cultivate an emotional intimacy that's easy to neglect when in physical proximity. Bailey came up with the idea of putting together a template for relationship cultivation, and as our relationship develops, we're adding to this template. Perhaps my next book will include this tool.

I don't know what the outcome will be for Bailey and me, but I hope that our friendship will continue to develop and deepen as we attempt to be in relationship in redemptive ways. I hope that you, too, will exchange healing and redemption in your relationships.

1. Stokes, *What Freud Didn't Know*.

PART 4

Grounds for Marriage Study Guide

How to Use This Study Guide

TO PEOPLE IN COVENANT CRISIS

Before I could feel comfortable publishing this book, I needed to find out how real people with real relationship problems might respond to it. My chief concern was that some might use the material to browbeat their partners. My next concern was whether the theology was reader-friendly enough for the intended reader.

So, I used the manuscript as the foundational text for a pilot therapy group, which consisted of one married couple and four individuals in various stages of relational breakdown: one was in the process of filing for divorce, two others were considering the option of divorce, and one had been divorced for eight years.

Over the sixteen weeks that we used to cover the material, several comments came up over and over again that, unbeknownst to my clients, addressed my concerns. First, my clients frequently described how the material in *Grounds for Marriage* and in this guide helped them to personalize the information, shifting their primary focus away from their partners and onto themselves. As one client succinctly emphasized, "This is a *self*-help book."

My second concern was alleviated, as well, when my clients articulated their understanding of the concept of "covenant." Although they expressed relief to have a fresh look at scripture, they also expressed frustration that they had never been taught about covenants in their various communities of faith, either in the past as they were growing up or in the present wherever they attended services. Many said that if they'd had this information taught and modeled long before, it would have spared them and their loved ones years of pain.

Perhaps your experience will be similar, but whatever it is, I hope this study guide will: 1) help you understand what happened to cause your relationship to break down, including what both you and your partner contributed to its collapse, and 2) help you understand and personalize the concept of "covenant."

I also hope that this workbook will simplify a typically complicated and painful evaluation process without being simplistic. This workbook may be able to help you envision what loving well might look like in your particular situation, especially if it looks differently than you've always imagined. To do something in a way that you've never done before requires great courage, and I hope these materials will help you find resources within you that you didn't know you had.

Doing the work in this guide won't be easy, so I recommend setting aside significant blocks of time to answer the questions thoroughly. Also, it's usually more beneficial to answer one question completely rather than many questions superficially, especially when everything in you wants to avoid facing painful realities at all. Know that as you search your soul with honesty, you're not alone. Others have done this hard work, too. Some of my clients said that going through this book and workbook was the hardest therapy work they'd ever done. So please be kind to yourself as you do this work. When it feels like you can't go on, put the book down until you're ready to search your soul again.

TO COUNSELORS, PASTORS, EDUCATORS, AND OTHER PEOPLE-HELPERS

If you're a people-helper, please try to understand that no one wants to see his or her relationship fail. Such a process usually leaves a person with overwhelming shame and sorrow. Those who have the courage to evaluate their relationships honestly should be commended, not condemned. I've never known anyone who went through a divorce who would describe it as "the easy way out," though this is a widespread accusation. More commonly, people stay in harmful relationships much longer than is good for any of the parties involved.

Your compassion is essential as you work with people who think something is wrong with them, or that God will hate them, no matter how harmful the circumstances, if they separate from a partner.

It's important that you spare people in pain simplistic solutions to complicated problems, and that you refer them to other professionals if the dynamics involved are more complex than you're trained to address.

As you work with individuals in covenant crises, the questions in this guide can help you invite people into an honest evaluation of their relational breakdown. The best thing you can do in this process is to teach them *how* to think for themselves, rather than tell them *what* to think. If you encourage them to make their own choices, it may take them longer to reach conclusions, but they'll be able to own them, without blaming you for their choices. They may not land where you want them to, but that's not your responsibility. They have to live with their choices; you don't, so whatever choices they make must be theirs.

If they don't choose what you wish they'd chosen, it may be easy to feel like their choice reflects badly upon you. However, if you're secure enough to allow them to make personal choices that you might not make, then you're secure enough to let go of wondering what others may thing of your work with couples that are in this covenant evaluation process.

When people make poor choices, even while they seem to be engaging in honest evaluation, it'll be important to check your judgments at the door to keep the dialogue open. The artful process of helping folks discover truth for themselves will be challenged when you see people in pain making choices that will cause them more pain. Keeping them in the pain may feel counterintuitive at times, but "it's when we're on the brink of personal collapse that we're best able to shift the direction of our soul from self-protection to trusting love."[1] Touching the depth of our pain can soften us and open us up to legitimate sources of life.

This guide can help you ask hard questions that encourage those with whom you work to face the pain of their lives with courage and honesty. If they choose to do this, your challenge will be to simply let folks feel their pain, and to be *with* them in it, without trying to rescue them from it, attempting to fix them in any way, or abandoning them in the process. This will require tremendous patience, courage, and humility on your part.

May this material help you practice with whatever balance of tenderness and strength you'll need for each unique situation.

---

1. Crabb, *Inside Out*, 234.

Introduction

1. Have the Biblical teachers in your history used a *pre*scriptive or a *de*scriptive approach to scripture? If they used both approaches, how did they choose which approach to use with particular scriptures?

2. What approach do *you* take when you try to understand and interpret scripture? Why?

3. When you interpret scripture, how closely do you follow the three hermeneutical guidelines laid out in this section?

    a. A text cannot mean what it never meant (refers to historical-cultural context):

    b. Context is king (refers to grammatical context):

    c. Genre is critical (refers to literary context):

4. What is it like to know that trying to make sense of the scriptures is more complicated than you may have thought?

5. With which of the three focus questions do you identify? Why?

    a. *How can intimate human relationships reflect intimate relationship with God?*

    b. *How can I help people heal from old wounds and turn from harmful ways of being so that they are free to be in a covenant relationship with God and with a covenant companion?*

    c. *How can a person heal from old wounds and then turn from harmful ways of being so that he or she is free to be in a covenant relationship with God and with a covenant companion?*

6. The author acknowledges that her own marriage failed. In your view, does this add credibility to this work, or does it take it away? Explain. What might you be able to learn about your situation from someone who has been through the process of a divorce?

7. What do you think the author means by "reading the text" of our lives? What do reading a book, understanding a person's life stories, making sense of a work of art, and interpreting a legal document have in common?

8. Before you read the material, consider the title and subtitle of this work. What do you think and feel are grounds for marriage? What feelings do the title and subtitle call up in you?

9. The author says that she wants to present a high view of marriage. What do you think she means by that?

10. Is there anything else in the Introduction that stood out to you?

FOR GROUPS:

1. Bring in a letter to or from a friend that you feel comfortable sharing. Exchange letters and try to interpret the meaning. How are your interpretations based on the assumptions of your own life?

2. Share a story from your own life in which you made a mistake that you feel would be a valuable teaching tool for others.

3. Homework: Watch the film *Vantage Point*, paying attention to the interpretations various characters make based on their unique perspectives. Discuss what you can learn from this film about making sense of life. How does this movie inform the concepts of interpreting text, soul, and culture?

Feelings and Thoughts about Group Interaction:

Chapter 1

Happily Ever After—A Match Made in Heaven?

A True Treaty

1. What is your initial reaction to the idea that covenant is conditional?

2. Do you seek to *please* God? Or do you try to *appease* him? Explain the difference.

    When I seek to please God, I . . .

    When I try to appease God, I . . .

3. In your own words, describe the difference between *penance* and *repentance*. Describe a story from your own life that demonstrates each of these concepts.

4. How can you seek to understand scripture for yourself? Why is this important in your life? Why is this especially important with regard to the practices of marriage, divorce, and remarriage?

5. What is the consistent message of the scriptures regarding how we should treat one another? Why are we to treat people in this manner?

6. What has been your experience in the faith community with regard to holding powerful people accountable to treat less powerful people with utmost reverence?

7. How do you determine what balance of strength and tenderness you should have in different circumstances of various relationships?

8. How does your partner reflect, mirror, image God?

9. What would it look like to treat your partner with dignity for a whole day? What would it look like for your partner to treat you with dignity for whole day?

10. Respond to Stone's statement that, "our behavior toward one another, along with our requirement for respect from others, reveals our spiritual health."

11. How well have you and your partner been living up to the calling to treat each other *even better* than you treat anyone else? Explain.

12. Respond to Allender and Longman's statement that, "The goal of marriage is to reveal God."

13. To what degree have the following impacted the strength of your relationship:

    a. Past baggage:

b. Contempt for differences:

c. Failure to grow:

14. Describe a time when you witnessed one person treating another with careful reverence and respect. What was this experience like for you?

15. Describe a time when your partner treated you with great dignity. What was this like for you? Describe a time when you treated your partner with great dignity. What was this like?

FOR GROUPS:

1. Discuss what an ideal partnership would be like for you.

2. Every relationship and covenant has conditions, consequences and rewards. Discuss the differences between the conditions, consequences and rewards of various kinds of relationships: with a store clerk; with a registered sex offender; with a homeless person; with your children; with your partner; with your mother; with your father; with your brother; with your sister; with your friend; with someone who has betrayed you.

3. Read Isaiah 1:17. How might this verse apply differently to the various individuals in your life?

4. In pairs or triads, practice the "Couple's Dialogue" exercise. (Use Appendix A for help until the format becomes second nature.)

5. Homework: Identify one person this week, and internalize the concept that this person is a sacred creature, made in the image of God. Determine how you'll treat this person this week. Share this with your group so that they can hold you accountable.

Feelings and Thoughts about Group Interaction:

Chapter 2

Happily Never After—Mates By Mistake?

A False Treaty

1. What have you learned (through modeling or other means) or been taught directly about marriage, divorce, and remarriage? What is this teaching based upon?

2. Name the various covenants in your life. What are their unique stipulations?

3. List the people in your life who have hurt you deeply. How have they done so? If you suspect that you're engaging in relationships that re-create the dynamics of these relationships in an attempt to get them to resolve more positively, describe the patterns you're identifying.

4. How do you feel about the possibility that some marriages are made by unconscious human error, not by God's ordination?

5. The author describes how she attempted to make life work on her own. Have you done the same thing? How? What is it like to acknowledge this?

6. In your own words, explain how love is unconditional but relationship is not. What is required for intimate relationship with God?

7. What strikes you most about the discussion of the covenant addressed in Malachi? Why?

8. What strikes you most about the social context of ancient Jewish marriage? Why?

9. What common conclusions about marriage and divorce do Jesus and Paul make?

10. What marriage vows did you and your partner make to one another? How well or how poorly have you kept these promises? How well or how poorly has your partner kept these promises?

For Groups:

1. What promises did you make to the people in this group when you agreed to be part of it? Did you agree to strict confidentiality? To attend regularly? To participate fully? To be on time? What are the consequences for breaking these promises? The rewards for keeping them?

2. Bring in pictures of your wedding or your wedding video to share with the group. Pay particular attention to the wedding vows, and to the symbols that you chose for the ceremony and for your early life together. Discuss the meaning of these.

3. What have you done to safeguard your covenant together?

Feelings and Thoughts about Group Interaction:

Chapter 3

God's Love Languages

1. What Hebrew words about covenant are most intriguing to you? How so?

2. How is the picture of God's relationship with his people presented in this chapter similar to or different from what you've learned in the past? How does it sit with you?

3. To what degree are you and your partner mutually vulnerable? How well do you know one another's dreams, desires, hopes, pains, old wounds . . . ? To what degree do you want to know and be known by your intimate partner? How frightening is it to consider being fully known by this person?

4. How can you go about letting your inner self be known by your partner?

5. What are some of your old wounds that seem to get triggered in your relationships? What are some of your partner's old wounds? How do you know? What can you do to avoid triggering your partner's wounds, now that you're aware of them?

For Groups:

1. Create a human sculpture of what genuine covenant would feel like to you.
2. Draw a picture of what it feels like to be injured in an old wound.
3. Create a collage that represents mutual vulnerability.

Feelings and Thoughts about Group Interaction:

Chapter 4

E.Q.: Don't Be Home Without It

1. How well do you recognize your emotions in the moment? Do you struggle to verbally describe your emotions?

2. Describe a situation when tuning into your emotions saved the day, either yours or someone else's. Describe a situation when failing to tune into your emotions caused damage.

3. How do you balance, or manage, your emotions? (Remember, managing your emotions isn't simply cutting them off, stuffing them, or expressing them without regard to others.) What do you typically do with emotions like anger, anxiety and depression?

4. How would you rate your ability to control your impulses? How would you rate your self-motivation? How have these qualities manifested themselves in your life?

5. Look up the words *empathic* and *hypervigilant* in the dictionary. How does each word fit you? How is each demonstrated in your behavior? Can you think of a time when you used your empathy in the service of loving well? Or in the service of self-protection? Can you think of a time when you used hypervigilance to protect yourself, even when you were in a safe environment?

6. What do you know about the attunement between you and your mother when you were a baby?

7. What did you learn as a child about emotions and feelings—yours and others? How?

8. How well would you rate your skill of handling relationships? Explain.

9. What were your gut reactions to the stories of Gabby and Neil, and of the author and Chip?

10. How well do you and your partner handle your relationship together? How well do you tune in to each other's emotions? What is your typical response when your partner becomes emotional or stuffs his or her emotion?

11. In your own words, describe what it means to be created in the image of God. What are the implications of this concept in your relationship with your partner? Your kids? Your friends? Your mother? Your father? Your siblings? How does the principle of punishment fitting the crime apply to each of these relationships? How do you think it should apply to you in each of these relationships?

For Groups:

1. Divide into pairs and role-play emotional intelligence in a variety of scenarios. Use this time to practice possible situations with relationships in your life.

2. Homework: Find your wedding video and wedding photos. Bring them for some possible activities for your next group session.

Feelings and Thoughts about Group Interaction:

Chapter 5

'Til Homicide Do Us Part

1. How similar were your wedding vows to the author's? How did you decide on the details of your wedding and on the promises you made to one another?

2. In your own words, explain what you promised to do until death? What did you not promise to do?

3. Looking back on the life of your marriage, how well have you and your partner kept your wedding promises to each other? How long did you intend that these vows would last?

4. Rewrite your wedding vows to reflect what your marriage has actually been like.

5. If you could write your own wedding vows now, what would you write?

6. How do you and your partner repair breaches of relationship? If this is less than ideal, how would you like repairs to be made?

7. How well do you nurture fondness and admiration for your partner? How well does your partner nurture fondness and admiration for you?

8. How do you and your partner cultivate romance?

9. Describe a situation in which your partner allowed you to influence him or her. Describe a situation in which you allowed your partner to influence you. How often does this happen? How can you practice this before the next group session?

10. Name a few of the problems in your marriage that may be unsolvable. Write out a dialogue for one of these issues that incorporates the five guidelines to help move from gridlock to dialogue: 1) softly approaching the conflict; 2) using repair attempts effectively; 3) monitoring yourself during tense discussions so as to avoid escalating beyond a productive level; 4) reaching mutual compromise; and 5) becoming more tolerant of each other's imperfections.

11. What hopes, aspirations, wishes, and dreams of your partner are you not respecting? How can you listen to one of your partner's dreams, offer your partner financial support of that dream, and then become part of that dream? How could your partner do this for you?

12. What are some traditions that you enjoy with your partner? What are some traditions that you'd like to establish?

13. How have you broken your promises to your partner? What would it look like to return to those promises? What promises to you has your partner broken? What do you need for relationship to be fully restored in these areas?

14. What pressures and hardships from *outside* the relationship have you and your partner weathered together? What pressures and hardships from *within* the relationship have you weathered together? What difficult circumstances and situations have you or your partner endured from within the relationship that *aren't* within the category of hardships, but that instead represent broken promises? How do you distinguish between these categories?

For Groups:

1. Role-play gridlocked conversations. Practice relating in a way that moves you from gridlock to dialogue.
2. Share your wedding videos and pictures. Discuss how well you kept the promises you made on your wedding day. How well has your partner kept his or her end of the bargain?

Feelings and Thoughts about Group Interaction:

Chapter 6

Naked and Unashamed

1. In your own words, try to describe what healthy sexuality is all about.

2. How did your family of origin demonstrate the masculine and the feminine? What did you learn from this? How would you like to change these views in your life?

3. How did others outside of your family impact your sense of masculine and feminine?

4. How well do you know, appreciate, and live out your feminine or masculine strengths? Describe a time when you felt most alive as a woman or man. Describe a time when you felt your gender was disdained or unappreciated.

5. If you or your partner is unsatisfied with your intimate relationship (emotionally and/or physically), what needs to change in order for the two of you to enjoy one another sexually? In your view, what are some steps that you and your partner can take to make these changes?

6. What parts of the author's sexual history did you most connect with? What parts seemed foreign to you?

7. What have you learned about yourself and about sexuality as a result of the sexual experiences that you've had throughout your lifespan? How does the content of this chapter impact those ideas?

8. How have you lived out in your partnership the things you learned (or didn't learn) about sexuality?

9. What can you learn from the way the sexual histories of Chip and Jade interacted?

10. What would an ideal sexual relationship be like for you?

11. Create a sexual development chart for yourself, using the columns in the book: healthy sexual development, my sexual development, views/lessons, behaviors/functions/responses, and hopes.

12. Read the fables in Appendix E. Which sections do you relate to the most? What emotions do the fables stir up in you?

13. How have you disdained your own femininity or masculinity and that of your partner? What can you do to amend this wrong and change how you relate in the future?

14. Write your own story in fable form.

For Groups:

1. Pair up and gaze into one another's eyes for five minutes. Discuss how this exercise affected you.
2. Describe what healthy sexuality is all about to a partner.
3. Share your fables with each other.

Feelings and Thoughts about Group Interaction:

Chapter 7

A Decalogue to Diagnose Hardening of the Heartery

A Toxic Condition

1. Describe what you think and how you feel about the concept that God's love is unconditional, but intimate relationship with him is conditional. Describe what this reality makes you think or how it makes you feel.

2. How was your process of covenanting with your partner similar or dissimilar to God's process of covenanting?

    a. Establishing clear covenants and conditions

    b. Enforcing the conditions when covenant is broken

    c. Creative attempts to address the issues of broken covenant

    d. Clearly warning and then following through with repercussions when covenant is incessantly broken and unrepaired

e. Following through on the condition of divorce when repair proves to be undesired by the other party

3. How has your loyalty to your partner been divided? How has your partner's loyalty to you been divided? What would it take to repair these breaches?

4. How have you and your partner evidenced hardness of heart in your relationship with one another?

5. If you have relational issues that should have been addressed long ago, what has prevented you from addressing them? To what have you been more committed than to total honesty and truth? How can you become more committed to truth and honesty?

6. What parts of the Decalogue seem harder to do than others? How can you enlist your group members to help you follow these principles?

7. What do you see as your contribution to the breakdown of your relationship?

8. What do you see as your partner's contribution to the breakdown of the relationship?

9. What's the point of an honest appraisal if there are no guarantees that your relationship with your partner will be reconciled?

10. Of the six signs of hardheartedness, which are present in your relationship?

    (1 = Never; 2 = Seldom; 3 = Sometimes; 4 = Often; 5 = Always)

    a. Harsh Start-ups   1   2   3   4   5
    b. The Four Horseman
          i.   Criticism   1   2   3   4   5
          ii. Contempt   1   2   3   4   5
          iii. Defensiveness   1   2   3   4   5
          iv. Stonewalling   1   2   3   4   5
    c. Flooding   1   2   3   4   5
    d. Body Physiology   1   2   3   4   5
    e. Failed Repair Attempts   1   2   3   4   5
    f. Bad Memories   1   2   3   4   5

11. What can you do this week to avoid contributing to further hurt, harm, and relational breakdown?

12. Consider the four signs that indicate the final stages of a relationship. How present are these signs in your relationship?

    (1 = Never; 2 = Seldom; 3 = Sometimes; 4 = Often; 5 = Always)

    a. You see your relationship problems as severe

                                                1   2   3   4   5

    b. Talking about things is fruitless and you fail to seek help outside yourselves   1   2   3   4   5

    c. You lead parallel lives   1   2   3   4   5

    d. Loneliness   1   2   3   4   5

    What do you want to do about this?

13. How has your childhood history impacted your choice of partner and your relationship with your partner? How has your partner's childhood history impacted his or her choice of you, and how has it impacted your relationship together?

14. What can you do to own and feel your contribution to the breakdown of your relationship?

15. Read the short prophecy of Malachi on your own (preferably in *The Message*). What feelings arise as you read this book?

16. What feelings arise as you read Jade's description of her relationship with Chip in this chapter?

FOR GROUPS:

1. Brainstorm ways to creatively address the issues of broken covenant in your partnership.
2. Role-play. Practice hard conversations using soft start-ups and direct complaints, avoiding the Four Horsemen.
3. Read *Intimate Allies*, by Dan Allender and Tremper Longman. Discuss together.

Feelings and Thoughts about Group Interaction:

Chapter 8

Repentance: Surprisingly Soft and Shame-Free

1. In your own words, define what this chapter describes as repentance. How is this similar or different from what you have been taught about it?

2. Describe a time when you were sorry for the pain you caused someone. What did you do about it? Using the principles in this chapter, what should you have done about it? Describe a time when you were sorry for the pain you'd caused God. What did you do about it? What should you have done?

3. What gods have been more important to you than undivided relationships with God, yourself, and others? (What have been your addictions, compulsions and attachments?)

4. With whose story do you identify more: Emily's, Elizabeth's, Merry's, Paul's, or Kim's? How so?

5. Respond to: "While people can make behavioral change without repentance, they cannot repent without behavioral change." Is either of these parts missing in your relationship between you and your partner? What do you need to do about that?

6. What would repentance look like in your situation? What would it look like if there were a shift inside you concerning your perceived source of life?

7. If you were to end your relationship with your partner, what changes would you anticipate for you and for your partner as individuals in regard to healing and repentance?

8. If you believe that staying in your partnership would be more damaging than extricating yourself from it, what prevents you from moving toward separation? What can you do to get help with this decision?

9. Draw a picture of what your marriage would be like if it were healed. Draw a picture of what you envision your marriage will be like in five years if it continues as it is.

For Groups:

1. Discuss how you might be able to tell if someone were sincerely repentant or not.
2. How could your partner tell if you were repentant? How could you tell if your partner were repentant?
3. What would it look like if your hearts were softened to one another?
4. Draw a picture of what repentance looks like.

Feelings and Thoughts about Group Interaction:

Chapter 9

To Have and to Fold

1. What were you taught about quitting as a child? What were you taught about delaying gratification? Do you stand by those lessons? Why or why not?

2. What were you taught about "quitting" a marriage? How is the content of this chapter similar or different than what you were taught about quitting?

3. How is the content of this chapter similar or different than what you were taught about confrontation?

4. What would it look like if you were to treat your partner with dignity, regardless of how he or she belittles you? (Keep in mind that treating one person with dignity may look very different than treating another person with dignity. People who harm without repentance need to experience appropriate consequences in order to send the message: "You're not behaving like a person with dignity and you're not treating others like they deserve dignity. I hope these consequences put you in touch with your dignity and the dignity of others again.")

5. What emotions were stirred when you read about how the author ended her relationship, desiring to treat both herself and her husband with dignity?

6. If you were to divorce and then regress emotionally to the time before you met your partner, what would you expect to find yourself thinking, feeling, and doing? How can you respond well if this were to happen?

7. Imagine what you would be like with a softened heart. Imagine what your partner would be like with a softened heart. Describe this.

8. If your partner were to confront you, what issues would he or she address? If you were to confront your partner, what issues would you need to address?

9. What would it feel like to confront your partner? Are you ready to do so? Why or why not?

10. In your own words, describe what the Bible says about confrontation.

For Groups:

1. Discuss how you can tell if you're ready to confront your partner or not.

2. Use the following points to write out a brief complaint with which your partner might confront you. Then write another one from you toward your partner.

    a. This is what you did.

    b. I hold you responsible.

    c. This is how it hurt me.

    d. I will no longer be silent.

3. Discuss how you would determine what kind of method of dissolution is best for a couple who is divorcing.

Feelings and Thoughts about Group Interaction:

Chapter 10

Grounds for Parenting: What About the Kids?

1. Respond to Gottman's words about caring for your children when your partnership is broken: "A peaceful divorce is better than a warlike marriage."

2. If you were to divorce your partner, how might you explain this to your kids in an age-appropriate way?

3. What do you think your children have learned about relationship as a result of your partnership? What scars might they carry as a result of these messages? How might they be impacted in the future? What can you do now to help your children heal or learn from your example?

4. How can you use your divorce as a teaching opportunity for your children?

5. If you choose to divorce, what is your plan for helping your children process this over time?

6. When children are involved, how can a person determine whether or not he or she should remain in a partnership?

7. What feelings arose as you read the story of the author's father mistreating her mother? If you had been her mother's best friend, what would you have advised her to do?

8. When parents don't honor one another well, what may preoccupy their children's minds? If a child doesn't have to spend precious mental energy on the parents' conflicts, what will he or she be able to spend his or her energy thinking about and doing?

9. What would you say to someone who tells you that he or she is only staying married for the sake of the kids?

FOR GROUPS:

1. Discuss the dynamic between your parents in your family of origin. What did you learn about relationship from this dynamic? How might your partnership be teaching your children the same things?

2. What messages would you want your children to receive about how to treat a partner and how to require respectful treatment? How will they receive these messages?

Feelings and Thoughts about Group Interaction:

Epilogue

Head and Heart: Reunited, and It Feels So Good

1. With which part/s of the author's letter to twenty-first century believers did you most identify?

2. What are your feelings about choosing relationship over doctrine?

3. In your opinion, what is the church's role in preparing couples for partnership and for married life? How well has the church done this? What might your church do to minister better in this area?

4. Is your relationship with God more in your emotions or in your mind? Are you satisfied with this? If not, what will you do about it?

5. How would you describe your prayer life? What is your reaction to the conversational prayer life described by the author?

6. Describe how your body feels when you're angry, sad, hurt, afraid, excited, joyful, overwhelmed, and confused. How can tuning into the language of your body help you connect with God, yourself, and others more deeply?

7. If you already *feel* your relationship with God deeply, what do you need to do to engage your *mind* in this relationship? If your relationship with God is more *thinking*-oriented, what do you need to do to engage your *feelings*? How might changes in these areas improve your intimacy with God, yourself, and others?

8. What "truths" do you hold that keep you distant from others, or others distant from you? What do you want to do about this?

9. Experiment: Be curious instead of critical for one day. Describe your experience.

For Groups:

1. Identify some of the doctrinal differences between group members. Tell stories of how you came to these various beliefs.

2. Imagine how, this week, you can reach out to someone who has different beliefs than you do. Report your experiences in the next session.

3. Share your experiences about what happened when you committed, for one day, to be curious instead of critical.

Feelings and Thoughts about Group Interaction:

Afterword

Happily Ever After?

1. The author acknowledges making a mistake in a romantic relationship because she misread the unspoken messages about the man's unavailability. What mistakes do you think you may be prone to make if you aren't careful?

2. The author continues the story of Bailey Green from chapter 7 to illustrate several points. The first point is about control. How does it feel to consider giving up control concerning your romantic connections? Or have you been passive in your approach to relationship and need to take a more active role?

3. How are you developing your integrity? How will this help you spot other people of integrity?

4. Write out a description of who you are. Based on this description, what kind of person might be a good fit for you?

5. If you were to regress to the mindset in which you formed a romantic betrayal bond, what might you find yourself thinking, doing, and feeling? What is your plan to resist forming another betrayal bond?

6. Respond to, "Your vulnerability is your strength." What feelings does this statement call up in you? How can you be open but cautious when you enter a romantic relationship?

7. The author's wish is that, you will "exchange healing and redemption in your relationships." How can you be a healing agent for others? How can you invite others to be a healing agent for you?

FOR GROUPS:
1. Share your descriptions of who you are. Give and receive feedback.
2. Discuss how your group members have been healing agents for one another. What can you learn from these relationships that you can take into relationships beyond the group?

Feelings and Thoughts about Group Interaction:

PART 5

Practical Tools—Appendices

Appendix A

Active Listening Skills

Note: One person presents one issue at a time.

1. Person #1 (Speaker) expresses the problem and talks about the feelings around it.

2. Person #2 (Receiver) (okay to stop and mirror the content in small segments)
   - Mirrors what speaker says, as verbatim as possible
   - Is that it? Did I get it right?

     (Yes - move on; No - do it again)
   - Is there more?
   - When there's no more, gives a nutshell/summary
   - Is that it? Did I get it? (Yes - move on; No - do it again)
   - What can I do to help? What do you need from me?

Adapted from: Hendrix, Harville, Ph.D. *Getting the Love You Want*, New York: Henry Holt, 1988.

Appendix B

Trial Separation Agreement Form

Trial separation is either: (1) a time of constructive re-evaluation and clear decisions or (2) a poorly planned time, after which a decision is inevitably made anyway. The most constructive trial separation begins with a clear, specific agreement between the spouses. If you're embarking upon trial separation, it's essential to address the concerns below. Couples who are separated and cannot agree on the answers to these concerns should recognize that they're progressing toward divorce. I highly recommend that you complete this work with the help of a trained professional counselor or mediator.

INSTRUCTIONS: (1) Find a quiet location on "neutral ground" where you won't be interrupted, (2) allow enough time for the husband and wife to answer these questions separately, and (3) discuss each question until you reach an agreement. Be very specific and concrete in your answers. Be flexible in seeking agreements and compromises.

1. Plans for your financial arrangements and living arrangements for this period?

2. Specific plans for visits, dates, or other contacts between husband and wife?

3. Plans for counseling (individually and/or together)?

4. Plans for discussing the separation with your children? Plans for custody? Plans for visitation?

5. Will you date other people during this separation? Yes___ No___

6. Is there anything that could happen to cause one or both of you to end the separation and proceed immediately to divorce? Be specific.

7. What specific problem(s) or issue(s) led to this separation?

8. What changes will each spouse need to make to renew the marriage commitment? Attach additional pages, if needed.

Appendix B

Husband	Wife

9. Length of Separation? How did you come to this conclusion?

We have reached agreement on our answers to these questions.

Husband _____   Date _____

Wife _____   Date _____

Appendix C

Sample Confrontation Letter

Dear Chip,

I hardly know how to express what I need to confess to you. I just realized what I have to say last night when preparing to do my counseling homework assignment, which was this letter, expressing my needs and longings. Writing this letter put several loose ends together for me.

After I jotted down some notes, I began. "Dear Chip, my childhood buddy," I wrote. But I couldn't go on. There was something about that phrase that didn't seem quite right, and my stomach churned within me. Certainly we had met when we were young, and I've often said that we married as kids. This is partially true, but the phrase "childhood buddy" seemed just a bit too young to truly describe our reality at eighteen and nineteen. Then I realized that my childhood buddy was my brother *Davie*, and I knew why my stomach was churning. When I met you, I experienced you as lost, dazed, dreamy, insecure, childlike, sexy, wiry. I experienced you as Davie; I'd unconsciously found a "brother" to revoke his abandonment of me when I stopped the sexual abuse. Who you *really* were, neither one of us knew, but that didn't matter to me. I'd found a way to both rescue my brother (for whom I've always felt compassion, with his unfortunate hand of cards) and to get him to love me. If I could rescue you, and if you could love me, you'd fill my brother-hole. My heart sank when I realized this last night, and I wanted to throw up. I hadn't fallen in love with you, Chip. I'd fallen in love with Davie. I've known for a long time that I've objectified you in demanding that you heal my father wounds, but I hadn't realized that I've demanded that you heal my brother wounds, as well.

So, I have to confess, and it gives me much sorrow to do so, that on October 22, 1988, I didn't marry *you*. I married someone whom I hoped would be a brother surrogate. I didn't marry a unique, young, male image-bearer of God whose life was sacred ground; I married, in my subconscious, a young man who, to me, was an image-bearer of my brother whom I idolized. I didn't fall in love and establish a true covenant with you; I fell into a classic trauma bond, "a highly addictive attachment to the people who have hurt you," as described in *The Betrayal Bond* by Patrick Carnes.

Several details of late also point to this sorrowful reality. Remember my interaction with Pierre [graduate school professor]? I was concerned that Pierre's playful "smart ass" comment about me after I'd left the room might have meant that he had engaged in a power play ... and won. I was concerned about losing my "playmate" over a power struggle. The feeling of being played by an authority figure to both engage and exploit me was a familiar one [a throwback to sexual abuse scenarios orchestrated by Davie], and the interaction with Pierre triggered an old reaction in me, despite Pierre's lack of malice in his good-humored comment. I had to acknowledge that I was still hanging on to one last hope that Davie would connect with his harm of me and initiate reconciliation in our relationship. I knew that I'd lost my childhood playmate when I was thirteen years old, but I hadn't let him go emotionally. Unconsciously, I've been living in fear of losing Davie completely, and now it's painfully clear to me. My emotional attachment to Davie hasn't been fair to you; I've required that you take his place, which has prevented me from simply letting you be who you are. I've had you playing a role in my story, a role you should never have had to play.

Another piece that completes this picture is the dream I had this past Monday night. In my dream, a boy with a long face (like you) relentlessly pursued me, sexually. I had a sense that I was already "spoken for," so I resisted this guy, even though I was attracted to him sexually. That I was already attached, to whom was not clear, made the "forbidden fruit" seem sweeter. Then when this long-faced guy pursued me for the sole purpose of pleasuring *me*, I could resist him no longer. When I woke up, I broke into spontaneous sobbing. The seemingly incongruent phrase that kept coursing through my mind was, "I don't want to lose my childhood buddy. I don't want to lose my childhood buddy...." I've never cried like that after a dream.

I wondered whether this childhood buddy, this guy to whom I was attached, might have been you, but somehow that didn't seem accurate because it felt like you were the one *pursuing* me, and that I was already attached to *someone else*. Something didn't add up. Then, after writing that original opening line to this letter ("Dear Chip, my childhood buddy"), I realized that my prior attachment was to Davie, and that my attraction to you has really been an attempt to get Davie, my childhood playmate, to whom I've been trauma bound through betrayal, to love me again. I've been unconsciously demanding that you take Davie's place. I also realized that if I wanted to have a (sexual) relationship with this long-faced young man who wanted to give me pleasure (the only guy who ever pleasured me, like this guy did), I'd have to lose my childhood buddy . . . I'd have to let Davie go if this new young man was going to have the chance to pursue me.

I don't know if you feel the implications of this. I don't know if you've connected with what it feels like to be objectified, used, exploited, consumed, and unappreciated for your own uniqueness, but I know exactly what that feels like, because it's the most painful part of my history. My whole childhood was about being used to satisfy this or that need of someone else. I was never Jade . . . no one ever really knew who Jade was, because she didn't matter. She was always enlisted in the service of someone else—to make him or her look good or feel good. I wasn't a person; I was an object. And when I was old enough to do the same thing, I did, and you became the biggest casualty in my desperate quest to regain my brother's love.

Chip, I'm so sorry for what I've done to you, and I don't know what to do with this new understanding. There's no way to go back and change how I've hurt you, and there's no way to make it up to you. I can only say that I sorrow deeply over having used and exploited you in this way. It was unfair, unkind, and cruel. I've stomped around on the holy ground of your soul for half your life, with little regard for the sacred place on which I've trampled with such irreverence.

It feels like you've done the same thing to me. I conveniently fell right into your lap. Since then, you haven't relationally pursued me with generosity or with reckless abandon because you didn't need to; I made it easy on you so that you wouldn't abandon me. If I'd been harder to get, or to keep, I don't think we'd be together today, because you rarely go out of your way to pursue things that don't come easily. I provided you with an opportunity to get some personal needs fulfilled, and I became a live-in sex partner, a housekeeper, a cook, a computer operator, an assignment completer—all of which you've received with a sense of entitlement and with little or no appreciation. I don't have a sense exactly who you married on October 22, 1988, but I know it wasn't me. It couldn't have been, because neither of us knew who I was. I can tell you who I am now, and I don't know if you will like that person. But I do know that you've used me as I've used you, and neither of us has insisted that we acknowledge and honor one another as unique human beings, imprinted with the insignia of God.

We began our relationship by playing (running, playing ping pong, etc.), and we moved quickly into making out and heavy petting. I remember making out with you when you came to my father's funeral. I remember being in a tree stand with you in the woods and thinking, "What am I doing? I'm here to attend my father's funeral, and I'm making out with Chip. I must be an awful, desperately selfish person that I care so little about my Dad." It was then that I remember initiating a sexual experience with you in a field. I was so amazed that you'd break a commitment with Jenni and drive 400 miles to be with me that I wanted to thank you in the only way I knew how to thank a guy for his companionship: a sexual favor. And like all the other guys before you, you didn't resist. You say that this event didn't happen at my father's funeral, and I've been willing, against my better judgment, to concede that it occurred later—maybe at the family reunion a couple months after that.

Being in relationship with you has created a self-doubt that, for a short time, left me questioning the data in my journal. I'm glad I have this journal because it reminds me that just because you don't *want* to believe something happened doesn't mean that it didn't. My journal restores sanity to me because being in relationship with you has been crazy-making. Because you don't want to believe that you hurt me, you've tried to re-write history, and I almost believed you, against everything that was screaming out inside of me. If it weren't true, why would I imagine that the event of our first sexual contact happened at Dad's funeral, when this makes me look the worst and darkest I could possibly look? Moreover, offering you a sexual favor at my Dad's funeral would be consistent with the sexual events that had transpired in my history, as sexual favors had guaranteed me companionship with my brother and his friends. In order to not be alone or abandoned, I yielded my body. Doing the same with you would be entirely consistent with the conditioning I had had about sex and boys: "sex equals companionship."

When I first allowed myself to face this part of our history, I didn't even assign you any blame. I'd pretty much initiated the genital contact in the incident, so I figured it was my fault.

Anyway, *when* it happened is less important than the fact that it happened *before we even knew one another*. What it confirmed to me was my fear that guys were all the same, that their penises ruled them. How beautiful it would've been if you'd foiled my attempts to pleasure you sexually. How different our lives would've been if you'd said something like, "Jade, sexuality is a beautiful thing. It's precious and magical and holy and sacred, and I'm tempted to take you up on your offer right now. But that would compromise my masculinity and my leadership in our relationship, which is still very young, and it would tarnish the most tender and vulnerable part of you. It's not that I don't want you, because I do, and if you're to share your body with me someday when we really know each other and have pledged our lives to one another, I'll be proud to have protected you from my own capacity to overpower you and your beauty. Until then, I want to get to know you—Jade. Who are you, what makes you sad, angry, afraid, joyful, or passionate? What makes you laugh, cry, and ache? How did you become who you are? How do you hide from relationship, and how do you express love? What do you want your life to amount to and why? I want to hold out for your body until I know and love your soul. For now, allow me to just hold you and comfort you while you mourn the loss of your father."

I realize that these are words that neither one of us could've even imagined at the time. But the problem is that you didn't value sexuality, either yours or mine, any more than I did, and the rest of our dating life included a great deal of sexual play and being in situation after situation where I had to say "no" to your sexual advances. That was a painfully familiar position for me to be in. During the sexual abuse years, I had no voice with which to say "no," because I was so desperate for relationship. Finally, when I did say "no," I got what I'd feared all along: abandonment. The phrase with which I left Ryan, "I can't do this anymore," is one that tumbled out of my mouth through gut wrenching sobs not too long ago, when I stopped fending it off in regards to our relationship, the dynamics of which leave me feeling like I've participated in my own exploitation. I finally allowed myself to connect with the unthinkable: you, too, had used me. Chip, you've exploited me for my body, for my intellect, for my abilities, for the parts of my personality that you've found useful, for my income earning potential. You, too, have made an object out of me.

We not only disagree on the timing of our first sexual experience, we also disagree on when I first told you that I'd already been sexual with boys. (In our ignorance, we didn't call it sexual abuse back then.) You say that I didn't tell you about my sexual abuse history until the summer before we got married. In reality, I told you about it very early in our relationship, because I remember going into my dorm room after you berated me about it. I remember being afraid of how you would respond, but I felt that you should know the truth if you were going to be involved with me. Your response left me feeling deeply ashamed and numb. That's when all the fighting began, and it was the subject of the intense fighting we had the summer before we got married. It seems that it has become the issue that has discolored and deformed our entire relationship. The fighting has continued ever since (with a shift to a lower intensity and frequency when I began my spiritual journey about eleven years ago), and I'd guess that many of our fights over little things were really masking resentments that go back to this original issue, as well as to the rejection I felt from you at that time. In all fairness, although I've never berated you for your sexual involvement with girls prior to our relationship, I've carried distrust of you because of the nature of those relationships. So I'm sure that our fighting was also motivated by my unconscious misgivings about that.

The fighting we did before we got married continued afterward, and during one of these fights just three months into marriage, you said that you'd rather have sex with any one of the women on TV than with me. This didn't draw me to you sexually. When I'd comment about your checking out other women in my presence, you'd get furious and defensive. You've told me that the romance left our relationship for you very early in our marriage, if not before. And just recently, you said that you're not attracted to me. Comments like those repel me from you, they don't compel me to you, sexually or otherwise. They haven't made me dislike *you*, however; instead, they've drawn me to dislike *myself*. We haven't been sexual very often over the years because I can't trust, knowing how you really feel about me, that you'll care for my most precious and delicate possession: my sexuality and my femininity. The biting comments that you've made about my body and my personality, the way you've handled sex between us, and the lack of tenderness you've shown me over the years have left me feeling rejected and in danger. These things also leave me wondering, "If Chip was so repulsed by me, why did he ever seek me out for sex? If that's how he felt, he must have only wanted sex to satisfy himself, not to make love to me." And that's exactly how sex has felt. How could I feel safe having sex with you, knowing how you really felt deep down? My low interest in sex wasn't a rejection of you, but a playing out of the rejection I felt coming from you. You could leave this relationship feeling desirable; I, on the other hand, feel undesirable. I'm afraid that others would find my body and my personality repulsive.

You've said that there were many times when I wasn't present during our sexual encounters. I admit that this is true. Given my history of sexual abuse as a child, this would make sense. I'm not making excuses for it; I'm simply acknowledging the truth of my fear of being used and my need to protect myself from further harm. I have to add to that mix, however, that you didn't go out of your way to ensure my sexual safety and comfort. You, too, have wounded me sexually. Your comments and your interest in sex despite our lack of emotional intimacy showed that you weren't a safe person to have sex with. I admit that I was often sexual with you even when I didn't feel safe, so as not to lose you. That was a very old pattern, as I'd given sexual favors many, many times so that I wouldn't be alone or abandoned. I stopped that pattern a year and a half ago, and when I did, all you talked about for months afterwards was how angry you were that we weren't having sex. You weren't bothered by our lack of intimacy, just by our lack of sex. Now that I'm living less and less by my old, codependent scripts, I'll likely lose you and your companionship, just like I lost the companionship of my brother and his friends when I finally got up the courage to end the abuse. The evidence seems to be screaming that you, too, were using me for sex all these years. It's a logical conclusion based on the data.

Given your sexual compulsion issues, Chip, you weren't present with me sexually, either. Your fantasy life either made you dissatisfied with me or gave you a way to stay engaged when you were disgusted with me or with my body. Perhaps this wasn't always true, but it was certainly true much more often than not. This hasn't compelled me to you. Sexual issues have been some of our biggest points of contention. Before we got married, I said to myself, "If we have issues that we need counseling about, I hope it won't be sex. I don't think I could handle talking about sex." Funny that I worried about that even before we got married. And then when sex became one of our biggest problems, I tried to ignore it until I could no longer pretend that the "elephant in the room" was something else. I've acknowledged this, and I am willing to accept that I have deeply failed you, sexually and otherwise. You aren't willing to do the same.

At one point when I was begging for us to go to counseling, you said that counseling was my god, and you refused to go. You've resented me for doing what we needed to do to get some honesty in this relationship, and you want to control why we break up. "If we break up," you said, "it won't be because of sexual issues." Too late. You can't just make problems go away by saying they don't exist. You have to deal with the problems at hand, and that's what you've refused to do. You say you have compassion for me, and based on the first page of your "Knight's Response" to my fables, I do believe you're sorrowful that I was hurt by my dad and by my brother. However, you stopped writing the knight's response right at the point when you would've had to account for your harm of the princess.

I've never accused you of conscious harm because I know that you have a good heart. I have a good heart, too, but even with my good heart, I've done some very shameful and harmful things out of unconscious motivations, as you can tell by my confession that opened this letter. Shame draws people to do things that are contrary to their natural personalities. The unconscious, shame-based processes in unhealthy people like you and me even compel their choice of spouse, and it's really embarrassing somewhere down the line when you put it all together. At least it has been for me, but I have to accept the data, no matter how ugly it reveals me to be.

You've reached conclusions about yourself *despite* the data, instead of allowing the data to inform you about possible unconscious motivations that may not paint you in such a pleasant light. For example, when you were having sex with people before we met, you were hardly considerate of those women all the time. In my mind, this isn't enough evidence to conclude that you aren't goodhearted. Instead, it's evidence to me that you were attaching some meaning to sex that was never meant to be attached to it. Perhaps you thought that "if someone will have sex with me, I must not be unlovable," "sex equals love, intimacy, or connection," or that "sex will make me alive." I don't know exactly what motivated you to have sex without intimacy, but these are the kinds of unconscious messages about sex that motivate people who don't understand true intimacy. These misunderstandings don't make people bad, but they do lead them to make hurtful choices. You aren't even willing to consider the possibility, despite the evidence, that your motives in wanting to be sexually involved with me before we were ever truly intimate suggests that your view of sexuality wasn't healthy. And your disregard of the evidence tells me that you'd rather reconstruct your own history than deal with the history that is recorded in my journal, which validates the history that I know in my heart.

While sex has been a constant thorn for us, our sexual issues merely scream that there are issues outside the bedroom that divide us. For example, your childhood lack of confidence and sense of inadequacy has led you to control and manipulate your world, including me, to make sure you never had a problem you couldn't handle. Hence, your compulsive need for order. I'm a very neat person, but you'd never know it by the way you've criticized me and insisted that I'm messy. I'm weary of being disapproved and judged, and I'll no longer protect you from the messiness of life. I've lived with your criticism, your judgment, your control, your rejection, your disdain, because I didn't live up to the image to which you want me to conform. Remember when you said that going to your mom's house as a teenager felt oppressive? That's what it's felt like for me in our own home. I've often dreaded coming home from work or school, wondering what would be wrong with me or my things, or if I had or hadn't done something. You've tried to control how I drive, where and how I park, what I do with my mail, what I look like, how I dress, whether or not and how I exercise, whether I use nose drops to clear my nose so that I can sleep or not, how I spend my time and my money, what I like to do for recreation, how much I get paid, how I run my business, my personality, my car. I've felt bullied, micromanaged, and loathed, and I've had to edit myself to keep your world as comfortable and compulsively neat as possible, so as to avoid your criticism. I don't know what image you're trying to mold me into, and I don't quite know why you're doing it, though I do have my theories; I only know that I can't be whatever image that is. I'm either too much or not enough, and I can't live like that.

You assume the worst about people's motives, and I'm no exception. If I'm such an untrustworthy person, why would you want to be in relationship with me, anyway? The truth is that I've been the most trustworthy person you know. I've protected you when I should have exposed you, longed for your healing and wholeness, and tried to encourage you to pursue it. You, however, have often questioned my healing process, mocked how committed I am to it, criticized it, and tried to sabotage it. I can no longer live with your coldness toward me, your refusal to take responsibility for hurting me, and your inability to feel what it's been like for me to be hurt by you. Now that I have friends who enjoy me, who seek me out, who are generous toward me, and who value me, I realize that I've been living in a desert for the last seventeen years. With these friends, I don't have to fight to be seen; I don't have interactions with them that leave me in need of counseling; I don't wish that I could escape from their presence; I don't fear that I'll be criticized; I don't wonder if they'll love me, even when they see my darkness; I can be honest with them, and I don't have to explain to them over and over again how they've hurt me; they can come to me with criticism or hurts that I've inflicted, knowing that I'll seek to understand and to make amends. I have people in my life with whom I can be completely honest, and I know that they won't think less of me; I don't spend hours in the middle of the night racked with sobbing, feeling like I'd rather die or be alone than to have to fight to be seen in relationship with them; my friends take responsibility for their harm of people, including me, and they don't try to defend themselves in order to maintain a false image of themselves.

This is the opposite of how I feel with you, and it's taken its toll. I'm more damaged now than I was before being with you. I can't imagine being in a relationship with another man because I feel like no one would be able to have anything but disgust for me or my body. I resent that you've caused this insecurity. I feel like I'm too much to handle and that my intellect, motivation, energy, and wonder at life are too threatening for a man, so I'm facing a life of being alone. I think, deep down, that these are lies that are the residue of being in relationship with you, but I can't be sure, so at this point, I'd rather live alone than risk trusting again. You've left me feeling like I'm so fragile and damaged that others will be poisoned in relationship with me, because I'll require that they never "bruise" me in ways I've been "bruised" before. You've not only bruised me in ways that I've been bruised before, but you've left your own, brand new wounds. The tragedy is that you don't take responsibility for either kind, and I've no energy left to try to explain what your responsibility is (which was not my job to begin with). My trying to fix you and us, has been governing me in relationship with you, and I need to be willing to surrender it all.

I've told you about the dream I had in which I was in a huge dining room that was kind of dark and had only one piece of furniture in it: a plain dining room table with a plain, white table cloth, on which sat an ornate vase. As I looked at the vase, a breeze rushed into the room and caught it, sending it careening toward the floor. In order to save this delicate vase, I rushed to keep it from hitting the floor. As I did so, I either heard a voice or sensed it—whether within me or from outside of me, I don't know—but the voice said, over and over, "Let it fall. Let it fall. Let it fall." So I let the vase fall to the floor, and it shattered into little pieces. That's when I woke up, and I knew that I had to let fall my relationship that I was trying so hard to save. I've been trying to make it work, trying to control what I cannot control. I can only be responsible for myself, and I have to release you to be responsible for yourself. It has done you no favors for me to act as if I'm the only problem, or even the biggest problem, in our relationship. People tend to marry those who are at the same level as they are in terms of woundedness. That implies that you came into the marriage just as wounded as I did, and I cannot *make* you heal and become whole.

Another issue that has divided us is that you spend a great deal of time second guessing yourself and what people think of you, trying to avoid true intimacy with me and with other people. You've isolated yourself from people over the years so that you now have virtually no friends. I've gone along with this because I didn't want to rock the boat or insist that we have people over if you weren't comfortable. You want to *have* pursuers but you don't want to *be* one. You say that you want true relationship, but when people pursue you, you go out of your way to avoid real relationship or to sabotage it. You pay lip service to desiring intimacy, such as described in the Parker Palmer book you recommended, *To Know as We Are Known*, but you do the opposite of what the book describes. Instead of moving toward the messiness of real relationship with the Motemann's, for example, you backed away as soon as you felt like they weren't accepting you because of their constructive feedback. You assume that people are malicious, and you do everything possible to avoid what you interpret as their rejection. You're terrified that people won't like you if they think you have a dark side, so you refuse to take responsibility for your harm of people. You said you were "done with Gary" when he has only tried to welcome and include you, such as when he asked you to join him on a spiritual retreat, a trip that ten other men would have loved to have taken with him. If he hurt you in any way, you needed to address it with him, rather than just writing him off. But blaming others for your own issues is your typical mode of operation. For example, because you haven't been transformed by your counseling experience, you blame Kyle, instead of accepting your healing process as your own responsibility.

It's discouraging that you haven't been honest with Kyle about your experience of him and of counseling. You've complained over and over about how you don't know what this process is all about, and you don't know if it's doing any good. You've expressed to me feeling misunderstood by Kyle and have reported misunderstanding him. When I suggest that you mention these kinds of things to him, you refuse, because you don't want Kyle to think less of you. Because you haven't leveled with him on your own, I'm in the position to "tell on you" because your lack of forthrightness clouds the truth of what's going on between us. The other day, you said that your impression of Kyle is that he wants couples to talk about their problems so that they can get in bed together. I wish it were that simple, but real relationships are much more complex than that. If you don't want messy, you'll have to stick with false intimacy, either with a real person who doesn't desire true intimacy or with an image in a picture or fantasy. You've avoided dealing directly with your sexual compulsivity, the roots of which continue to be your contribution, however unintentionally and unconsciously, to our failure in relationship.

Speaking of unconscious motivations, we've done a lot of fighting over the years that I suspect was driven by our unresolved and unconscious inner conflicts. One thing about which we've often fought is your incessant dreaming. Dreaming about things that you never intend to do, your discontent, and your lack of gratitude for the blessings we have leaves me feeling unnoticed, unknown, and unappreciated. I don't feel treasured or cherished. I feel incidental, an intrusion in your life, something to be shifted here and there, so that I can be used or shelved as needed. You've mostly worked part time in our relationship, and very little of your leisure time has been spent thinking about me or considering ways to foster relationship between us. This job has been left up to me, and I resign that position. The time that you've had over the years to think usually has been spent constantly worrying about things that will likely never happen, and I've come to believe that you'll never be able to focus on us—something that *did* happen. If you'd spent as much energy working on our healing and yours as you do on worrying, we'd be in a much better place than we are.

Another issue that has distanced me from you is your divided loyalty. Though I don't know exactly with whom or with what I've been competing for your heart, I do know what it has felt like to be in this competition. I've felt alone when you haven't been able to feel my pain, when you've defended others against me, and when you haven't protected my heart or my interests.

I'll no longer compete with whomever and whatever I've been competing for your heart. I'll no longer play a *role* in your life. I haven't been able to be your lover because you haven't been able to sustain any kind of vulnerability with me. I long to be intimate, emotionally and sexually, with someone who knows and loves who he is (and who I am), and who will share his heart with me. I know that you're in the process of discovering who you are, and I know that this process is a long and arduous one. I wish you the best in it. But I can't be satisfied with only part of you. I won't share you with your parents, with old girlfriends, with old memories or with fantasies, airbrushed images, objects, or television. I can't live with your divided loyalty, a loyalty to a way of being that comes from a wounded past. I can't live in a relationship that isn't exclusive. I may be available when you've resolved your loyalty issues, but I can't be sure.

One of the deepest divisions and deepest heartaches for me has been that when I tell you of my pain, you look at me blankly and confused. I know in those moments that we're oceans apart, and I've come to believe that we'll never be walking the same path. It's the same feeling I get when I realize that my own family members don't get me, don't know how to love me, and don't try. You asked me recently how I can feel so deeply for you, and I didn't understand that question. I responded, "How could I not? I care about you, Chip, and that means to me that I can empathize with your suffering." Because you haven't empathized with the suffering you've caused me suggests that you don't care about me and can't look at the world through my eyes. Our relationship has failed, in part, because of your inability to enter my world. If you'd been able to identify on the heart level with what it's been like to be used, and to be used by you, we might've had a future together.

For example, you said recently that if you made me cry, you always felt really bad and tried to give me a hug. This just isn't true. Because you've been so insensitive to my tears, I no longer even cry them around you. I've shed most of my tears, and there have been torrents of them, in private, because with you they're only met with resistance and defense. For example, when I came home from the EMDR 2 training, you refused to help me with a simple chore, and when I burst into tears of overwhelm and exhaustion, you were cold toward me. That was more typical of your response to my tears about your harm of me. You can usually handle my tears about other people, but when it comes to how *you* have hurt me, how *your family* has hurt me, and very recently how *my own family* has hurt me, you only get defensive.

When you describe your remorse in Moab over hurting me, you forget that before you went to church to talk to the elders, you turned your back on me and walked out while I was sobbing my guts out on the bed. It shouldn't take this kind of pain to get you to see me, and it's just not true that you embrace me when I cry over the way you've hurt me. If that were true, we wouldn't be in counseling today. The truth is that I've wept in the closet, in the shower, in my bed in the middle of the night, at work, in Target. These are tears that you don't see, and I leave your presence if I have to cry over something painful in our relationship, because you don't have compassion on my pain if you feel that it's about you or about someone in our families. When I do address how you've hurt me, you get angry or defensive and say, "How long do I have to be saddled with the voids left by Jade's history?" Because you don't address the voids left by your own history, you remain more loyal to your wounded past than to me, and this has divided us.

I used to envision what it would be like for us to move through a healing process and come out whole and together on the other side, and I've shared that vision with you. The dream had a really great ending. However, I can no longer imagine that "working through" is possible for us. I've lost my vision.

I'm weary of being the "bigger man," or the stronger one, in the relationship. Until now, you've been content to leave the healing to me, as if I were the only problem. But I'll no longer believe that lie, a lie that you've endorsed, because there's too much evidence to the contrary. Good for you for pursuing your own healing at this point, even though I had to put our relationship up as collateral in order for you to do so. I wish you the best in it. I've longed for you to be the leader of the healing between us, but since you haven't been, I hope that you'll give everything you have to heal on your own.

Appendix C 305

I mentioned earlier that I could define clearly who I am so that you can decide for yourself if you want to be in relationship with me—not just in relationship, but in relationship *with me*. So here's who I am. I'm a curious combination of intelligence and play, philosophy and frivolity, beauty and sweat, humor and solemnity. I enjoy words and word play, and I live in wonder of being alive. Almost every day, I find myself in awe of something or someone, and my heart swells with gratitude for being alive and for being on this spiritual journey. I love color and whimsy and laughter. I also love tears and grief and pain and anger . . . whatever emotion is appropriate for the situation. I love being human. I feel deeply, and I think deeply. I'm intrigued by theology and ideas and the size of the universe. I've thought a lot about many things, and I've arrived at an opinion on many topics. I see the big categories of life, like relationships and love, in much simpler terms than I used to, but I find that the living of simple concepts is much more complex than I ever imagined. I love paradox, metaphor, and the story of Jesus. I cry over commercials, movies, and worship songs. I pray myself to sleep at night, and I cry a lot then, too. I haven't read my Bible in I don't know how long, and my relationship with God is stronger than it's ever been. I love animals, and when there's a natural disaster, I have more empathy for them than I do for people. I grieve for the underprivileged, the victim, the fatherless, and the widow. I long for justice, I love mercy, and I deeply desire to walk humbly with God. I love God so much that I've laid down my deepest longings and dreams at his feet, and he loves me so much that he's created and granted me a dream that's bigger than I could've ever imagined.

I love running, hiking, reading, and sleeping under the stars. I love to try exotic ethnic foods, and I love feeling out of control on roller coasters. I get a big kick out of people's clumsiness, especially my own, which is why I dissolve in tears and laughter when I watch America's Funniest Videos. I hate playing Risk, what I call "the ultimate game of betrayal," but I love playing cards and non-conquest board games with friends. I enjoy having people over for a meal and community—good food and good conversation gives life to me. I'm a wild and strong woman, who is really easy to tame, if you understand what makes my heart beat. I have charisma and charm, I'm inviting and captivating, and most people like me as soon as they meet me.

I'm self-motivated, highly achieving, intuitive, empathic, emotionally and mentally intelligent, introspective, and deeply spiritual. I love people, especially one-on-one or in very small groups; their stories fascinate me. I long to love well, and I know that to do so is an art that I'm just beginning to learn. It takes a great deal of emotional effort to learn to be human and to love well; the learning curve is huge. But I have a tenacity that keeps me in this learning process no matter how hard it is. I'm a survivor of emotional, spiritual, sexual, and (vicarious) physical abuse, and I live with those wounds. They're healing well, and the pain of them is now being redeemed in the lives of others. This leaves me in wonder.

I also live with sorrow over the pain that I've sewn into your life and into the lives of many others by my own unresolved pain. My heart is soft toward your pain, and I've longed for your heart to be soft towards mine. I've also longed for you to find out who you are, and to share yourself with me. I've longed for you to lead us into the future with both strength and tenderness, with non-cocky confidence, and with masculine strength and protection. I've longed to share camaraderie with you in dealing with our past wounds, before and after we met one another. I've longed to admire you because you aren't afraid of life, or of an honest appraisal of past and present hurt, including the pain of your family of origin, the pain you've caused me, and the pain I've caused you. I've longed to admire you because you know what you want, and you pursue it; because you can articulate your feelings; because you honor and fight to protect my heart and the hearts of others who've been hurt; because you understand and value the unique gifts of masculinity and femininity; because you enjoy showing affection in many different ways; because you're secure in who you are; because you're sorrowful in your heart about how you've used me; because you grieve for me about how that has felt for me; because you treat sex as a holy experience between two image-bearing human beings in a covenantal personal encounter with one another; because you take ownership of your issues; because you show your appreciation for the possessions that God has given us. I've longed to work through our stuff so that we could minister together and bring healing to others who've been bonded to trauma. I've wanted to believe in that miraculous possibility, but I don't know if that's healthy or not, because I don't know if it's realistic to hope that people with our particular differences can be in love and at peace with one another.

That describes some of my internal world. As for the external, my body, I have three tattoos that are very meaningful to me because they represent different aspects of my personality. I have deep, expressive blue eyes, an easy smile, plum-colored hair, a softball player's body, including about twenty pounds of extra fat that no longer responds to "dieting" like it used to (a word I no longer use to refer to food manipulation) or to exercise (which I do regularly), and I have a passion for jogging (which I used to call running) that I don't think I'll ever shake . . . nor do I want to. My body is in better shape today than it will be tomorrow and every day after that for the rest of my life.

With that said, I have to acknowledge that I can be the opposite of all my good qualities. I can push people away by my defensiveness, my strong opinions, and my insecure pride. I've often used food, education, and books to numb my pain and to withdraw into hiding. I violate relationship in ways that only people who are in relationship with me know, and I need to be called on my relational failures by people who love me, people who are both strong and tender, people who believe in what I can be, and who don't allow me to settle for what I am. I'm terrified of poverty, and to fend it off, I've worked too many hours, and I've bought cheap things. I want to be taken care of, but I want to have control over whether I'm poor or not. Having to be in control is one of my biggest hang-ups, and I'm guessing that it's the most significant way that I violate relationship. I try to be tough, even though I'm naturally tender-hearted. I try to be nice, and I have to remind myself that, often times, being nice has little to do with being kind. I try to be competent, so that I don't need anyone, and I find myself alone when I most need other people. I try not to be a burden to anyone and find that people can't get close to me because I resist their help and their care. Because I mistrust people who offer me kindness, I sometimes misinterpret their gestures of blessing. It's hard for me to believe that anyone would desire to sacrifice for me, so I make sure that they're never in a position to do so, robbing them of opportunities to care for me, and robbing me of opportunities to feel cared for. I avoid idleness and unproductive moments, because the fear of being considered lazy holds me in bondage. I'm not sure exactly where this panic comes from, but it's no fun for people who desire to relax in relationship with me. (I'm glad to say, however, that I'm making progress on these things as my relationships with friends bring healing to my heart.)

I'm still sexually broken, but I don't know how badly. I think I'll have to be in a sexual relationship to find that out for sure, but I know that I still don't trust you in that area, nor do I feel that it's safe to do so because of your as yet unresolved sexual issues. I've had a hard time trusting myself, as well, so I've probably seemed either indecisive or dogmatic at times, and this must've been maddening to live with. I can be critical of others and the world when I'm feeling insecure or frustrated in relationship. My way with words at these times can be biting, ugly, belittling, and cruel. I'm not proud of these things, and I don't want them to be a part of my life. You, probably more than anyone, have felt how I violate relationship.

That's me. Take me or leave me . . . literally. If we're honest with ourselves, I have to admit that you made this choice a long time ago, and I'm just now bringing it into the light. You've made it clear by action, by inaction, by words, and lack of words, that you aren't attracted to me and that you don't want me. If you want something badly enough, you do everything you can to get it or to keep it, even if it makes you look foolish. Guys do pretty wild "mating dances" to attract the ones they love, both before and after marriage. Your passivity in regards to nurturing our relationship has been a silent scream that you don't want me, and I'm only now allowing myself to hear what you *haven't* said or done. You've pursued me sexually, but not relationally, and this has been deeply painful. You've also explicitly stated your lack of desire for me. I'll no longer try to make you love me because this is an impossible task. It's too demeaning and wearisome to have to fight to be cared for, and I can't *make* you care for me.

I've wondered if something was wrong with me that made it so hard for you to care for me, but I'll no longer blame myself for what is your responsibility. Whether you own your responsibility for hurting me or whether you feel sorry for hurting me or not, you deserve to know from me *how* you've hurt me, just as I appreciated knowing from your own lips how deeply I'd hurt you with my own divided loyalty, as I was more loyal to my work than to you.

However, I broke my loyalties to my wounded past when, in June 2004, I severed all historical loyalties to anyone and anything but you. I put all my eggs in one basket, which was a great risk, since there was nothing in our relationship that would assure me that I'd end up with you. But I had to lay it all down and finally "leave home" emotionally if I ever wanted to be able to truthfully say that I did everything in my power to give you my heart. Since then, my heart has been fully yours, if you wanted it, but you haven't accepted my invitations to true intimacy. Your loyalty to me remains divided. You're more loyal to a way of being that comes from your wounded past and the people in it than you are to me and to the possibility of having true relationship. A marriage covenant must be an exclusive relationship, a quality that hasn't characterized our relationship. I can no longer be sexually intimate if I'm not emotionally intimate with my partner, and this isn't asking too much.

I've longed for you to know who you are, and to be in a relationship where you can share intimately, but it seems that you don't want to risk what it takes to be intimately known. You don't pursue it. Your actions show that you can't be (or simply don't want to be) what I long for in an intimate partnership, and our relationship needs to be redefined. From my viewpoint, to love each other well is to insist that we find healing and wholeness and to be more committed to the truth and to each other and to each other's growth than to a treaty that was false from the beginning. Given that neither of us was aware of the forces that would be against our union, agreeing to be marriage partners was like the leaders of two warring countries agreeing to peace when neither has the power to really pull it off. I regret that neither of us insisted on figuring this out many years ago, because we might've been able to save what seems irreparable to me now.

I do hope that this process has helped to clarify what went wrong between us, from my perspective. I didn't want to hurt you by telling it, but I do feel that it was important to explain one last time the harm that you've done to me, because you've often said, "I just don't get it. You haven't explained it well enough." I'm not inarticulate, and no one else in my life has such a hard time understanding me, but at least now it's down in black and white, and you've heard it from my own lips. Perhaps I'm still trying too hard to elucidate everything clearly, which may explain the length and redundancy of this letter.

Please know that it gives me no joy to call you on these failures because I know how sensitive you are to criticism; this letter will likely feel like rejection, even though it's only meant to bring clarity and to give you the bill that you've racked up over the years. I've come to believe that you won't change in relationship to me. I no longer believe that the eroded trust can be repaired. This is sad because *trust is established by repair of its violation*. In other words, you don't have to be perfect in a relationship, you just have to be willing to acknowledge and feel sorrow for when you aren't.

I wish I could continue to accept all the blame for our issues, because that would keep me in control. But it wouldn't serve the truth.

Although you've had little intimacy in your life, I'm probably the one person on this earth who knows you best, and I hate to feed your mistrust of people by calling you on the ways you've harmed me. You've wanted to avoid being accused, and I've refrained from doing so in order to keep you from feeling bad about yourself, which I now realize was a doomed effort, because you already feel bad about yourself, and nothing and no one seems to be able to convince you of your value and uniqueness. But I can no longer protect you from your own responsibilities, and I'm sorry for having tried to do so all these years. I'm sure that it's only added to your lack of motivation to take responsibility for your life, and this hasn't been kind to you at all. I thought that, by not telling you about these things and trying instead to encourage you all the time, I might be able to fill up the voids in your life created almost forty years ago. How presumptuous and misguided of me. This has allowed you to avoid taking responsibility for the emotional damage you brought into the marriage and for your healing from it, and because you haven't done this without my insistence, it's clear that you refuse to own your own load of baggage.

In a nutshell, I don't believe that I've been asking too much; I've certainly not been asking more of you than I've required of me. All I've wanted is that it matter to you when you hurt me, particularly when old wounds are involved. I've needed you to take full responsibility for your life—for your emotional damage and for your harm of me—from your heart, and you haven't done so. You think that if you injure an old wound, you're not responsible for the hurt. I, on the other hand, feel that wounding someone in an old injury requires a person to own a *larger* portion of damage, such as when I neglected you in favor of work, just like your Dad did. This injury would've been bad enough if it had been a wound that I'd created on my own. It was doubly bad, however, that you'd already been wounded like that, and I was kicking you in the old injury. When I connected with how deeply I'd wounded you in this familiar way, I wept like a baby, and I immediately set out to change my behavior. My heart had been broken on your behalf, and I grieved for the harm I'd inflicted upon you for sixteen years. Remember the scar on my leg from an old injury that still stings like the dickens whenever it gets bumped because the nerves are still exposed? When someone bumps it and I wince in pain, they feel especially bad that they've hurt something that's already vulnerable. It's the same with emotional pain: it's natural to feel even worse for inflicting harm on what's already raw.

I've needed you to take responsibility for the gashes that you created in my heart, especially the ones that inflicted harm on already painful places, but you've refused to. I've also needed to be enjoyed for who I am, but you've mostly criticized me, over and over again. I've needed you to show appreciation for the things I do or bring to the relationship, but you've mostly shown either that you feel entitled to them or that you disdain them. I've longed to be known, approved, accepted, liked, and enjoyed. Though I've longed for it, I don't need it to be whole. I'm a whole person without you—I don't need someone to complete me. I *desire* to be in an emotionally and sexually intimate relationship, but only with someone who is living into and out of who he is, and only with someone who wants that for me. I've needed you to regard me with reverence and tenderness as a fellow creation, one who bears the feminine image of God, and you haven't done so. Remember when Uzzah touched the Ark of the Covenant and was immediately struck down? Clearly, we're not to treat sacred things with irreverence. You haven't regarded me as a sacred being, and you haven't treated me with reverence. I've needed you to be strong and lead us into healing, but you haven't stepped up to the plate. Your passivity and your avoidance have been every bit as damaging to our relationship as the residual effects of my having been sexually abused.

I've needed you to deal with your own wounds so that they don't continue to harm us, but you haven't decided that our relationship was more important than everything else. I've hoped that our work with Kyle would help us beat the odds, but I'm afraid that we waited too long to deal with our wounds, and gangrene has set in. I've hoped to see redemption and reconciliation in our story so that we could live together in covenant relationship, and so that we could offer hope of reconciliation to those who are trauma bound as we've been. But I guess I'll have to settle for being able to relate to the grief of those who haven't succeeded in dealing with old issues so as to be able to strike up a true covenantal bond.

I know that you, too, will walk away from this relationship deeply hurt, by the wounds I've inflicted upon you. I'm so sorry, Chip, that we weren't able to repair the damage we created together, and I'm sorry that you, too, will take these wounds into your future relationships. I once had a client who showed me a scar on her arm that her husband had inflicted when he was angry with her. When I saw the scar, I wept. "This woman is going to live the rest of her life with that scar on her arm," I thought, "a reminder that someone valued her so little that he thought it acceptable to mark her body." I'm afraid this is what we've done to each other, but our scars are on our hearts. We haven't born well the weight of one another's glory, and we've violated the image of God in each other in many ways, not the least of which I've illustrated for you in the fables that I wrote and shared with you. Because of that violence, our hearts will limp on with our brokenness into future relationships.

This is a tragedy, but it seems to me that we need to cut our losses before we incur and inflict more. If someone can convince me that splitting up at this point is a big mistake, I might reconsider, but it seems like the most merciful thing we can do at this point. Something shifted in me when I read the more than seventeen years of journal entries detailing the pain and problems in our relationship. Our relationship has been suffering since before we were married, and the problems we have now are the same ones we had then; we haven't resolved even one issue.

Having stayed together for seventeen years, I don't feel that splitting up at this point is a rash decision. However, in North Carolina, people have to wait a year after filing divorce papers to actually finalize them. I'm willing to agree to the waiting period, unless you'd prefer not to wait that long. At this point, it does seem to me that we'd only be prolonging the inevitable, but if we do decide to give it a year, we need to live in separate residences in order to be free enough to clearly evaluate the decision.

Because I've lived too often by the axiom that "some things are better left unsaid," it may seem by this letter that there was nothing good in the relationship. This isn't true, and I'm thankful for some good gifts that I'll always have from you. I'm thankful for your teaching me to be financially wise; I'd probably be in credit card debt just like my mom if it weren't for you. I've also learned from you how to relax and how important vacations are. We've been to some really cool places and have seen some of God's great handiwork that I'd never have known was out there if it weren't for you. Basically, you've taught me to be more intentional with my resources, both financial and physical. We've been through hundreds of school assignments together, and I'm grateful for your support and sacrifices when my nose was lost between the pages of a book or my fingers were pecking away on a paper.

We've grown as individuals more in the last three years than we have probably in our entire lives. The growing pains have been hard, but I'm enormously proud of both of us. Our hard work has resulted in three graduations for me during our seventeen-year history and another graduation for you. Thank you for being there for me at those graduations. We've weathered some intense storms, not the least of which was eight years of infertility. I've never experienced such deep pain and sorrow and confusion in all my life, and I'm thankful for every moment you dug deep within yourself to offer me comfort when all seemed dark and dismal. (I guess the greatest consolation in our failed attempts to have children is that we're not dragging innocent, little people through this crisis, and I'm thankful for that.) I'm also thankful that you have a deep and intimate relationship with God, a relationship that's growing deeper with your recent reading of books from the mystics. It gives me comfort to know that as difficult as it is for you to be close with people, you do have an intimate relationship with God. I'm glad that you'll never be completely alone, even if you decide to remain isolated or to avoid true intimacy with people. I do wish your inner healing had spread to our relationship, but you seem only to be getting harder toward me, even as you've become a bit more compassionate toward others.

I'm proud of you, Chip, for what you're doing in your business; it's a business that seems to fit you well, and I hope that you can eventually put to rest all the worrying you do that your employees will quit and leave you destitute. I hope that you can marvel at what you're creating so that you can simply enjoy the entrepreneurial spirit that's built into you.

I've been both enriched and wounded by our relationship. I only wish the balance of those two had been different.

With deep sorrow,
Jade

Appendix D

The Decalogue (Ten Commandments) of Honest Appraisal and Personal Responsibility

1. *Take personal ownership of anything and everything that you've contributed to the breakdown of the relationship.* Don't demand that your spouse take ownership of his or her contribution in order for you to take ownership of yours. This process may require the help of a counselor, pastor, or honest friend who isn't afraid to help you identify your own contribution to the marital breakdown, but who recognizes that marital breakdown takes two.

2. *Commit not to engage in arguments, but to simply collect data and come to reasonable conclusions based on the behavior you witness.* Use this time to collect data about yourself and your own harmful style of relating, as well as about your spouse and about his or her style of relating. Use your journal, prayer, meditation, and other soul-searching techniques to find comfort as you absorb the criticism, contempt, entitlement, dependence, avoidance, passivity, denial, insensitivity, rejection, passive aggression, defensiveness, stonewalling, blame-shifting, incessant worry, negativity, lack of compassion, lies, disregard, inattention, carelessness, distance, coldness, indifference, obsessions, or whatever other attitudes or behaviors are toxic in the relationship. Again, third party help is often invaluable here. Absorbing the pain of the relationship isn't intended to be permanent, but it is necessary for the evaluation period. Who knows, your spouse may even respond positively to the change in your demeanor. If not, I must warn you that he or she may become even harder toward you, because we tend to become either softer or harder; we don't remain neutral.

3. *Refuse to cover your hurt with anger (or your anger with hurt), and stop holding your partner responsible for your emotions.* Commit to naming what is true (my spouse is being contemptuous, defensive, critical, insensitive, and I'm tempted to be passive aggressive toward him) with regard to the dynamics of the relationship, and allow yourself to feel whatever emotions are appropriate for every situation. (If you typically hide your hurt behind anger, allow yourself to feel hurt. If you typically hide your anger behind hurt, allow yourself to feel angry.) This is simply being honest about your pain, allowing yourself to feel your raw emotions.

4. *Refuse to dump your hurt or your anger with your partner onto others.* You've probably gotten into the habit of dumping your frustration with your spouse onto your friends who offer you sympathy and compassion. If you deny yourself a forum to receive this sympathy, you'll come face to face with your pain. Once you can no longer deny it, you'll have to deal with it instead of deflect it.

5. *Refuse to try to control your partner's healing process.* In order to love the other person well, you have to let her succeed or fail on her own. Completely let go of your over-functioning, your avoidance, or whatever your typical mode of operating in the relationship is. This principle requires that you relinquish any control, overt or covert, that you have over your spouse. You have to let go and allow the other to freely choose whether or not to be in relationship with you.

6. *Refuse to believe the lie that either you or your spouse is the only one contributing to the breakdown of the relationship.* You're probably triggering each other. Even the most innocent party will be able to identify some contribution to the dysfunctional dynamic. Evading the issues, avoiding one's own pain, spiritualizing, enabling, and trying to be the savior are some of the toxic contributions of seemingly innocent parties.

7. *When the other person's behavior doesn't match his or her words, commit to reading and believing the behavior, no matter how painful the truth might be.* When we have competing desires, we pursue what we *most* want. If your spouse wants to change things, not just rearrange things, he or she will seek help on his or her own voli-

tion. This may be one way to gauge the level of commitment (or lack thereof) that your spouse has to you and to the relationship. Remember, the nation of Israel "honored God with their lips, but their hearts were far from him" (Isa 29:13, NIV). Their behavior belied their true feelings.

8. *Open your heart to feel the pain of the other, particularly the pain that keeps him or her bound to a way of being that comes from a wounded past.* "Hurt people hurt people." If you can't find compassion for your partner's bondage, without condescension, you're likely still holding him or her in contempt. If you want your partner to feel your pain, you have to be willing to feel your partner's. When you enter your own pain and allow God to minister to you in it, you'll begin to feel the pain of your spouse. Be aware that it's easy for an empathic person to set aside compassion for his or her own experience in favor of feeling for others, which is sometimes an unconscious way to avoid one's own pain. It's also easy for empathic people to not only feel compassion for someone but to take responsibility for making that person feel better. Refuse to fall into the trap of setting yourself up as your spouse's savior, which isn't compassionate at all in the long run. People need to have the freedom to choose for themselves, either poorly or well, and it's compassionate to let them do this. It may hurt, but severe mercy, administered with gracious confidence, is the best medicine in many circumstances.

9. *Be open to unconventional sources of revelation and epiphany* (i.e., dreams, your body's stress symptoms, someone you dislike, a collision of events, an old journal entry, an experience in observable nature, etc.). Be open to God's voice as he may speak in unexpected ways, being careful to listen with your heart, not just with your head. I'm always amazed by the myriad of ways that God communicates with people when they allow themselves to listen with their hearts. If you listen with your spirit, your core, which requires that you delve into the deepest pain in your spirit, you'll find God there, and his voice becomes clear. He's not a voice in your head. He's a spirit, and he communicates to your spirit through his spirit.

10. *Commit to sharing your heart with your spouse, even if he or she stomps all over it.* Become completely vulnerable to your spouse and open your heart to emotional intimacy with him or her. Understand, also, that you'll only be able to do this when your personal healing journey leaves you strong enough to hold onto yourself, even if your spouse doesn't receive you well. Give your partner one more chance to show genuine interest in the relationship. Of course, "one more chance" will eventually become "one last chance" for the offending party to join in a genuine repair process. (Note: If your spouse is abusive in any way or is emotionally checked out, I suggest that you only share your heart with your partner with third party help.)[1]

---

1. Stone, Jade G. *Grounds for Marriage*, Eugene, OR: Wipf & Stock: 2011.

Appendix E

Twin Parables

THE SWORD AND THE STONE: A FABLE ON FEMININITY FORSAKEN

Once upon a time, a baby girl was born to parents who were confused about the most important things in life. The little girl was a lady princess, as all little girls are, but her parents didn't teach the little girl about her dignity and her beauty. Instead, they taught her about humiliation (calling it humility) and about plainness (calling it beauty).

The little lady's father said, "Girls are fragile and simple-minded. They need us sword-bearers to ensure that girls make it through this evil world without getting hurt. Because of us sword-bearers, girls don't have to think about life. In fact, thinking is a dangerous thing for a girl to do because she's not designed to think. She doesn't really know how, so when she tries, she gets herself in trouble." The little lady princess's mother mindlessly nodded, affirming her husband's words.

The little lady princess thought about what her father had said, and decided that the reason it didn't make sense to her must be because she wasn't supposed to be thinking about anything. So she kept her mouth shut and tried not to think about it too much, which was very hard for her to do because thinking seemed to come naturally to her, even though her father said that girls weren't designed to do it.

There was also another thing that made the little lady confused: the stunning precious stone in her pocket. The little lady's father said, "Your gem is weak and fragile, and talking about it makes it disintegrate." Since it was shameful to talk about, the little lady princess decided that something was wrong with her gem. She kept it hidden and never spoke a word about it. As time went by, she began to believe that if her gem was brittle, she must be a lowly maiden, rather than a lady princess, which is a shame, as there are no such things as lowly maidens.

Not only were these parents confused about precious stones, but they were also confused about swords, such as those of her father and of her older brother, who was in training to be a noble knight, as all little boys are. "The sword," her father said, "is for keeping order in the world. Without the sword, the ladies of the world would start thinking too much and would cause the evil in the world to take over."

The little lady princess was confused by her father's words, because it seemed that her father used his sword to *give orders* rather than to *keep order*. And, as her mother never questioned the way her father wielded his sword, the little lady thought that she must not let anyone know how much thinking she did or that few of her parents' beliefs made sense to her, because thinking was considered sword-worthy, not gem-worthy, and it was evil for a girl to act like she had a sword.

So the lady princess closed her mouth and her pocket, but she couldn't keep her mind from spinning.

One day, the lady princess's brother and his friends asked her to expose her gem to them. She had been taught that good little girls should obey sword-bearers, so the little lady princess complied. She figured that this was the price to pay for the honor of companionship with sword-bearers who were strong and powerful and able to protect her from herself. The two boys, who hadn't been taught about beauty and dignity or about nobility and valor, grabbed the gem and struck it with their swords, marking the gem with a deep gash. Immediately, the little lady princess became numb with shock, but she had obeyed the sword-bearers, so she figured that she had done the right thing.

She decided that her gem really was fragile and weak and vulnerable to the sword, and she believed that it was worthless. "I'm such a fool to think that my gem was valuable," the little lady thought. "Where did I get such a silly idea? Besides, I'm honored to be allowed in the presence of my big brother and his friends. It's a small price to pay for a lowly maiden to be rewarded with the company of these strong knights-in-training."

Many, many times, the lady princess's brother and his sword-bearing friends requested her to expose her gem, and every time, they gashed it with their swords. Before long, the gem was no longer shiny, clean, and bright. Instead, it was dull, tarnished, and chipped. The little lady princess began to forget how beautiful and precious the gem was, partly because she'd never really known.

Then one day, the little lady princess's father died unexpectedly. *He can't give orders anymore,* the little lady thought with relief. But she wept because he'd never be able to *keep order,* either, and he'd never protect or hold her precious gem with care.

To the funeral came a young noble knight-in-training, a dashing sword-bearing friend of the lady princess. This friend came from a great distance to support the little lady, and she was stunned that a sword-bearer would genuinely care for her enough to travel so far.

When the two were alone, the little lady princess thanked the young knight in the only way she knew how: she revealed to him her gem. Like all the sword-bearers she had ever known, he, too, struck her gem with his sword. Although his mark was softer than the other blows her gem had received, the little lady princess couldn't distinguish this mark from any of the others. She didn't know that this young noble knight was confused about gems and swords, and that when she had offered her gem so readily, the young man, in his confusion, had impulsively brandished his sword against it. He didn't know that gems were to be protected by swords, either.

When the young man returned his sword to its sheath, neither he nor the lady princess saw the chip that the gem had made to the sword's blade. Neither realized that the young man's sword had been dulled by the little lady's gem. As the sword, brandished so carelessly, had tarnished the lady's feminine dignity, so the gem, exposed for all the wrong reasons, had chipped the young man's masculine nobility.

In their ignorance, the little lady and the young knight continued to damage each other's most valuable possessions until one day, a magician came upon the forlorn young lady princess in the woods. The Wise One seated himself on a log beside her.

"Your face is so sad," the Wise One said, and he lifted her chin with his white-gloved hand. The young lady looked into his eyes and saw tenderness and compassion.

"I'm so ashamed, Wise One," she said, "but I don't know why. I just don't like myself anymore." Tears welled up in her eyes and spilled down her cheeks. The Wise One gently wiped one away with his finger.

"This tear speaks of great wrongs. Perhaps you've lost your gem?" the Wise One inquired. "Perhaps you've lost what is most valuable to you?"

"Oh, no. I still have my gem," the little lady assured him. "Here it is, right here." And she pulled the gem from her pocket. "But it's all tarnished and marked up now. It really isn't worth anything."

When the little lady looked up, she was alarmed to see tears falling from the Wise One's eyes. "What are *you* crying for?" she asked, and she reached up to wipe the tears from his cheeks.

"Please. Allow these tears to fall. They honor the blows to your gem," the Wise One said.

The lady princess was confused. "But what good is my gem? It's weak and fragile and frail."

"It's delicate, dignified, and precious," the Wise One solemnly but gently corrected. "And enchanting," he added, with a twinkle in his eye. "This gem is who you are. It's dazzling and magnificent and mysterious, but it's been treated shamefully. It's time for your gem to be polished and repaired."

The Wise One took the gem into his gloved hands, wiped the tears from his face, and cleaned the gem with his tears. Then he gently rubbed the gem between his gloved palms. When he held the gem out in his palm for the little lady to retrieve, it was shiny, bright, sparkling, and unblemished again.

The little lady gasped. "It's more beautiful now than it ever was."

"Take good care of this gem, my little lady," the Wise One said. "It's the most precious thing you have. It's your femininity, your sexuality, the core of who you are. It is you."

"Oh, I will!" the little lady exclaimed. "Thank you very much."

"You're most welcome."

Suddenly, the lady princess was struck by an awful thought. "But what about the knights? They can take my gem and destroy it again with their strong swords."

"Yes, they can," the Wise One agreed. "But there are some knights who understand what their swords are for."

The little lady was confused. "What are they for?" she asked.

"They're for protecting the magic and the dignity of gems," said the Wise One. "The beauty of gems is great, and the enchantment of them can strip a knight of his masculine nobility, if he doesn't know that his sword is given to him to protect the vulnerability of gems."

The little lady remembered the first time she'd offered her gem to her knight. She had wanted to thank him for caring for her, so she'd offered him her most precious possession. Not knowing that his sword was given to him to protect her gem, the knight had marked it like all the sword-bearers she'd ever known. And in misusing his powerful sword, he'd become captive to it and to how powerful the gem could make him feel, tarnished though it was. He stole what counterfeit beauty he could from the gem, rather than use his sword to bring out its true beauty by anointing it with honor.

"I took his masculine nobility and he took my feminine dignity," the little lady mused sadly. "I stripped him of the protective power of his sword, and he stripped me of my vulnerable beauty." The Wise One nodded. "Is there any way to repair that tragedy?" the little lady asked tearfully. "Is there any way for me to give back and protect his masculine valor and for him to give me back and protect my feminine vulnerability?"

Again, the Wise One nodded. "It'll be hard work, because you've been wounding each other this way for a long, long time. You'll have to learn to believe in your magical femininity and in his valiant nobility, and he'll have to do the same. It's not easy when you've been living for so many years by the lies you were taught. But you're not alone. I'll be here to guide you and to direct you and to remind you of the true purpose for gems and swords."

"So if swords are for protecting gems, what are gems for?"

"Ah. Good question, my little lady. Gems give beauty and magic to the world. Yes, gems are delicate—not fragile; they're precious—not frail. But they have the power to make this world an enchanting place. Without knights and princesses who treasure and cherish precious gems, this world would be overcome by the power of misused swords. But noble knights who value precious gems fight to preserve their unique magic. Swords and gems must work together to protect the masculine strength and nobility of the sword and the feminine softness and beauty of gems. One can't survive without the other. Both are destructive if they aren't properly cherished, and both are more beautiful than anything else in the whole world if they're given due honor and respect. Each gem and sword has the power to curse or to bless."

"I wish I'd protected my feminine dignity and my knight's masculine nobility, and I wish he'd done the same."

"You wounded each other deeply that day, my little lady. But it's not too late to go back. Do you know what you would've wanted your noble knight to do when you offered him your gem?"

The little lady thought for a moment. "I would've wanted him to take my hands, close them around my gem, and say, 'Your gem is beautiful, precious, magical, captivating, holy, and sacred. It's so stunning, even though it's marked, that I'm tempted to mark it with my own sword. But that would compromise my nobility, and it would tarnish your dignity. It's not that I don't want to admire your gem, because I do, and if you're to share it with me someday when we truly know one another, I'll be proud to have protected your gem from my own sword and its capacity to overpower you and your beauty. So I can't accept your offer. I want to get to know you: a very special lady princess. Who are you? What makes you sad, angry, afraid, joyful, or passionate? What makes you laugh, cry, and ache? How did you become who you are? How do you hide from relationship and how do you express love? What do you want your life to amount to and why? I want to hold out to enjoy your gem until I know and love your whole soul. Please return your gem to your pocket. I want to shield it from my sword, which can be as fiercely destructive as it can be valiantly protective. I want to use my sword to guard your gem. For now, allow me to just hold and comfort you while you mourn the loss of your father.' That's what I wish he would've said."

Tears flowed down the young lady's cheeks as she imagined how beautiful such a moment would've been, if her young knight had protected her most precious possession, if he'd simply held her as she cried for a father who'd wielded his sword to destroy. Had the story unfolded like that, their lives would've been very different.

The Wise One interrupted the lady princess's reverie. "It's not too late. You can be different in this relationship starting now. You can determine to settle for nothing less than nobility and dignity, nothing less than valor and beauty, nothing less than courage and vulnerability, nothing less than the true purpose of swords and gems. You need not accept substitutes."

"And you'll help me to do this?" The lady princess doubted her own strength and resolve to be true to her gem and to her knight's sword.

"You can always find me here in the woods," the Wise One assured her. And the two grasped each other's hands and looked deeply into each other's eyes.

"I'm most grateful," said the little lady, "and I'll always be indebted to you. I wish there were something I could offer you in thanks."

"To honor the magic of your gem and the valor of your knight's noble sword is thanks enough. Were everyone to do that . . ." The Wise One's voice trailed off wistfully.

And with that, the little lady returned to her chateau to contemplate the words of the Wise One. *Things are going to be different if I revere the valor of my noble knight and his sword and if I honor myself and my precious gem,* she thought.

And the lady princess began her future with hope.

THE SWORD AND THE STONE: A MYTH ON MASCULINITY MARRED

Once upon a time, a baby boy was born to parents who were confused about the most important things in life. For example, the little boy was a noble knight, as all little boys are, but his parents didn't teach the little boy about his strength and his valor. Instead, they taught him about hiding (calling it "being nice") and about shame (calling it "being good").

The little boy's father was unkind to the little boy's mother, and his mother absorbed her husband's contempt. She'd grown up watching her own parents belittling one another, so the boy's mother had decided never to engage in conflict of any kind, particularly around her children. So, the little boy learned that conflict must be avoided at all costs, that there was no need to respect women, and that women weren't supposed to require that they be respected.

Furthermore, in the name of niceness, the boy's parents avoided difficult emotions, too, and the boy got the message that his emotions weren't important. He learned that keeping up an image and the appearance of peace was more important then being honest in relationships. Because of these unwritten rules, his household was mostly void of meaningful engagement. It was pleasant enough on the outside, but it was emotionally empty on the inside, and the boy longed for his parents to pursue him, invite him into intimate conversations, and guide him through the difficulties of life and relationships. He was a sensitive boy, a boy of deep emotion, but no one in his family was interested in emotions, so he was lonely all the time, and he often rocked himself to sleep to the sound of radio music performed by people who, even though he didn't know them, seemed to be as full of emotion as he.

Neither his father nor his mother ever so much as mentioned to the boy that he was designed to be a valiant knight, and that he was in training to one day protect and cherish a lady princess. Somewhere inside of himself, the boy sensed his valor, but, having no one to talk to about it and no words even to speak of his confusion, he tried to learn what he could about his nature. Without guidance, either through direct teaching or indirect modeling, the boy was left on his own to figure out the most important things in life, especially how to value himself and how to treasure a lady who might one day be his princess.

When the boy was an impressionable and lost eleven-year-old, the boy's family moved from one land to another, and the boy was torn from everything he'd ever known—everything that felt secure in his life. Without guidance, the boy found himself in this unknown land with no idea how to make friends and no one to talk to about it. He was dreadfully lonely, and he had no idea how to make his world better.

The boy desperately needed his father to train him in the ways of knighthood. But his father was too busy for the boy.

Before long, the boy began to seek guidance and value outside of his family; he talked to the new friends he managed to make in the new land. These friends were also knights-in-training, as all little boys are, but they also had no idea that they had royal blood coursing through their veins.

Their biggest questions involved how to be in relationship with young ladies, and because they had never been taught in any way how to treat a lady princess well, or even that they were worthy of such respect, the boy and his friends were left to learn by trial and error . . . mostly error.

The boy, now old enough, but hardly wise enough, to be called a young man, entered into a few relationships with young lady princesses in ways that didn't honor his or their royal status. Particularly, the young man was especially curious about the gems that he knew young lady princesses kept hidden somewhere in the folds of their clothing. He sensed that they could enchant his loneliness away, so he was drawn to see these gems, and he went searching for them. But, because he hadn't been taught about their value, he sometimes tried to steal them from the lady princesses.

The young man didn't realize how priceless such gems were to lady princesses and how hurtful he was when he wielded his sword, demanding to see them. He didn't realize that these gems were only to be seen if he'd cherish them as he'd cherish the most precious hidden treasure he'd ever imagined. He didn't realize that his sword was designed to protect these gems, not to possess them.

Before long, the young man realized that that these gems had the power to bewitch him; they had a power over him that he couldn't resist in his loneliness, and he was ashamed of his weakness. He sensed that his sword and his strength were given to him for a higher purpose, but he had no idea what that higher purpose was, and he had no idea how to find out.

By this time, the young knight had married a lady princess, who was also uninformed about the most important things in life. In their ignorance about knights and princesses, the two deeply wounded each other time and time again.

One day after his lady had refused to show him her gem, the young knight fled into the woods in his confusion and frustration. He sat down on a log and held his head in his hands.

After some time, the young knight sensed that he wasn't alone, and he looked up. Seated next to him was a magician.

"You look confused," the Wise One said, and he lifted the young man's chin with his white-gloved hand. The young man looked into his eyes and saw tenderness and compassion.

"I'm so ashamed, Wise One," he said, "but I don't know why. I just can't figure out what's wrong in my relationship with my lady princess." Tears welled up in his eyes, and spilled down his cheeks. The Wise One gently wiped one onto his finger.

"This tear speaks of great wrongs. Perhaps you haven't been valuing your sword?" the Wise One inquired. "Perhaps you haven't been protecting your treasure?"

"I don't know," the young man said. "I don't know what to do with my sword, and I'm not sure that I have any treasure to protect."

"Ah. You need a bit of guidance, I see," said the Wise One. "Allow me to tell you about the valor of your sword and about the treasure of your lady's gem."

The Wise One took a deep breath. "Your sword is the most valuable thing you own. It's given to you to keep order in the world and to *protect* the beauty of gems. It's your masculinity, your nobility, your valor, your greatest honor . . . if you use it properly. Gems are vulnerable to swords that aren't used properly, however, and it's easy to mar the delicate beauty of precious stones. But there's nothing like the power of a sword, used properly, to protect their dignity and enchantment. When you use your sword to protect gems, it's the most honorable thing you can do with the power of your sword. However, it's also possible to use this power to *possess* gems, and to possess them fails to honor their beauty, magnificence and mystery. Swords, you see, are designed to protect the dazzling enchantment of precious stones."

The young knight remembered the first time he'd urged his lady princess to show him her gem. When she'd held out to him her most precious possession, he'd been disappointed to see how tarnished and marked it was. Not knowing that his sword was given to him to protect her gem, the knight had marked it like all the sword-bearers she'd known before him. And in misusing his powerful sword, he'd become captive to it and to how powerful the gem could make him feel, tarnished though it was. He'd stolen what counterfeit beauty he could from the gem, instead of using his sword to bring out its true beauty by anointing it with true honor.

"I took her feminine dignity and she took my masculine nobility," the young man mused sadly. "I stripped her of her vulnerable beauty, and she stripped me of the protective power of my sword." The Wise One nodded. "Is there any way to repair that tragedy?" the young man asked tearfully. "Is there any way for me to give back and protect her feminine vulnerability and for me to take back and protect my masculine valor?"

Again, the Wise One nodded. "It'll be hard work, because you've been wounding each other this way for a long, long time. You'll have to learn to believe in your valiant nobility and in her magical femininity, and she'll have to do the same. It's not easy when you've been living for so many years by the lies you learned. But you're not alone. I'll be here to guide you, direct you, and remind you of the true purpose for swords and precious stones."

The young man took in the Wise One's words and contemplated them deeply. "I never realized how important my sword is, or how much power I possess, either to bless or to curse."

"You've had no idea how important your sword is in keeping order in this world and in protecting the most precious treasure of lady princesses. Perhaps you'd let me see your sword?"

The young knight slowly and shamefully unsheathed his sword. He was painfully aware of the chips, chinks, and scratches in the sword's blade.

The Wise One carefully ran his white-gloved fingers over the sword. As he did so, each mark disappeared, and the blade was restored to its original sharpness and splendor. When he was finished smoothing out the nicks, the Wise One held the sword up, like an offering, to the woods. The smooth, sharp blade glinted in a ray of sunshine filtering through the trees.

"From this day forward," the Wise One said, "I declare that this sword, restored to its original majesty, be enlisted only in the fight against evil. May it ever be used to wrest order from chaos and beauty from ashes."

Then he reverently returned the sword to the young man who sat mesmerized by the miracle he'd just witnessed. Overcome with gratitude, the knight allowed his tears to stream down his face. Never before had he realized how important he was and how invaluable his sword was in the battle against evil.

When he finally could speak, the young knight said, "Wise One, I'm forever indebted to your wisdom and to your kindness. Thank you for showing me the value of my sword. I'll honor it well, and I'll use it to protect and to treasure the gem of my lady princess."

"Take good care of your sword, my young knight," the Wise One said. "Always remember that it's the most precious thing you have. It's your masculinity, your sexuality, the core of who you are. It is you."

"Oh, I will!" the young knight exclaimed. "Thank you very much."

"You're most welcome."

Suddenly, the young knight was struck by an awful thought. "But what about the gems? They can take my power and destroy it with their enchanting magic."

"Yes, they can," the Wise One agreed. "But there are some lady princesses who understand what their gems are for."

The young man was confused. "What are they for?" he asked.

"Gems give beauty and charm to the world. They're delicate and precious, and they have the power to make this world an enchanting place. Without knights and princesses who treasure precious gems, this world would be overcome by the power of misused swords. But noble knights who value precious gems fight to preserve their mysterious magic. Swords and gems must work together to protect the masculine strength and nobility of the sword and the feminine softness and beauty of gems. One can't survive without the other. Both are destructive if they aren't properly cherished, and both are more beautiful than anything else in the world if they're given due honor and respect. Each sword and gem has the power to curse or to bless."

"I wish I'd honored my masculine valor and my lady's feminine dignity, and I wish she'd done the same."

"You've wounded each other deeply, my young knight. But it's not too late to go back. If you could do it all over again, what would you do differently when your lady princess agreed to show you her gem before you knew one another?"

The young knight thought for a moment. "I would take her hands, close them around her gem, and say, 'Your gem is beautiful, precious, magical, captivating, holy, and sacred. It's so stunning, even though it's marked, that I'm tempted to mark it with my own sword. But that would compromise my nobility, and it would tarnish your dignity. It's not that I don't want to admire your gem, because I do, and if you're to share it with me someday when we truly know one another, I'll be proud to have protected your gem from my own sword and its capacity to overpower you and your beauty. So I can't accept your offer. I want to get to know you: a very special lady princess. Who are you? What makes you sad, angry, afraid, joyful, or passionate? What makes you laugh, cry, and ache? How did you become who you are? How do you hide from relationship and how do you express love? What do you want your life to amount to and why? I want to hold out to enjoy your gem until I know and love your whole soul. Please return your gem to your pocket. I want to shield it from my sword, which can be as fiercely destructive as it can be valiantly protective. I want to use my sword to guard your gem. For now, allow me to just hold you and comfort you while you mourn the loss of your father.' That's what I'd say."

Tears flowed down the young man's cheeks as he imagined how beautiful the moment would've been if he'd protected his lady's most precious possession, if he'd simply held her as she cried for a father who'd wielded his sword to destroy. Had the story unfolded like that, he would've shown her that swords don't have to be wielded to overpower, and their relationship would've begun on an honorable foundation.

The Wise One interrupted the young knight's reverie. "It's not too late. You can be different in this relationship starting now. You can determine to settle for nothing less than nobility and dignity, nothing less than valor and beauty, nothing less than courage and vulnerability, nothing less than the true purpose of swords and gems. You need not accept substitutes."

"And you'll help me to do this?" The young man doubted his strength and resolve to be true to his sword and to his lady's gem.

"You can always find me here in the woods," the Wise One assured him. "You don't have to fear your loneliness, and you don't have to be dependent on gem-bearers to take your shame and loneliness away." The two clasped each other's hands and looked deeply into each other's eyes.

"I'm most grateful," said the young knight, "and I'll always be indebted to you. I wish there were something I could offer you in thanks."

"To honor the noble valor of your sword and the magic of your lady's precious gem is thanks enough. Were everyone to do that . . ." The Wise One's voice trailed off wistfully.

And with that, the young knight returned to his chateau to contemplate the words of the Wise One. *Things are going to be different if I honor the precious gem of my lady princess, and if I revere the valor of my noble sword*, he thought.

And the young knight began his future with hope.

APPENDIX F

Annotated List of Resources

HERMENEUTICS

Fee, Gordon, and Douglas Stuart. *How to Read the Bible for All Its Worth*, 3rd ed. Grand Rapids: Zondervan, 2003.

This book is an excellent, easy-to-understand look into the basics of sound, biblical interpretation. It's been revised and updated to keep pace with current scholarship, resources, and culture. It also includes a list of recommended commentaries and resources.

———. *How to Read the Bible Book by Book: A Guided Tour.* Grand Rapids: Zondervan, 2002.

This book can be used as a companion book to *How to Read the Bible for All Its Worth*, or it can be read as a stand-alone. The book provides both zoomed-in and zoomed-out looks at each book of the Bible in its cultural-historical-grammatical-literary context.

Klein, William, et al. *Introduction to Biblical Interpretation.* Nashville: W Publishing Group, 1993.

This book is much more detailed than *How to Read the Bible for All Its Worth*, and its more technical style may make it less accessible to some. However, it's an excellent resource for responsible interpretation, addressing literary, cultural, social, historical, and personal issues that impact our understanding and application of a text. The book also provides an annotated list of additional resources.

Osborne, Grant. *The Hermeneutical Spiral.* **Downers Grove: IVP, 1991.**

This resource, at first glance, may seem daunting. However, it provides a comprehensive introduction to biblical interpretation and includes sections on general interpretation, genre analysis, responsible application, preaching, and the problem of constructing meaning. For more advanced study, this resource is an excellent one.

Sproul, R. C. *Knowing Scripture.* **Downers Grove: IVP, 1977.**

In this resource, Sproul provides a basic introduction into the world of responsible interpretation. His style is simple (not simplistic), and he presents the science of interpretation in a way that is accessible to the layperson. He also gives practical guidelines for applying the science of interpretation.

Vanhoozer, Kevin. *Is There Meaning in this Text?* **Grand Rapids: Zondervan, 1998.**

In this resource, Vanhoozer tackles post-modern uncertainty with regard to meaning and interpretation. The book is divided into two parts; the first examines the controversy around deconstruction of author, text, and reading; the second defends the concept of intrinsic meaning in a text as intended by the author of a text. From the lenses of theology and philosophy, he treats the topics of metaphysics, methodology, and morals of interpretation. This book isn't for the faint of heart, but it's an excellent resource for those who would enjoy a scholarly look at the subject of interpretation.

EMOTIONAL HEALTH

Allender, Dan, and Tremper Longman, III. *Bold Love.* **Colorado Springs: NavPress, 1992.**

Allender and Longman team up to present a fresh look at what Proverbs says about love and forgiveness. This book challenges a milquetoast brand of love. Instead, the authors present love as active, unpredictable, cunning, and creative. "There is nothing redemptive about a love that just accepts people for who they are," say Allender and Longman.

Crabb, Larry. *Inside Out*, 10th anniversary ed. NavPress: Colorado Springs, 2007.

First published in 1988, the book addresses simplistic solutions of the modern faith community to the problem of woundedness, and calls us to integrity, honesty, and intimacy with God and others. Crabb contends that it's impossible to love well if we don't engage the pain and unconscious motivations of our hearts that keep us bound to a self-protective style of relating.

Goleman, Daniel. *Emotional Intelligence*, 10th anniversary ed. New York: Bantam, 2005.

Though this isn't a faith-based book, it's an excellent resource on human relationships and what makes them work well or poorly. The wisdom presented in this book is backed by research about the brain and human behavior. It's a must-read for people who want to be relationally smart.

May, Gerald. *Addiction and Grace*. San Francisco: HarperCollins, 1988.

In this book, May explores the physiology and psychology of addiction, and then presents a hopeful solution through grace and contemplative spirituality.

Peck, M. Scott. *People of the Lie*. New York: Simon & Schuster, 1983.

In this book, Peck does a superb job of marrying psychology and theology in a way that exposes the psychology of evil and provides hope: "Evil can be conquered only by love," which requires a paradox of "tolerant and intolerant, accepting and demanding, strict and flexible."

Peck, M. Scott. *The Road Less Traveled*. New York: Simon & Schuster, 1978.

For an introduction into the world of human psychology, this book is an excellent resource. Peck encourages his readers to face reality at any cost if they want to be mentally well. He discusses the nature of loving relationships with God, self, and others. I would recommend reading this one before reading any of Peck's other books.

Stokes, Timothy B., Ph.D. *What Freud Didn't Know: A Three-Step Practice for Emotional Well-Being Through Neuroscience and Psychology.* New Jersey: Rutgers, 2009.

In this book, Stokes combines research in neuroscience and psychology to explain how the amygdala records, stores, and activates emotional memory loops and imagery associated with painful events, especially those of childhood. Integrating ideas about mindfulness, habitual thinking, and insight imagery, Stokes provides tools to help people who have experienced trauma build resiliency and inner peace. Stokes' warm writing style can appeal to both general readers and practicing mental health professionals.

INTIMATE RELATIONSHIPS

Adams, Kenneth. *Silently Seduced.* **Deerfield Beach: Health Communications, 1991.**

This resource defines covert incest and describes the long-term impact of this damaging kind of parent-child relationship. Adams' perceptive insight provides emotional incest victims with a framework to understand what happened to them, how their lives and relationships continue to be affected, and how to begin the process of recovery.

Allender, Dan. *Intimate Marriage Curriculum Kit.* **Downers Grove: InterVarsity Press, 2005.**

This video and study guide curriculum offer companion materials for *The Intimate Mystery*, by Dan Allender and Tremper Longman, III. The topics presented include marriage, communication, dreams and goals, family ties, forgiveness, masculinity and femininity, and sexual intimacy.

Allender, Dan and Tremper Longman, III. *Intimate Allies.* **Wheaton, IL: Tyndale House, 1995.**

Allender and Longman team up in this book to present a pattern for love and marriage as imaged by God in scripture. Combining scholarship and storytelling, the authors present a picture of marriage that helps the reader visualize what covenant is designed to look like as covenant partners navigate inevitable struggles and conflicts. You may be surprised by the practical but unconventional wisdom of this work.

———. *The Intimate Mystery*. Downers Grove: InterVarsity Press, 2005.

This book provides a helpful look at marriage from a zoomed-out perspective, discussing topics such as the purpose of marriage. Using Genesis 2:24 as a springboard for the theology presented in this book, Allender and Longman challenge partners to allow their marriage to draw them into an intimate relationship that reflects the kind of intimacy we can have with God.

Carnes, Patrick. *The Betrayal Bond*. Deerfield Beach, FL: Health Communications, 1997.

This book provides hope for people who are trapped in the cycle of highly addictive attachments to people who have victimized them, but who want to muster the courage to break these bonds and embrace healing and wholeness.

Gottman, John and John DeClaire. *The Relationship Cure*. New York: Crown Publishers, 2001.

This book presents five steps for building better connections with family, friends, and lovers. It takes some of the research from *The Seven Principles for Making Marriage Work* and other research and applies it to all relationships.

Gottman, John, and Nan Silver. *The Seven Principles for Making Marriage Work*. New York: Three Rivers Press, 1999.

This book is a must-read for couples who want to understand what creates intimacy in a relationship. Gottman and Silver present their findings from years of observing the habits of married couples.

Gottman, John, and Julie Gottman. *The Art and Science of Love*. Seattle, WA: The Gottman Institute, 2005.

This video workshop presents key principles from John Gottman's research to help couples build and maintain successful relationships. The workshop uses role-play and exercises to help couples apply the principles they learn in the workshop lectures.

Hendrix, Harville, Ph.D., *Getting the Love You Want: A Guide for Couples.* **New York: Henry Holt and Company, 1988.**

Although this is an older work, the principles and practical exercises in it are timeless. This step-by-step guide helps couples create a loving, supportive, and revitalized partnership. Hendrix is a pastoral counselor, educator, and therapist. In partnership with his wife, a psychologist and women's activist, Hendrix originated Imago Relationship Therapy, a unique healing process for couples, prospective couples and parents.

Mellody, Pia. *Facing Love Addiction.* **San Francisco: Harper SanFrancisco, 1992.**

This resource explores the toxic patterns of relating as played out by love addicts and avoidance addicts. Mellody offers practical, step-by-step guidance to help readers face painful realities, acknowledge and disengage from addictive behaviors, and address underlying symptoms of codependence.

THEOLOGY AND DIVORCE

Atkinson, David. *To Have and To Hold.* **Grand Rapids: Eerdmans, 1979.**

An older work, this book still provides a helpful perspective for those who may be confused about how to reconcile the issues of marital breakdown. Although the writing style is dated, Atkinson examines biblical teaching on marriage in a way that is accessible to lay people. He presents a historical sketch of religious attitudes on marriage, divorce and remarriage, and then presents theology on marriage as a covenant. He also provides practical suggestions for pastors who may feel torn between doing what's right, what's good, what's realistic, and what's popular.

Carter, Les. *Grace and Divorce.* **San Francisco: Jossey-Bass, 2005.**

Without compromising scriptural truth, Carter acknowledges the practical reality that many marriages are destined to fail. In view of this reality, he presents a gracious approach to those who may be experiencing the most painful event of their lives: divorce. Carter draws our attention to the spirit of the law and gives a way to minister to people that honors the character and mission of Jesus.

Instone-Brewer, David. *Divorce and Remarriage in the Bible.* Grand Rapids: Eerdmans, 2002.

In this book, Instone-Brewer questions whether we correctly read scriptures that address marriage, divorce, and remarriage. In light of first-century Jewish and Greco-Roman thought, the author shows how the original audiences for these texts heard them differently than we do today. Carefully exploring the background literature of the Old Testament, the ancient Near East, and ancient Judaism, Instone-Brewer constructs an interpretation of scripture regarding these subjects that's fresh and enlightening. For those who enjoy scholarly work, this book presents much of the author's doctoral research in first century rabbinic Judaism. It's a dense read, but it's extremely helpful in providing literary and cultural context for difficult scriptural passages regarding marriage, divorce, and remarriage.

———. *Divorce and Remarriage in the Church.* Downers Grove: IVP, 2003.

This book is much more accessible to the lay reader than the previous one listed, although I highly recommend both. In this work, Instone-Brewer presents much of the same information in a reader-friendly way and offers the same faithful, realistic, and wise guidance for the believing community today. Instone-Brewer does a masterful job of reconciling seemingly contradictory passages of scripture in a way that's hermeneutically sound and encouraging for pastors and parishioners alike.

At http://www.divorce-remarriage.com, David Instone-Brewer addresses many problems and questions regarding scripture and divorce. You can find much of what he presents in his books on his website. Also, he includes links to his published articles. Most uniquely, he presents several "visual sermon" ideas for both adults and children. A handy and helpful website.

DIVORCE RECOVERY

Ahrons, Constance. *The Good Divorce.* New York: Quill, 1994.

This book does a wonderful job of helping a parent going through a divorce to focus on the child's needs. Ahrons provides practical wisdom for parents who know that staying together would cause more damage than being apart.

Smoke, Jim. *Growing Through Divorce.* **Eugene, OR: Harvest House, 1995.**

This resource is practical and encouraging for people who are experiencing what may be the most difficult season of their lives. Smoke's writing style is easy to read, and he offers the specific guidance that's necessary when clear thinking is hijacked by pain and overwhelmed feelings. Although this book doesn't address marriage from a standpoint of covenant, it does provide both compassion and direction.

See the following websites for resources on how to navigate various aspects of the divorce process: http://www.divorceshoppe.com and http://www.schermediate.com.

CHILDREN AND DIVORCE

Bonkowski, Sara. *Kids Are Non-Divorceable: A Workbook for Divorced Parents and their Children Ages 6–11.* **Skokie, IL: ACTA Publications, 1987.**

This useful, practical guide keeps children and their parents connected during a time when relationships are particularly stressed.

Brown, Lauren, and Marc Brown. *Dinosaur's Divorce,* **Boston: Little, Brown, and Company, 1986.**

This book for preschoolers uses a dinosaur family to help explain divorce in a simple and straightforward way.

Gardner, Richard. *The Boys and Girls Book About Divorce.* **New York: Science House, 1970.**

This book addresses basic questions that preteens and adolescents typically have when their parents divorce.

Illsley-Clarke, Jean, and Connie Dawson. *Growing Up Again—Second Edition: Parenting Ourselves, Parenting Our Children.* **Center City, MN: Hazeldon, 1998.**

The expert advice in this book has helped thousands of readers improve their parenting practices. Now, the book is substantially revised and expanded, and it includes practical help for parents who choose to divorce.

Prokop, Michael. *Divorce Happens to the Nicest Kids.* **Warren, OH: Alegra House Publishers, 1986.**

This self-help book for children, ages 3–15, addresses various false beliefs with which children struggle as parents go through divorce.

(For additional books on divorce for both children and adults, go to http://www.divorceshoppe.com and click on the "Bookstore" link. Also go to http://www.schermediate.com and click on "Resource List." There are many excellent resources for kids and their divorcing parents. If you're a parent going through a divorce, your children need you to help them process their confusion, pain, and anger, while you experience these emotions on your own. You owe it to them to do your research so that you can provide them with loving, mature, and sensitive guidance, even as you grieve. Please be sure that your children have a variety of resources to help them sort through their feelings during this most difficult time. This list is just a start; it's in no way comprehensive, and written resources are only one means of help available.)

Bibliography

Abma, R. *Bonds of Love: Methodic Studies of Prophetic Texts with Marriage Imagery.* Assen, the Netherlands: Van Gorcum, 1999.
Adams, Ken. *Silently Seduced.* Deerfield Beach: Health Communications, 1991.
Ahrons, Constance. *The Good Divorce.* New York: Quill, 1994.
Alexander, T. Desmond et al., eds. "Repentance." *The New Dictionary of Biblical Theology,* 727. Downers Grove, InterVarsity Press, 2000.
Allender, Dan, Ph.D. "Desire and Ecstasy." *Intimate Marriage DVD,* Disc 2. Downers Grove: InterVarsity Press, 2005.
———. "Different Bodies." *Intimate Marriage DVD,* Disc 2. Downers Grove: InterVarsity Press, 2005.
———. *The Wounded Heart,* revised ed. Colorado Springs: NavPress, 1995.
Allender, Dan, Ph.D., and Tremper Longman, III, *Bold Love.* Colorado Springs: NavPress, 1992.
———. *Intimate Allies.* Wheaton, IL: Tyndale House, 1995.
———. *The Intimate Mystery.* Downers Grove, IL: InterVarsity Press, 2005.
Applewhite, Ashton, William R. Evans, III, and Andrew Frothingham. *And I Quote.* New York: St. Martin's Press, 1992.
Arterburn, Stephen, and Fred Stoeker. *Every Man's Marriage.* Colorado Springs: Waterbrook, 2001.
Associated Press (January 6, 2004). "Judge Dissolves Britney's 'Joke' Wedding." Online: http://www.msnbc.msn.com. Retrieved on 2007-03-03.
Atkinson, David. *To Have and to Hold: The Marriage Covenant and the Discipline of Divorce.* Grand Rapids: Eerdmans, 1979.
Augsburger, David. *Caring Enough to Confront.* Ventura, CA: Herald Press, 1981.
Barker, Kenneth L., and John R. Kohlenberger, III, eds. *NIV Bible Commentary.* 2 vols. Grand Rapids: Zondervan, 1994.
Carnes, Patrick. *The Betrayal Bond.* Deerfield Beach: Heath Communications, 1997.
Carter, Les. *Grace and Divorce: God's Healing Gift to Those Whose Marriages Fall Short.* San Francisco: Jossey-Bass, 2005.
Cate, Robert L., *Old Testament Roots for New Testament Faith.* Nashville: Broadman, 1982.
Chapman, Gary. *The Five Love Languages: How to Express Heartfelt Commitment to Your Mate.* Chicago: Northfield Publishing, 1992.
Crabb, Larry. *Inside Out,* 10th anniversary ed. Colorado Springs: NavPress, 2007.
Dillard, Raymond, and Tremper Longman, III. "Chronicles." *An Introduction to the Old Testament,* 169–77. Grand Rapids: Zondervan, 1994.
———. "Hosea." *An Introduction to the Old Testament,* 353–62. Grand Rapids: Zondervan, 1994.

———. "Malachi." *An Introduction to the Old Testament*, 437–42. Grand Rapids: Zondervan, 1994.

———. "Psalms." *An Introduction to the Old Testament*, 211–34. Grand Rapids: Zondervan, 1994.

Elwell, Walter A., Ph.D., and Philip W. Comfort, Ph.D., eds. "Covenant." *Tyndale Bible Dictionary*, 325. Wheaton, IL: Tyndale House Publishers, 2001.

———. "Knowledge." *Tyndale Bible Dictionary*, 789. Wheaton: Tyndale House, 2001.

———. "Love." *Tyndale Bible Dictionary*, 827–29. Wheaton: Tyndale House, 2001.

———. "Marriage, Marriage Customs." *Tyndale Bible Dictionary*, 861–64. Wheaton: Tyndale House, 2001.

———. "Sex, Sexuality." *Tyndale Bible Dictionary*, 1181. Wheaton: Tyndale House, 2001.

Fee, Gordon D., and Douglas Stuart. *How to Read the Bible Book By Book*. Grand Rapids: Zondervan, 2002.

———. *How to Read the Bible for All Its Worth*, 3rd ed. Grand Rapids: Zondervan, 2003.

Flanigan, Beverly. *Forgiving the Unforgivable*. Indianapolis: Wiley Publishing, 1992.

Fulghum, Robert. *All I Really Need to Know I Learned in Kindergarten*. New York: Fawcett Columbine, 1986.

Goleman, Daniel. *Emotional Intelligence*. New York: Bantam, 1994.

Gottman, John, Ph.D. *The Seven Principles for Making Marriage Work*. New York: Three Rivers Press, 1999.

Graber, Ken. *Ghosts in the Bedroom*. Dearfield Beach: Health Communications, 1991.

Gromacki, Robert G. *New Testament Survey*. Grand Rapids: Baker Books, 1974.

Hendrix, Harville, Ph.D. *Getting the Love You Want*. New York: Henry Holt, 1988.

Hindman, Jan. *A Very Touching Book*, revised ed. Baker City, OR: AlexAndria Associates, 1985.

Illsley-Clarke, Jean, and Connie Dawson. *Growing Up Again—Second Edition: Parenting Ourselves, Parenting Our Children*. Center City, MN: Hazeldon, 1998.

Instone-Brewer, David. *Divorce and Remarriage in the Bible: The Social and Literary Context*. Grand Rapids: Eerdmans, 2002.

———. *Divorce and Remarriage in the Church: Biblical Solutions for Pastoral Realities*. Downers Grove: IVP, 2003.

———. *Divorce and Remarriage in the 1st and 21st Centuries*. Cambridge: Grove Books, 2001.

Kehler, Byron. "Confronting an Offender." Class Notes. Guiding Survivors of Childhood Sexual Abuse Through Recovery. Milwaukie, OR: 2004.

———. "Sexual Development Chart." Class Notes. Guiding Survivors of Childhood Sexual Abuse Through Recovery. Milwaukie, OR: 2004.

Lewis, C. S. *Weight of Glory*, revised ed. New York: HarperCollins, 1980.

Maltz, Wendy. *The Sexual Healing Journey*. New York: HarperCollins, 2001.

May, Gerald. *The Awakened Heart*. New York: HarperCollins, 1993.

———. *Will and Spirit: A Contemplative Psychology*. New York: HarperCollins, 1982.

Mellody, Pia. *Facing Love Addiction*. San Francisco: Harper, 1992.

Neher, A. "Le symbolisme conjugal: expression de l'histoire dans l'Ancien Testament." *Revue d'Histoire et de Philosophie Religieuses*, 34 (1954): 30–49.

Ontario Consultants on Religious Tolerance. "Divorce and Remarriage: US Divorce Rates for Various Faith Groups, Age Groups, and Geographic Areas." religioustolerance.org/chr_dira.htm. Retrieved on 2010-08-06.

Peck, M. Scott. *The Road Less Traveled*. New York: Simon & Schuster, 1978.

Richards, Lawrence O., ed. "Choose." *New International Encyclopedia of Bible Words*, 160. Grand Rapids: Zondervan, 1991.

———. "Knowledge." *New International Encyclopedia of Bible Words*, 382. Grand Rapids: Zondervan, 1991.

———. "Love." *New International Encyclopedia of Bible Words*, 418. Grand Rapids: Zondervan, 1991.

———. "Repentance." *New International Encyclopedia of Bible Words*, 522. Grand Rapids: Zondervan, 1991.

Ryken, Leland et al., eds. "Marriage." *Dictionary of Biblical Imagery*, 537–39. Downers Grove: InterVarsity Press, 1998.

———. "Hard, Harden, Hardness." *Dictionary of Biblical Imagery*, 364. Downers Grove: InterVarsity Press, 1998.

———. "Repentance." *Dictionary of Biblical Imagery*, 705. Downers Grove, InterVarsity Press, 1998.

Smith, Ralph. *Old Testament Theology: Its History, Method, and Message*. Nashville: Broadman & Holman, 1993.

Smoke, Jim. *Growing Through Divorce*. Eugene, OR: Harvest House, 1995.

Sproul, R.C. *Knowing Scripture*. Downers Grove: InterVarsity Press, 1977.

Stokes, Timothy B., Ph.D. *What Freud Didn't Know: A Three-Step Practice for Emotional Well-Being Through Neuroscience and Psychology*. New Jersey: Rutgers, 2009.

Unger, Merrill F., ed. "Marriage." *The New Unger's Bible Dictionary*, 817. Chicago: Moody Press, 1988.

VanGemeren, Willem A., ed. "רחב." *New International Dictionary of Old Testament Theology & Exegesis*, vol. 1, 638–42. Grand Rapids: Zondervan, 1997.

———. "חסד." *New International Dictionary of Old Testament Theology & Exegesis*, vol. 2, 211–18. Grand Rapids: Zondervan, 1997.

Vine, W.E., Merrill F. Unger, and William White. *Vine's Complete Expository Dictionary of Old and New Testament Words* [computer file], electronic ed., Logos Library System. Nashville: Thomas Nelson, 1997.

Young, William P. *The Shack*. Portland, OR: Windblown Media, 2008.

Youngblood, Ronald F. et al., eds. *Nelson's New Illustrated Bible Dictionary* [computer file], electronic ed., Logos Library System. Nashville: Thomas Nelson, 1997.

www.ingramcontent.com/pod-product-compliance
Lightning Source LLC
Chambersburg PA
CBHW070554300426
44113CB00011B/1909